The Visionary Window

The Visionary Window

A Quantum Physicist's Guide to Enlightenment

AMIT GOSWAMI

Quest Books
Theosophical Publishing House

Wheaton, Illinois ◆ Chennai (Madras), India

Quest Books
The Theosophical Publishing House
PO Box 270
Wheaton, IL 60189-0270

www.questbooks.net

Library of Congress Cataloging-in-Publication Data

Goswami, Amit.
   The visionary window: a quantum physicist's guide to enlightenment /
Amit Goswami. – 1st Quest ed.
      p.   cm.
"A publication supported by the Kern Foundation."
Includes bibliographical references.
ISBN-13: 978-0-8356-0793-3 (hardcover)
ISBN-10: 0-8356-0793-3 (hardcover)
1. Quantum theory—Religious aspects.   2. Religion and science.
I. Kern Foundation.   II. Title.

BL265.P4 G67 2000
215—dc21   00-058581

ISBN-13: 978-0-8356-0845-9 (softcover)
ISBN-10: 0-8356-0845-X (softcover)

5   4   3   2   *   05   06   07   08   09   10

Printed in the United States of America

To Swami Vishnuprakashananda
of Rishikesh, India
and
Swami Swaroopananda
of Paradise Island, Bahamas

Contents

Illustrations

Preface

The institutional separation of science and spirituality began in the seventeenth century in the West when the philosopher René Descartes divided reality into mind (the domain of religion) and matter (the domain of science). This division spread to Asia through the British domination of the East in the eighteenth and nineteenth centuries. The separatist paradigm of science, developed further by Newton and others, gave way, however, in the twentieth century to a new paradigm, quantum physics. This new understanding has created a window in the boundary wall separating science and spirituality. This book is one of the early explorations of this promising window.

The word *quantum* means a discrete quantity, and it (rightly) elicits images of tiny submicroscopic objects. Indeed, it is with submicroscopic phenomena that quantum physics began. But after almost a century of using it to delve into the mystery of matter, it is clear that quantum physics by itself is not complete; the observer, consciousness, is necessary to complete it. Logic dictates, as I demonstrate, that this consciousness, necessary for the closure of quantum physics, is the same consciousness that mystics throughout the world and recorded history have encountered. This cannot be a coincidence.

Thus opens the visionary window, the opportunity to invite into science the idea of consciousness as the ground of all being and to recognize it as the metaphysical basis for a new paradigm of science—a science within consciousness.

For many decades materialists have attempted to subjugate the spiritual territory, to explain away spirituality as an emergent epiphenomenon of matter and material interactions. As a result, spiritual philosophers, especially in the West, have become somewhat defensive. Part of their defense has been to chart out territories: science applies to "lower" aspects of reality, to the behavior of matter and life and mind; spiritual philosophies and religions apply to the "higher" aspects of reality. But this Cartesian "truce" has outlived its usefulness and reflects an unnecessary insecurity.

The same defensive wisdom tried to maintain the science/spirituality divide by claiming that science changes and therefore it is not to be trusted as a path toward the eternal spirit. I agree that spirit is eternal, and science must be based within the truth of eternal spirit. But within the eternal spirit, there is the question of cosmology and its evolution, which spiritual traditions themselves are forever trying to decipher. This is where science can be a valuable co-contributor.

The triumph of the separatist Newtonian paradigm was its success in explaining the cosmos without God, without consciousness—or so it seemed. But then paradoxes kept showing up, and anomalous data, not only in quantum physics but also in biology and psychology. It is a fact that Newtonian biology cannot explain life or health or cognition.

The new science within consciousness acknowledges the role of consciousness in cosmology and in the evolution of the cosmos, including biological evolution. This I promise to demonstrate. The new cosmology, not surprisingly, is found to be quite consonant with the ancient vision of spiritual traditions, which is helping to build it. And reassuringly, the current Newtonian paradigm of science remains valid within its established arena of applicability.

The book is not only about the contribution of spiritual traditions in building a new integrative science; in the last part of the book I show that the new science can repay its debt by helping us understand the efficacy of spiritual practices. Give-and-take between science and spirituality thus applies all the way, as it should for the two most comprehensive endeavors of humanity.

The cartography of inner space I offer is complete and satisfying and is consonant with all the spiritual traditions of the world. However, for setting forth this map, I have used many Eastern concepts and terms (most often Sanskrit) simply because the Eastern terminology is very precise in this realm.

In *The Self-Aware Universe* I argued, convincingly I hope, that consciousness is the ground of all being and that this metaphysics is a more inclusive and appropriate one for present and future science. In the present book I show how the new metaphysics can deal with what Ken Wilber and others call the great chain of being—from nonlife to life to beings with mind to soul to spirit. With this extension of scientific cosmology and the new breakthroughs of thought developed in this book about the methodologies of science and spiritual traditions, I then show that an integration of science and spirituality is now an accomplished fact. In this way, if *The Self-Aware Universe* can be compared to Newton's breakthrough that started modern science, *The Visionary Window* can be compared to the subsequent developments by Maxwell and Einstein that completed the classical physics worldview.

Perhaps the greatest challenge of living in the world today is compartmentalization, torn as we are between two competing worldviews—one the godless, rationalized creation of the old separatist Newtonian science, the other the spiritual knowledge that resonates abidingly in our hearts. I offer this book to you, the reader, as a guide to the practice of quantum yoga. *Yoga* means to yoke—to join or add.

When the quantum is added and integrated into the Newtonian worldview, you not only have a new, more complete worldview, you have integrated your spiritual heart with your scientific head.

I am grateful to many people for help with this project. The philosopher Dr. Deviprasad Chattopadhyaya initiated the idea of the book by encouraging me to write a monograph on the subject of science and spirituality for a Government of India philosophy project that he heads. I would like to thank Drs. Robert Tompkins and Henry Swift for careful readings of the manuscript and various helpful suggestions. Discussions with Dr. P. Krishna and Swami Swaroopananda were very helpful in shaping the final manuscript. Margaret Free's help with the editing and Jan Blankenship's secretarial help are also acknowledged. Thanks also to Carolyn Bond for an editing job well done.

I would also like to thank Don Ambrose for some early help with the figures and Madonna Gauding for the final rendition of the figures. I also thank my editor at Quest, Sharron Dorr, and the editorial staff for an excellent job in putting the book together.

I would like to thank Rajiv Malhotra and The Infinity Foundation and also Barbara Stewart for support for part of the period of writing this book.

I also wish to express my sincere gratitude to all who have helped me grow in spirit; to name only a few: Ram Dass, John Lilly, Arthur Young, Richard Moss, the late Franklin Merrell-Wolff, Joel Morwood, Ligia Dantes, Satyanarayan Sastry, Swami Dayananda Saraswati, Swami Vishnuprakashananda, and Swami Swaroopananda. Finally, I am grateful to my wife, Dr. Uma Krishnamurthy, with whom my spiritual practice is thoroughly entangled, for many helpful discussions on the subject of emotions.

Foreword
by Deepak Chopra

I have rarely read a book that gave me so much hope for the future as the one you are now holding. Its author offers brilliant answers to the most gripping questions that have ever been asked. I am tempted to call them the questions of children, though mystics, saints, artists, philosophers, and madmen never let go of them. Where do we come from? Do I have a soul? Who created the world? What happens after death? Why is anything real? In all societies these ultimate mysteries are buried under the debris of everyday life. We get and we spend, we marry and we work, and yet inside ourselves, at that delicate frontier where the heart peers over an invisible horizon onto eternity, we have not confronted what is real. At best, society appoints a priesthood to be the caretakers of "the big questions." As individuals we live on the hopes that our souls will escape being troubled by those questions too much.

This form of escapism is deeply troubling. One of the most humane themes in this very humane book is Professor Goswami's feeling of loss, his regret that our deep spiritual yearning has been put on hold. And who would not agree? When Christ said, "The truth shall set you free," or Socrates said, "An unexamined life is not worth living," or the ancient Upanishads said, "You are That, I am That, and all this is That," each sage and master assumed that these were the most important words anyone could hear. They weren't just meant for priests. And they weren't just meant for a long-ago time in a faraway place.

Professor Goswami has heard all these words—and many more like them—and has decided to unravel them with a scientist's care, reason, and rigor. He is fortunate in having a foot in two worlds, being both a lifelong student of Indian spirituality and an accomplished physicist. Many books over the past twenty-five years have tried to blend East and West, to reconcile nirvana and nuclear physics. Some have been successful on the poetic plane, giving us beautiful images of dancing quanta that whirl in space like ecstatic dervishes. Other, more literal authors have soberly unfolded the parallels between Einstein's relativity and the Buddha's doctrines for the ending of suffering. Yet I can say with humility that none of us have equaled Professor Goswami, who casts his net far beyond mere images or intellectual parallels. He lays before us the one Reality that every seer and sage has proclaimed and then forces us to accept that science cannot succeed unless it recognizes that same unity. Across the event horizon the realm of space-time-spirit is waiting. As one of the boldest to step into the new world, Professor Goswami has set himself a breathtaking project, and nothing is shirked. Is the universe conscious, as the ancients proclaim? Is God in every atom? Does the soul communicate to us here in the material world? Is death not an ending but a creative act opening into new possibilities? Is creation the ultimate example of a quantum leap? All these possibilities, and many more, are set forth with great competence, passion, and cogency in these pages. I can hardly think of a "big question" that Professor Goswami does not illuminate with startling conviction.

The primary contention here is that consciousness is the ground of Being and the source of creation. Everything we see, hear, touch, taste, and smell is a spontaneous flow from the source. Life is all, and all is alive. Such a position was first stated thousands of years ago in

India, later to be echoed in one form or another by all the mystical traditions East and West. But in our time mysticism has reached a low ebb, driven back and seemingly defeated by materialism. The ruling priests of science are all but unanimous on one point: mind is a creation of the brain; therefore it is a shadow of reality, a mere epiphenomenon, to use Professor Goswami's term. We are machines that somehow learned to think. This is the argument of upward causation. First comes energy, then matter, then DNA, then cells, until as life creaks it painful way up the ladder, we reach the brain, at which point a random firestorm of chemical events, sparked by minuscule flickers of electricity, give rise to thinking, feeling, dreams, emotions, and all other aspects of the mind. If you had sophisticated enough instruments, you could peer into the brain and spot the exact electrochemical impulse that fools you into believing that you are in love, or that you have a soul, the illusion of illusions.

Cultural blindness has made us forget how strange this mechanistic view actually is, how far removed from the great river of human wisdom. Every spiritual tradition has declared its belief in downward causation: first came Unity, or all-pervading consciousness, which separated itself into an inner world and its outer picture. From this transcendent beginning life took shape, but in invisible form its seeds have always been present. Being was imbued with all that it needed for the spectacular unfolding of the cosmos: it had intelligence, creativity, total mastery of space and time, and the potential to diversity into infinite possibilities.

So are we machines that fooled themselves into thinking we had consciousness, or are we consciousness that built a machine so that it could experience the world (a world that is just ourselves in another guise)? The conflict between upward causation and downward causation has proved to be the ultimate holy war. Because his approach is by nature conciliatory, Professor Goswami doesn't dwell on the bloody battles that have divided science and the church. His goal is to show that both sides can win. If science pays attention to its own experimental findings, it must abandon crude materialism; and if the church gives up its equally crude myths, God will be available to everyone. I won't spoil the adventure of reading Professor Goswami's arguments, but will only say that there are many surprises in store for all dogmas here. The atheist will be just as humbled as the fundamentalist, but neither is humiliated. Professor Goswami proceeds with kindness—a rare courtesy of the heart—in saving both God and reason. His vision of one Reality and one consciousness opens the door to anyone who wishes to walk through. As a reader, you leave this book without having to buy into a new religion or having to feel that your cherished beliefs were ignorant and misguided. Finding the truth is not a matter of making anyone wrong, but of seeing how every belief can be expanded. Our besetting sin has been narrowness of vision, for all along both scientists and believers have been tapping into the same deep well of possibilities. Unity has room for all diversities.

I do not know if the term "quantum yoga" as used in this book will catch on, but it deserves to. The mass media widely proclaims that we are about to enter the age of the genome. In this new dawn the "blueprint of life" will be decoded and then manipulated for the good of all humans. Yet for many centuries a more mysterious code has waited be broken: "You are That." The code sounds so simple. "I am That." It sounds almost empty. "All this is That." These three sentences, first uttered over three thousand years ago in India, tell us more about human destiny and creativity, more about our dreams and abilities, than all three billion bits of the human genome. A technology that could solve the riddle of even one word—"That"—would liberate people from countless ills and suffering. "That" is the invisible, unbounded, ever-living, eternal, unborn, and undying source that this book so beautifully elucidates. The mystery of life, as Professor Goswami eloquently proves, is not contained in atoms or in any event our five senses are attuned to. We were not born in the furnace of the Big Bang but in the womb of creation, which still surrounds and nurtures us. Beyond time and space is the home of infinite possibilities, an upwelling of life, truth, intelligence, and reality that can never be diminished. It is as full as it ever was or ever will be. This is the promise of the ancient seers, and it holds good today. Knock and the door will be opened, not just to one wish, but to all that humanity could ever imagine.

CHAPTER ONE

Quantum Yoga: Can Science and Spirituality Be Reconciled?

I ONCE PARTICIPATED in a panel discussion in Berkeley, California, on the question "Can scientific and spiritual traditions carry on a dialogue?" The first speaker, an American Buddhist, expressed uneasiness. The two traditions have diverged so much, he said, that both may need to return to basics and start over; maybe then they can have a dialogue. I spoke next. I think I surprised him and probably many in the audience by saying that not only can there be dialogue, there can and will be complete reconciliation between the two traditions. In fact, I asserted, the reconciliation has already begun. How is this so?

When my Buddhist friend was talking about science, he meant science based on classical physics, the physics that Isaac Newton founded in the seventeenth century and Albert Einstein completed in the first decades of the twentieth century. And his uneasiness was justifiable. Most biology and psychology and virtually all of our social

1

sciences are carried out day to day on a Newtonian basis. Newtonian science has given us some strong prejudices—such as determinism, strong objectivity, and materialism—that are appropriate when we investigate the order of the outer world. But the purpose of spirituality and religion is to investigate our inner reality, to establish order in our inner life, where ordinarily disorder, conflict, and unease reign. The spiritual quest is to find happiness beyond the discord; it is an investigation of consciousness. Since spirituality requires that consciousness plays a causal role, it is difficult, if not impossible, to make room within objective, materialist science for spirituality.

This was May, 1996, and I, too, was right because science had changed. Classical physics was replaced in the 1920s by a new physics called quantum mechanics. And now, after seven decades, this new physics is causing a major revision in how we think of living systems and how we do biology and psychology and thus all social sciences (Goswami 1993; Herbert 1993; Stapp 1993; Eccles 1994). In the new paradigm there is a window of opportunity, a visionary window, through which to recognize that consciousness plays a major role in shaping reality; then spirituality can be reconciled with science.

The word *quantum* comes from a Latin word meaning quantity and signifies a discontinuously discrete amount. In classical physics all things vary in a continuous manner, but in quantum physics things change in both continuous and discontinuous ways. Continuous change is materially caused, even in quantum mechanics. But what brings about discontinuous change? If we posit that consciousness causes the change, we have the proposition that prompts the shift from a divisive paradigm to one that integrates science and spirituality (von Neumann 1955). But there is more to consider here.

We have made enormous progress in science; why have we not made similar progress in religion in spite of the efforts of spiritual traditions for millennia? In science, once a few scientists discover the laws of universal order, the job is done; the rest can read those scientists' work, and that is enough to be able to appreciate the harmony of the outer world. In the realm of spirituality, however, great strides have been made by figures such as Buddha, Plato, Lao Tsu, Moses, Jesus, and Muhammad. But their discoveries have not brought harmony and happiness to everyone. We remain by and large, even today, a violent and unhappy bunch. Why is this so? The objective of spirituality takes much longer to accomplish because one person's spiritual realization and happiness does not proliferate to others. Finding happiness and establishing inner harmony are fundamentally individual processes.

The Sanskrit word *yoga* means union, integration. I have coined the phrase *quantum yoga* to signify the integration of the quantum message into a comprehensive new worldview that unites science and spirituality in a personally meaningful way. This book is not only an introduction to the visionary window that quantum physics opens for us, but also a guide to the practice of quantum yoga leading toward personal enlightenment.

The word *dialogue* originated from two Greek words: *dia*, meaning through, and *logos*, meaning word; thus, *dialogue* generally means communication through words. Physicist David Bohm defined dialogue more significantly, as "a free flow of *meaning* between people in communication." Can there be dialogue between science and religion in this Bohmian sense?

Initially, a dialogue between science and religion seems rather unlikely. Both science and religion are endeavors in the search for truth. Both are based on the intuition that truth is unique, not pluralistic. The problem is that even when we haven't gone far enough in our search, we try to impose our limited truth upon others. This is what many exoteric religions have done traditionally; now science is doing the same thing, which has led to the present polarization of science and religion.

A Brief History of the Rift in the West

To grasp the meaning of someone else's system it is essential to understand the metaphysical basis behind that system. And there is the rub. The metaphysics of science, as developed mainly in the West in the last three hundred years, seems diametrically opposed to the metaphysics behind the dominant religion of the West, Christianity.

In brief, Christianity, as popularly practiced, holds that a nonmaterial power, God, created the world and has supervised its affairs ever since in order to align them with his purpose, which is good. But there is also evil, the banishing of which restores order and happiness in our inner reality. The purpose of religion is to help people conquer evil and follow goodness—God's way. We learn by experience: God rewards our good deeds and punishes evil ones. We also learn about good by loving God. We have free will to choose good or evil, to love God or not. We must have faith in order to choose good: faith in God's goodness, faith in the authority of the Bible, faith in the authority of religious leaders, and so on.

In medieval times in the West even material reality itself was neatly divided into earth, where imperfection reigns, and heaven, the abode of God and perfection. In this dualistic picture God is separate from the world and heaven is separate from earth. Popularly, heaven was understood as outer space: the abode of the moon, the sun, the planets, and the stars. Science grew out of the intuition of a few people—Galileo, Kepler, and Newton principal among them—that the laws that govern "imperfect" earthly movement and the laws that govern "perfect" heavenly movement in fact may not be different. First, they showed that heavenly movement is not perfect at all (for example, the planets are not perfect spheres and they move in imperfect ellipses, not perfect circles). Next they demonstrated that the same set of laws governs objects both on earth and in heaven (outer space). This led eventually to the bold claim that God is not needed to explain movement either on earth or in heaven, at least as far as the material world is concerned.

By the twentieth century, science's success had led to a series of metaphysical notions of reality based on science, each one antithetical to notions of popular Christianity. One of these ideas is strong objectivity, which was already mentioned—reality is independent of us, so our free will, our decisions to love God or to follow ethics, do not make any difference in the affairs of the world. Other ideas are material monism and its corollary, reductionism—all things are reducible to matter and to its elementary particles and their interactions. The dualism of God and the world was openly questioned: if the God-substance is different from the world-substance, how does God interact with the world? Therefore, it makes sense to postulate that there is only one substance, matter.

Classical physics, with such luminaries as Newton, Maxwell, and Einstein at the helm, introduced other philosophical prejudices. I have already mentioned causal determinism—if the movement of things, the way they change, is causally determined, there is no room for divine purpose. Another tenet is continuity—all movement is continuous. Still another tenet is locality—all causes and all effects are local, mediated by interactions or signals that travel through space in a finite amount of time. Continuity and locality make it difficult to conceive of any way that a nonmaterial agency could interact with matter. Any nonmaterial intervention would seem discontinuous and nonlocal from the point of view of the material world.

The success of science done under the banner of these metaphysical assumptions prompted one more, epiphenomenalism—all subjective phenomena, such as consciousness and self, are epiphenomena (secondary phenomena) of matter; they are merely ornamental, having no causal efficacy of their own.

ꜣerate of these six metaphysical tenets—objectivity, ꜧ and reductionism, determinism, continuity, locality, ꜧenalism—is called by various names: material realism, ꜧm, scientific realism. In sum, this view holds that only mattei ꜧ its correlates: energy and force fields) is real; all else is epiphenomenal.

In the early days of science, the physicist-philosopher René Descartes divided reality into mind and matter, mind being the domain of God and religion and matter the domain of science. Matter was postulated to follow physical laws. Mind was allowed free will and the power of dominion over the earth including plants and animals. The philosophy of modernism that Descartes promulgated defined the modern human: the prerogative of being human is to predict and control nature with the help of science and technology.

Since mind was God's domain, religion and spiritual transformation toward good at first continued to make sense within modernism. But because of the concept of epiphenomenalism, this temporary truce between science and religion came increasingly under attack. The argument was this: the material world contains both order and disorder, both harmony and disarray. For example, the periodic motion of the planets about the sun is harmonious, while according to the entropy law, entropy (the amount of disorder) always increases. Why can't the mental world be understood in the same terms? Unhappiness and sorrow (mental disorder) as well as happiness and joy (mental order) may be simply part of the natural law of matter—in this case the brain. There is neither the ability nor the need to transform. In short, religion is superfluous.

Furthermore, the methodology proffered by religions—faith—is diametrically opposite to the methodology developed by science. The scientific method is founded on trial and error: try it and see. Make a theory and verify it. Experiments, not authority, are the ultimate arbiters of truth. Science's widespread success speaks for the effectiveness of its methodology. In comparison, only a few have claimed to have achieved transformation through faith, and many of these accounts are debatable in the eyes of science. In this way modernism slowly gave way to postmodernism: existence was regarded as preceding essence or God, and the notions of spiritual good and order and any metaphysics that gave value to these notions was "deconstructed."

The defenders of religion—predominantly Christianity in the West—have not fared well against this frontal attack from science. Take the case of biology. Biologists in the West make a fairly good case against Christianity's teleological ideas of how God creates the world according to his purpose. They claim to understand all of life through Darwinian ideas of evolution, according to which chance mutations produce genetic variations and nature selects the fittest among them to survive. God's purposive intervention is not required; all is chance and the necessity of survival. The champions of Christianity respond to Darwinism with "creationism," pointing out gaps in the scientists' arguments. The most famous gap is the absence of continuous fossil evidence that shows how plants became animals or how reptiles became birds. But creationists posit only the Biblical account as an alternative to evolution: God created the world and all life within it in six days circa 4000 B.C. This account precludes any explanation of fossils at all, except as God's whimsy.

The religionists have fared no better in responding to challenges against dualism: if God and the world are separate, what mediates the interaction between the two? Such interaction, according to science, would require an exchange of energy; but according to the law of conservation of energy, the energy of the world is a constant. Any dualistic divine intervention must be a "miracle," in violation of the law of conservation of energy! Why, the materialists ask, should God be lawful in the affairs of the external world, but invoke miracles in the affairs of the mind, which after all must be a phenomenon of the brain? Why should we expect God to obey our rules? retort the religionists. The debate goes on.

How can there be a dialogue, a meaningful communication, between a scientific tradition that scoffs at such "unscientific" notions as miracles and teleology, and a religious tradition that abhors "scientism" (science practiced as religion instead of employing strictly scientific arguments against God)? The debate in the West has failed to penetrate this impasse. This is the basis of the pessimism of my Buddhist friend mentioned earlier.

Most unfortunately, the debate has led to cynicism regarding values. A lot of people in the West don't really believe that anybody can be *good* except a simpleton like the title character of the movie *Forrest Gump*. Imagine that Forrest Gump dies and goes to heaven, where Saint Peter stops him at the Pearly Gates. "Sorry. You have to answer three questions to get in," says Saint Peter. "The first question is, how many seconds are there in a year?"

"That's easy," says Forrest Gump. "Twelve."

"How did you get that?" asks a surprised Saint Peter.

"Count them. January second, February second, March second—"

"I see," interrupts St. Peter. "Well, I'll let you have that one. Now for the second question. How many days in a week start with a *t*?

"Four," answers Forrest Gump confidently.

"How do you get that?"

"Easy. Tuesday, Thursday, today, and tomorrow."

"Alright, I'll give you that one also," Saint Peter says with a chuckle. "But you must answer this one correctly. What is the name of God?"

"Andy," says Forrest Gump.

"What on earth gave you that idea?" asks Saint Peter in exasperation.

"I learned it singing hymns at church. 'Andy [and He] walks with me, Andy talks with me—'"

And with that, an amused Saint Peter ushers Forrest into heaven.

Simple-minded people tend to be good out of the belief that there is a heaven and there is God. Few sophisticates do, although they may sympathize with that belief and its values: it would be *nice* if society followed them. Religious values are merely inconvenient to the cynical many who are busy competing and taking care of "numero uno"; after all, isn't that what scientific realism is all about? As biological beings, isn't survival our only value?

The Story of the Rift in the East

Spiritual traditions in the East dance to a different metaphysical tune. Hinduism, Buddhism, and Taoism posit that a transcendent consciousness, rather than matter, is the ground of all being and that all else is epiphenomena, matter and self included. These traditions see the spiritual quest for unblemished happiness as the quest for the true nature of our being, our wholeness.

Eastern traditions solve the problem of dualism with the idea of transcendence and its proper understanding. Consciousness is both inside and outside the material, space-time reality. As transcendent— outside—it is pure consciousness, unmanifest. Immanent—inside—it appears split as self and the world, subject and object; but the split, the separateness, is epiphenomenal, brought forth by a mysterious force called *maya* in the Hindu tradition. I call this philosophy monistic idealism, but it is also called Vedanta in India and the Tao in China.

There is a monistic, mystical core in Western spirituality as well, called the perennial philosophy (Huxley 1970). The esoteric traditions in the West understand perfectly that consciousness, the ground of being, is transcendent; they also know what this means. "The kingdom of God is within you, it is also outside you" (Guillamont et al. 1959, 3). But populist, "exoteric" Christianity misinterprets transcendence dualistically, as consciousness, or God, separate from the manifest material reality.

To see clearly the diametrically opposite positions of material monism and monistic idealism, consider the story of the Greek king Milinda and the Buddhist monk Nagasena. The king wanted to know the nature of reality. Nagasena approached the king's chariot, untied the horses, and asked, "Are the horses the chariot, O noble king?"

"Of course not," replied the king.

Nagasena then removed the wheels from the chariot and asked, "Are these wheels the chariot, O noble king?"

The king replied again, "Of course not."

The monk continued stripping the chariot, asking if each part was the chariot, until all the detachable parts were dismissed. Nagasena then pointed to the chariot's chassis and asked one last time, "Is this chassis the chariot, O noble king?"

Once again the king replied, "Of course not."

So what is the real chariot? The material monists would say that there is no chariot without its reductive parts. The parts are the whole, and the chariot exists only as an epiphenomenon of the parts. Any chariot other than its parts is a "ghost in the machine."

But that's not the position of Nagasena or any other monistic idealist. Nagasena was demonstrating to the king that there is no self-nature in objects apart from consciousness, just as there is no self-nature in the chariot or its parts other than the material of which they are made.

A modern-day Nagasena, the Vedanta teacher Swami Dayananda, who lives in Saylorsburg, Pennsylvania, makes the same point when he holds up a gold bangle and asks his audience, "The bangle may think it is real, but is it?" Then he mischievously smiles and continues, "If the bangle is melted down and made into a gold necklace (reincarnation), it may even think itself superior to the gold bangles. But can that which changes be real? The unchanging, the gold, is the real thing. Bangles and necklaces are epiphenomena."[1]

The intellectual history of the East can be thought of as one long debate between three philosophical "isms"—dualism, monistic idealism, and material realism. Eastern dualists, like dualists in the West, believe that God and the world—God and ourselves—are separate. When we are with God, we are happy; so the dualists give us devotional and ethical practices to help us be with God, much as exoteric Christianity in the West does. The proponents of monistic idealism point out that their philosophy is based on investigation, that consciousness can be known directly in its inclusive suchness because "we are That." When we transcend the dualism of self and the world through direct knowledge, when we discover our wholeness, we become happy because our true nature is happiness. To monistic idealists, dualists have not looked far enough into the self. And the tenets of material realism, idealists contend, are either pure speculation or the results of incomplete investigation also. To this, material realists counter that it is foolish to base one's metaphysics on subjective experiences. And dualists scoff at the idea that separation of God and the world is the product of maya.

More recently, under the influence of the West, academic scientists in the East have legitimately demanded a mechanism for how the one and only consciousness becomes many. The spiritual traditions offer only the concept of maya as a vague force of epiphenomenal creation, but furnish no details comparable to today's scientific models. Moreover, in the East there is a traditional denigration of the world of epiphenomena in favor of the one reality beyond, an outlook that has only caused material misery in the lives of ordinary people. To the Eastern scientist this is further proof of the folly of spirituality: Look at the West, which has gained material prosperity by rising above spiritual superstitions. In response, the spiritual traditions of the East rightly point out that material pursuits have brought the West material prosperity no doubt, but they have also exacerbated mental poverty. Without spirituality, without the notion of one consciousness, the values that guide people's lives and sustain their societies cannot be justified. In fact, under relentless attack from science, these spiritual values are now being abandoned by many people all over the world, and this is causing chaos.

Seeking a Basis for Reconciliation

One track for a possible dialogue between science and religion has arisen from the observation that spiritual and material traditions often use similar metaphors to elucidate their concepts. In the seventies physicist Fritjof Capra wrote the influential book, *The Tao of Physics*, which delved deeply and revealed many parallels between concepts of modern science and spiritual traditions (Capra 1975). If modern science uses the same metaphors as spiritual traditions, perhaps science is already spiritualized to the extent it needs to be. Capra and others (for example, the founders of the deep ecology movement) have enunciated a new, ecological worldview with parallels to animistic views of certain forms of shamanism—God is immanent everywhere, all things are interconnected and alive in spirit. In this view, there is no need to think in the divisive, reductionist terms of Newtonian science nor to postulate a transcendent being.

This preference for the immanent vis-à-vis the transcendent grew out of a reaction to exoteric Christianity. The exoteric Christian worldview is distinctly dualistic—the perfect world of God in comparison to the vile and imperfect world of space, time, matter, and motion. Eve's eating the apple of knowledge was (mis)interpreted as a sin, and guilt became a major theme in Western thought. Guilt has persuasive power in Christianity but, justifiably, is considered inhibiting in modern Western psychology. Since the idea of a transcendent world was linked with the idea of collective guilt, transcendence itself became suspect to the modern Western mind.

Philosopher Ken Wilber sees the ecological worldview as the proponent of a descending-to-the-eco (ecology/world) "motto," in contrast to the ascending-from-the-ego "motto" of the Christian worldview (Wilber 1996a). According to Wilber, the Christian worldview emphasizes transcendence, an ascending from the concerns of the ego and the world, whereas the postmodern worldview promotes immanence, a descending from concerns about God and transcendence. But, as Wilber correctly says, reality is not dualistic; reality is a monistic integration of the immanent within the transcendent. Postmodern deep ecology, however, has been unable to integrate the ascending and descending aspects of reality. In fact, the social effect of this new-age brand of spirituality has been to enable opportunists to co-opt spirituality for selfish material pursuits.

Experimenting with another track for integration, many scientists have tried to extend traditional science to explain the subjective half of the world: consciousness, the self, spirituality, and moral values. For these scientists, explaining consciousness is a matter of understanding how the brain behaves as a complex material machine. Consciousness is an epiphenomenon of matter. These scientists ask: What in the brain's complexity makes it conscious or makes ethics relevant? Can an epiphenomenon of matter have the appearance of causal efficacy and even of creativity and spirituality?

Chaos theory also has shown promise as a context for a science/

spirituality dialogue. Chaotic systems are those that are so sensitive to their initial conditions that their behavior cannot be predicted for long; little inaccuracies or omissions in reading the initial values of positions and velocities multiply exponentially to make the behavior of chaotic systems appear creative. Small changes in the environment enable chaotic systems to display new, self-organizing behavior (order). Could spirituality be the apparently creative behavior of a chaotic system?

But if spirituality is an epiphenomenon of chaos and chaos is the norm, then once again the vision of religion—to replace suffering and disorder in our inner reality with happiness and order—is undermined. The spiritual vision makes sense only if happiness is the order and chaos, or unhappiness, is the epiphenomenon.

Furthermore, a reconciliation between science and spirituality in terms such as ecology or chaos theory is precarious. Wilber (1996a) argues the folly of founding spirituality on scientific notions. Science, he points out, is an evolutionary enterprise. New theories rise to invalidate older theories. A perennial philosophy cannot be based on such ephemeral notions as a theory of emergent consciousness in the brain. Back again to our impasse.

Can there be dialogue and eventual reconciliation between science and spirituality? Wilber is right. So long as we hold onto a material-based ontology, there is no scope for real dialogue, let alone reconciliation, for the simple reason that science deals with phenomena while spirituality is concerned with what is beyond phenomena.

The Integration of Metaphysics

The crucial question is: Must the metaphysics of science be based on material realism? The current paradigm of physics has in fact shifted beyond Newtonian science to quantum physics. Quantum physics is based on the notion of quanta—discrete quantities of energy and other attributes of matter, such as angular momentum. The consequences of this physics for the description of matter are deep and unexpected. For example, matter is described as waves of possibility. Quantum physics calculates possible events for electrons and the probability of each of these possible events, but cannot predict the unique actual event that a particular measurement will precipitate. So who or what precipitates the unique actuality from the myriad possibilities? Or, to use the physicists' favorite jargon, who or what "collapses" the possibility wave into the actual electron in actual space and time in an actual measurement event?

It took seven decades for us to see that this question, which I call the visionary window, has the paradigm-shifting consequence of reconciling science and spirituality. But the basic idea is extremely simple: the agency that transforms possibility into actuality is consciousness. It is a fact that whenever we observe an object, we see a unique actuality, not the entire spectrum of possibilities. Thus, conscious observation is a sufficient condition for the collapse of the possibility wave. Mathematician John von Neumann (1955) argued decades ago that consciousness is a necessary condition for that collapse. All objects obey quantum mechanics; this includes any machine we may employ to facilitate our observation. Any such measuring-aid machine, however, when coupled to a quantum possibility wave, makes up a larger wave of possibility that includes the machine. In order to initiate collapse, an agency is needed that is outside the jurisdiction of quantum mechanics. For von Neumann, there is only one such agency: consciousness.

This potent idea, however, became bogged down in a nasty debate because consciousness is misunderstood in the West. In Western materialism, consciousness collapsing a possibility wave is a paradox, because consciousness as an epiphenomenon of matter (the brain) has no causal efficacy; how can it cause a quantum possibility wave to collapse? And if consciousness belongs to a dual world, then all the objections against dualism previously cited come back to haunt us. It took all of seven decades for the light of monistic idealism to be brought in to clear up the matter.

Here, then, is my thesis: When we introduce consciousness as the ground of being, as transcendent, as one, as self-referent in us—which is what the spiritual teachers of the world have taught—then the quantum debate can be settled and the paradoxes resolved.[2]

And there is more. Positing consciousness as the ground of being calls forth a paradigm shift from a materialist science to a science based on the primacy of consciousness. In this science, matter has causal efficacy but only to the point of determining possibilities and probabilities. Consciousness ultimately creates reality, because the choice of what is actualized, event to event, is always up to consciousness. Therefore, consciousness can and does imbue reality with its creative purpose, as many Christian theologians (those who do not hold dogmatically to the creationist view) have intuited. This choice of actuality from possibility comprises the discontinuous change that I mentioned before. The world is *only seemingly* continuous, Newtonian, and material. In reality, it is discontinuous, quantum, and conscious.

Most importantly, such a science leads to a true reconciliation with spiritual traditions, because it does not ask spirituality to be based on science but asks science to be based on the notion of eternal spirit. Spiritual metaphysics is never in question. Instead, the focus is on cosmology—how the world of phenomena comes about. The new science can include subjectivity as well as objectivity, spiritual matters as well as material ones. This new science I call *science within consciousness* or *idealist science.*

The Integration of Cosmologies

In the Middle Ages, influenced by Aristotelian thinking, Christian belief maintained that the universe was anthropocentric. The earth was regarded as the center of the universe. Humans were regarded as superior to animals. These cosmological components of Western religion were demolished by science. Copernicus demonstrated that the sun, not the earth, was the center of the solar system. Later work took the demolition of Christian cosmology even further: the sun is only an average-sized star on the edge of one galaxy among a hundred billion other galaxies. We are insignificant on the cosmic scale. Scientists now make a good case for a big bang creation of the universe some fifteen billion years ago. From that initial creation, the evolution of galaxies, star systems, planets, and life are all seen as the play of chance statistical fluctuation. Darwin's argument that humans have evolved from animals and his further contention that all evolution is a mere play of blind chance and the necessity of survival further diminish the importance of being human and suggest that human pursuits such as religion are meaningless.

What is the exoteric Christian answer to the big bang? Since the big bang is a singularity in some theories of cosmology, and since a singularity is a breakdown of physics, the Christian scientist may see in the big bang the signature of the divine (Jastrow 1978). But there are also ways in physics to avoid the singularity (Hawking 1993). The most vocal Christian answer to Darwinism is still creationism, which, in view of the fossil data, does not make sense to the modern mind.

I argued in the preceding section that within esotericism (whether it is called Vedanta, mysticism, perennial philosophy, or monistic idealism) is the resolution of the ontological debate between science and religion. Does the esoteric ontology—consciousness as the ground of all being—offer a resolution of cosmologies as well? This is the subject of part II.

A number of coincidences in cosmology suggest that the universe evolves toward the manifestation of life and sentience—an idea that is called the anthropic principle (Barrow and Tipler 1986). When we do science within consciousness, we see that the anthropic principle makes perfect sense: the universe is a play of consciousness. It evolves towards sentience because its meaning is us (see chapter 5).

The gaps in the fossil record suggest to quite a few biologists that Darwinism is not the complete story of evolution (Eldredge and Gould 1972). Creationism also does not make complete sense; though the Christian contention that God intervenes in the affairs of the world, even in biological evolution, to align the world with purposiveness, is credible in a science within consciousness. Note, however, that in this science *purpose* does not mean final cause—an idea that conflicts with what we know about initial causes from materialist physics. But in science within consciousness, we can look at the fossil gaps as the signature of creative conscious intervention—purpose enters evolution creatively (see chapter 6; also Goswami 1997a).

The materialist cosmology is not wrong, but it's not the complete story. In the completion of the story the cosmological struggles of both science and religion are found to converge, and integration becomes possible.

The Integration of Methodologies

The methodology of religion is faith, while the scientific method is "try it and see the result." This great divide seems impossible to cross. If we consider the esoteric religious traditions, however, the divide between the methodologies of religion and science is not so great after all. In fact, there are obvious parallels. Although experiential and subjective, the esoteric traditions of both East and West also use the scientific method of "try it and see for yourself." They do not define the spiritual search as a matter of acceptance of dogma. Faith is reinterpreted not as blind belief in this or that system of knowledge, but as an intuition to be followed by a commitment to look, to investigate.

Science within consciousness allows us to see that both scientific and spiritual traditions have not emphasized an important aspect of their endeavors. When we emphasize this hidden component, it becomes clear that science and spirituality have been using the same method all along. What is this unrecognized component? It is creativity—the discovery of or insight into new meaning within old or new contexts (Goswami 1996). Until recently, scientists have been much too carried away with emphasizing the rational and continuous processes of scientific investigation. But creativity is nonrational and discontinuous. And science involves creativity in a major way. "I did not discover relativity by rational thinking alone," said the immortal Einstein. That comment does not fit within material realism, but so what?

Spiritual traditions have always known the importance of the nonrational—for example, the intuition that becomes faith—but they, too, have not universally emphasized the suddenness and discontinuity of spiritual insights. Science within consciousness enables us to develop a theory of creativity in which science is the result of creative investigation in the outer arena and spirituality is the result of creative investigation in the inner arena.

There may be a protest: Spiritual traditions don't follow one path, one technique; each has its own methods. In creativity, one starts with a burning question and the answer comes in sudden insight. This may describe how a seeker finds truth through what Hindus call the path of knowledge (*jnana yoga* in Sanskrit); but Christianity uses the paths of devotion to God and ethical action, and loving God and acting ethically are not what we normally identify as creative endeavors. Can all these methods be classified as inner creativity?

Is loving a creative act? Do ethics demand a protracted process, of which insight is the crown jewel? I argue that when we recognize creativity in love and ethics, the misconception that Christianity is dualistic evaporates. In other words, the dualism of exoteric Christianity comes largely from the methodology it uses. Because the methodology initially requires a separation between God and ourselves, we tend to forget that there is unity beyond the separation and that the method eventually takes us there.

So not only can we have a dialogue; I contend that the development of science within consciousness can give us an integration of science and religion, an integration of metaphysics, cosmologies, and methodologies. The majority of this book presents the details of this integration.

The Integration of Spiritual Traditions

I now want to raise a high hope. I submit that it is the absence of a good cosmology that has engendered divisiveness among religions. The world's great religions, united at their esoteric cores (see, for example, Schuon 1984), differ greatly in their exoteric expression because they present cosmology differently. Furthermore, in the absence of a science, they mythologize their cosmologies. My hope is that as a cosmological science within consciousness gains strength, these myths will give way to a re-illumination of the underlying unity of all religions.

Take the mythologized story line of the Christian cosmology.[3] Because Eve ate the apple of worldly knowledge and persuaded Adam to do the same, humanity knew separation and fell from the perfection of Eden. Then God sent his beloved and only son, Jesus, to return fallen humanity to Eden, to perfection. Thus Jesus is the only door back to Eden.

But the story of the fall from Eden comes from the Jewish tradition, which has a different take on how the story ends. Yes, declare the Jewish spiritual authorities, there will be a messiah at the "end of time" who will redeem humanity (or at least the chosen ones) to perfection, but Jesus is not he.

So battle lines are drawn. Jews feel that Christians are "less" because they have settled for a false messiah. Christians feel that Jews are "less" because they are "Christ killers." Moslems are repulsed by the whole "son of God" idea: God sends messengers only to remind humanity that God is their Lord. Moses and Jesus were both such messengers, but the last and the best messenger was Muhammad.

The Hindus seem to agree with the Christians that God can and does appear in human form, as "sons of God." Whenever the forces of evil seem to subdue the good, God incarnates as an *avatara* to elevate good over evil, however temporarily. Krishna was such an avatara; so was Buddha and so was Jesus.

Buddhists maintain, in still another twist of the same theme, that ordinary human beings can regain perfection through their own efforts. These perfected beings, instead of returning to "Eden," remain at its threshold as *bodhisattvas* until all humanity has so redeemed itself.

Postmodernism, the most recent development in Western thinking, has given us deconstructionism ("God is dead" and all metaphysics is false) and an ecological worldview in which God is fully immanent in the world itself. Eden is here, and there is no need to posit transcendence, the fall, and the spiritual journey of return.

So which is the correct story line? We can never settle this by debate, as past millennia have proven. However, I submit that as we gain an understanding of the cosmology of the human condition and the nature of the spiritual path, these disparate story lines will all be seen as expressions of one grand story. In other words, I believe that the integration of science and spirituality will enable the different spiritual traditions to acknowledge their underlying unity, a unity that the poet Rabindranath Tagore called "the religion of man." In Hinduism it is sometimes referred to as *sanatana dharma*, the eternal religion. Diversity of religions will of course remain, but superimposed on an underlying unity.

The Organization of this Book

Part I of this book introduces quantum mechanics methodically and demonstrates how it demolishes the tenets of material realism. It also shows how an analysis of the quantum measurement question leads to the same picture of consciousness that spiritual teachers have described for millennia.

Part II establishes the main premises and assumptions of the new paradigm with a view to developing a more general cosmology than the materialist one. I trace the origins of the division of the world into secular and sacred. I then take up the creationists' issues and demonstrate creative purposiveness in biological evolution. Finally, I delve into cosmology in its most general form and show that it is consonant with the spiritual traditions' vision.

What is the use of science within consciousness? Does it help to understand that the methodology of spiritual traditions is fundamentally the same as that of science? Does it help to establish ethics on a scientific foundation—a science of ethics? In part III, I show that it does. Does the new science help us understand the spiritual quest for unblemished happiness and the resolution of the quest? Can the new science be used to reconcile some of the deep divisions between spiritual traditions and even the deep divisions within us individually? I go into all these questions in part III.

One may ask, isn't the idea that consciousness is the ground of all being just another metaphysical idea? Shouldn't we think twice before declaring this the termination of our search for truth? Esoteric religions agree that no verbalizable metaphysics can be the final truth, for the final truth can only be discovered directly by each of us. However, some metaphysics are more inclusive than others and therefore are better fingers pointing to the moon of truth. This book demonstrates that the metaphysics of monistic idealism can encompass material realism and dualism.

In India, although the main thrust of spiritual thinking has retained a nondual theme, the expressions of that theme have varied widely. Buddha taught emptiness (*shunyata*); the Upanishads and the philosopher-sage Shankara taught "one without a second" (*ekam eva advitiyam*); Sankhya philosophy espoused reality as dual, a play of individual consciousness (*purusha*) and matter (*prakriti*); and Tantra and the Puranas sang the glory of the many, God immanent in the world. No story line is left out; all are included because all embody the search for truth. Again, no truth discovered by one is imposed on any other except as an encouragement to look. Can we revive this inclusive attitude once again, this time bolstered by a new integration of (mainly) Western science and (mainly) Eastern spirituality—an attitude that enables us to understand the different roles of limited views united in the search for truth? Following the best intuitions of all traditions, scientific and spiritual, let us all search, with mutual respect, for the one truth, each free to choose our metaphysics on the path in accord with our stage, ability, taste, and need.

Notes

1. For a taste of Swami Dayananda's wonderful exposition of Vedanta, read his *Introduction to Vedanta* (1993).

2. This subject is treated in detail in my book *The Self-Aware Universe: How Consciousness Creates the Material World* (1993). Chapter 3 of the present book presents a succinct and up-to-date summary.

3. I am grateful to Joel Morwood for a discussion of the ideas in this section.

Part I

The Quantum Leap

The Fall of Materialist Ontology

M ODERN SCIENCE has backed
spiritual traditions and their associated tenets into a corner by provid-
ing a viable alternative worldview that explains phenomena without
relying on any spiritual metaphysical notions whatsoever; this fact is
well known. What is not so well known is how far quantum physics
has pushed conventional material-realist science and some of its dic-
tums into a corner. To understand quantum physics' achievement, we
should take a look at the principles of material-realist science that it
has refuted. During its three-hundred-and-fifty-year history, conventional science has adopted the following as dogma:

- CAUSAL DETERMINISM: The world is a determined,
  clockworklike machine. Every change, every movement of an
  object is determined by the object's initial conditions (position and velocity) and the material forces that act on it. René
  Descartes, who split reality into a dual world of mind and
  matter, anticipated determinism. Isaac Newton developed the

physics underlying it. But it was the French mathematician Pierre Simon Laplace who first clearly enunciated determinism. Laplace wrote a book on celestial mechanics, perhaps the first book of its ilk that did not mention God as a causal agent. This caused a scandal of sorts in the French court. Even Emperor Napoleon was intrigued, eventually summoning Laplace and asking him, "Why haven't you mentioned God in your book?" Laplace is supposed to have replied, "I haven't needed that particular hypothesis."

- CONTINUITY: With causal determinism came the hypothesis that all movement, all change is continuous.

- LOCALITY: All causes (and their effects) are local, which means that they propagate in space with a finite velocity over a finite amount of time. In other words, simultaneous action at a distance is impossible. Einstein discovered that material objects obey a speed limit, the speed of light, which is some 300,000 kilometers per second. Thus Einstein may be considered the father of this particular dictum.

- STRONG OBJECTIVITY: The material world is independent of consciousness, that is, of us, the observers. This idea has its roots in the thinking of Aristotle.

- MATERIAL MONISM AND REDUCTIONISM: Everything is made of matter (atoms or elementary particles) and its correlates (energy and force fields), and every phenomenon has a material origin to which it can be reduced. The physicist Richard Feynman said that if everything was destroyed and we were allowed to preserve just one idea from today's scientific civilization, that idea would be "everything is made of atoms"—so strong a believer was he in the idea of material monism.

- EPIPHENOMENALISM: All subjective phenomena—indeed, consciousness itself—are epiphenomena of matter. *Epi* means
  secondary; thus *epiphenomenon* refers to the secondary effects
  of underlying material interactions, effects that in themselves
  have no causal efficacy. Epiphenomenalism is a clear and necessary offshoot of material monism. According to this view,
  all causes percolate upward from the elementary particles of
  matter in a simple hierarchy: elementary particles make atoms, atoms make molecules, molecules make living cells, cells
  (neurons) make the brain. At each level, new phenomena come
  into play—life at the cellular level and consciousness at the
  level of the brain—but they are really epiphenomena, reducible to the elementary particles and their interactions. All
  causation is upward causation.

Notice that each of these doctrines is ultimately not provable.
How do we prove experimentally that all phenomena are material? For
example, how do we demonstrate that thoughts are material phenomena? Moreover, we haven't studied *all* phenomena. Some of these
material-realist doctrines, such as objectivity, determinism, and epiphenomenalism, fly in the face of our common sense: we undeniably have
subjective experiences, we undeniably are conscious, and we certainly
assume that we have free will. To scientist colleagues who promote
epiphenomenalism to me I respond, "If you believe you are an epiphenomenon, then why do you take yourself so seriously?"

In fact, why do intelligent people take these doctrines seriously?
Even many quantum physicists are caught up in material-realist thinking and vainly try to explain away the radicalness of the quantum
message. The success of science and its spawn, technology, is somehow
thought to be associated with the validity of these doctrines. Modern
science developed primarily in the West, where early scientists literally

had to risk persecution from religious dogmatics in order to study nature. But now that science has its autonomy, why continue the battle of dogmas when truth is our objective, not whose dogma is right? We must give up habitual acceptance of the material-realist doctrines because, frankly, quantum mechanics has proven some of them to be outright wrong and has cast grave doubt on the validity of the rest. In particular, continuity, determinism, and locality have been proven wrong. Let's start our discussion of quantum physics by examining how the experimentally established principles of the new physics negate these dogmas.

Beyond Continuity: Quantum Leaps

Continuity is in fact a commonsense and necessary assumption of science. Look at the environment around you and then close your eyes for a second. When you open your eyes, how do you know that you are seeing the identical environment (granted that it looks the same)? You are making the assumption of continuity.

Scientists were lulled into the assumption of continuity because the phenomena of the macro world, even under scientific scrutiny, by and large do not seem to violate that assumption. Moreover, the assumption of continuity enables us to study physics mathematically, objectively, and logically.

But quantum physics, from its very inception, has beaten the doctrine of continuity to a pulp. Max Planck, the German physicist who discovered the idea of the quantum at the end of the nineteenth century, saw that energy is exchanged not continuously but rather finite bit by finite bit. A quantum of energy, as he called it, is the smallest amount of energy that can be exchanged between two bodies.

The Danish physicist Niels Bohr developed a model of the atom in which the idea of discontinuous movement became quite vivid—as baffling a picture as that is. An atom consists of electrons moving about an atomic nucleus. According to Newtonian physics and the doctrine of continuity, electrons that rotate must continuously emit light, gradually losing energy and orbit and eventually falling into the nucleus. So a "classical" atom, one that obeys the principle of continuity, is not stable—which is in contrast to our experience. Niels Bohr realized that the atom is stable because the electrons emit light not continuously but only when they jump from a higher orbit to a lower one. If they are in the lowest orbit, there is no lower orbit to jump to; hence the atom is stable.

But consider what this implies about the quantum jump in order for the theory to work! Bohr had to assume that the orbits are the only places where the electrons can be; they are not allowed in between. So how does an electron jump orbit? It disappears in one orbit and reappears in the other, never traveling through the space in between. Can you imagine jumping from a high rung of a ladder to a low rung without passing through the space between rungs? This is Bohr's picture of the quantum jump (fig. 1).

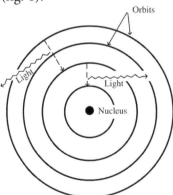

Fig. 1. Quantum jump in the Bohr atom. When an electron jumps orbits, it does not go through the intervening space.

The discovery of quantum mechanics—more than a decade after Bohr developed his theory—revealed that the electron's quantum-leaping ability originates from its wave nature; electrons are waves of possibility. When we are not observing an atomic electron, due to its interaction with the electromagnetic field the electron becomes a superposition of being in two (or more) orbits at once—albeit in possibility. When we observe the electron, the possibility of it being at two (or more) places becomes the actuality of being in one place momentarily—and simultaneously a light quantum is emitted. This collapse of the electron's possibility wave to the actual electron we see takes place instantly. It is discontinuous; there is no local collapsing through space at a finite speed over a finite time. The discontinuity of the quantum leap remains.

Erwin Schrödinger was a co-discoverer of the new quantum mechanics—in particular, of the equation that the quantum possibility waves (more formally called wave functions, or coherent superpositions) obey. Since he was dealing with waves, which are supposedly a continuous phenomenon, Schrödinger initially thought he had eliminated discontinuity from physics. Alas! When he visited Bohr in Copenhagen, Bohr showed him otherwise. So upset was he with Bohr's undeniable logic that he blurted out, "If I had known that these discontinuous quantum leaps were here to stay, I'd never have discovered quantum mechanics."

James Frank and Gustav Hertz long ago provided experimental verification that atomic energies exist as discontinuous energy levels, that the electron is not allowed to take on any energy in between these discrete values. The existence of a spatial discontinuity in the electron's quantum leap is best revealed in the phenomenon of quantum tunneling or barrier penetration, observed in transistors, for example—the electron's ability to leap over a barrier that is energetically impenetrable (classically speaking). The quantum electron has this ability because it disappears on one side of the barrier and reappears on the other side, never going through the barrier. (Thus *tunneling* is in fact a misnomer for this phenomenon.)

One down, two to go.

Beyond Determinism:
Uncertainty, Probability, and Possibility

The physicist Max Born was the first to interpret quantum objects as waves of possibility—the square of their wave amplitude (the maximum value of the wave disturbance) gives the probability of finding the object in a particular actuality. If we measure an electron possibility wave (technically called a wave packet), we sometimes find the electron here, sometimes over there. Over a large number of experiments, the probabilities of finding the electron in various positions form a distribution in the familiar shape of a bell curve (fig. 2a).

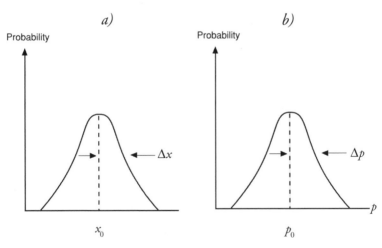

Fig. 2. (a) The position probability distribution (Δx) of an electron; (b) The momentum probability distribution (Δp) of an electron.

What does it mean that the electron's behavior is probabilistic, that we can predict only the probability of the electron being here or there, but not its definite position? If we cannot predict things definitely, where is determinism? Determinism is out the window. Werner Heisenberg, the other co-discoverer of quantum mechanics, elucidated the indeterminacy of the physical world in the uncertainty principle: we cannot measure with utmost accuracy both the position and the velocity of a quantum object simultaneously.

The bell curve distributions give us a quantitative view of the uncertainty principle. Figure 2a illustrates the probability of the position of the electron. Similarly, if we plot the probability for the velocity or momentum (which is mass multiplied by velocity), we get another bell curve (fig. 2b). Each of these bell curves defines a width, a range of deviation on the average from the most probable value (the peak value). These widths define the uncertainties of the quantity described by the probability distribution. The position bell curve gives the position uncertainty; the momentum bell curve defines the momentum uncertainty.

Now we can state Heisenberg's uncertainty relation quantitatively: the product of the position and momentum uncertainties is greater than or equal to a constant of nature, designated as h. This constant was discovered earlier by Max Planck, who called it the quantum of action. This quantitative law has been verified by myriad experiments.

Why is the uncertainty principle important? It reveals that we cannot determine both position and momentum (velocity) simultaneously with utmost accuracy; therefore, we can never determine those coveted initial values of Newtonian determinism: initial position and initial velocity. And without accurate initial values, it is impossible to predict the trajectories of objects in motion, even with accurate knowledge of the causal forces (even if the Newtonian laws held true). Like Humpty Dumpty, once determinism has taken this great fall, no efforts can put it together again—uncertainty prevails.

One word about Planck's constant *h:* The uncertainty principle makes it clear that *h* fixes a scale of nature, the scale at which quantum effects are normally large. It just so happens that *h* is a rather small quantity, thus camouflaging the quantum effects—the uncertainty and the possibility-wave nature—of most macro objects. The possibility wave of a macro object spreads between measurements, but it spreads very slowly—so slowly that it is appreciable only at time scales comparable to the age of our universe (fifteen billion years).

Nevertheless, make no mistake: even macro objects are quantum possibility waves. They do spread. Recently, thanks to the accuracy of measurement possible today with laser technology, a one-ton apparatus was found to spread in a short time by one hundred thousand trillionth of a centimeter.

Two down.

If material forces and material causes cannot completely determine the future, there is room in the world for creativity and for free will. But to assume that quantum objects have free will or that they are creative in any way would be sloppy thinking. The fact is, the behavior of quantum objects *is* determined behavior—determined by the mathematical equation of Schrödinger; but what are determined are not trajectories, as Newton and Laplace thought, but possibilities and probabilities. This still allows us the statistical determinism necessary for the prediction and control of large numbers of objects—the primary focus of conventional physics. (Consider, for instance, that a macro object the size of a thimble holds 10^{23} molecules of water.) Creativity enters the scene in the case of the single quantum measurement, the collapse of a single event. When consciousness collapses actuality from possibility, there is room for free will, for creativity, and for divine purposiveness.

Beyond Locality:
Quantum Nonlocality and Transcendence

Why is the locality assumption so important to science? Imagine standing before a water fountain and the water suddenly surging and splashing you. Perhaps there was turbulence in the flow of water, or perhaps there was a little gust of wind. One could study the situation and maybe even write a paper on chaos theory at work here. But suppose somebody coughed in New York and caused water to move in Seattle! Could one do science under such circumstances?

I hope your answer is no. Science warmly welcomed Einstein's confirmation of the locality assumption with his theory of relativity. This theory gave us the speed of light as the limit for the speed of material objects—no influence in space and time ever travels faster than the speed of light. So all influences are assumed to be local, taking a certain amount of time to travel through a certain amount of space. This assumption enables us to keep track of what influences are important in a particular situation.

But quantum mechanics violates the doctrine of locality. In quantum mechanics, the discontinuous collapse of a sprawling possibility wave is instantaneous and therefore nonlocal. At first this seemed to be all theory; how can we experimentally verify that an object really extends over vast distances in possibility but collapses to a point of actuality instantly when we measure it? Thanks to the work of physicists David Bohm and John Bell, it is possible to think of nonlocally correlated quantum systems. Parts of these systems can move in possibility very far from each other, and yet when we collapse one part by measuring it, the other part instantly collapses in a state that gives away its secret nonlocal correlation (Bohm 1951; Bell 1965). For instance, consider two correlated electrons that start together but subsequently move in opposite directions. When one is collapsed in a state with an indicator pointing "up," the other is always found collapsed in a state with the same indicator pointing "down." Clearly, the correlated electrons dance to the same tune, instantly and without any local signals.

Three down, and the materialists are out!

One does not have to see a violation of Einstein's theory of relativity in this nonlocal collapse. The possibility waves reside in *transcendent* potentia, in a domain that transcends space and time. Nonlocal influence is transcendent influence; it influences manifest reality but involves no signals in space-time. A nonlocal influence operates from outside space-time but has influence within space-time. About the transcendent world one of the Upanishads declares: "It is within all this; it is outside all this." Can this be? Yes, it can, when we understand transcendent as nonlocal in quantum-mechanical terms.

Physicist Alain Aspect and his collaborators, who experimentally verified nonlocal correlation between quantum objects (Aspect et al. 1982), were the first ones to carry out what today we hail as experimental metaphysics. They not only proved nonlocality but also confirmed the existence of a transcendent domain of reality beyond the material domain of space-time. This is in direct contradiction to the one-material-world assumption of material realism and is in direct support of the idea of transcendence found in all spiritual traditions.

Objectivity, Materialism, and Epiphenomenalism

So, thanks to quantum physics, we have direct experimental proof that continuity, determinism, and locality do not hold. For the negation of the other tenets of material realism—objectivity, material monism, and epiphenomenalism—quantum mechanics is strongly suggestive but not quite definitive (yet). This is the reason, in part, that material realism is still a valid "ism" in some people's minds.

Is the world independent of us? Or does what we see depend in some crucial way on us, on our choices? Physicist Niels Bohr helped us see that we do play a crucial role in shaping reality.

Quantum objects are transcendent waves in potentia, but they collapse as localized particles when observed. How can we experimentally ascertain their wave nature in transcendence? Easy, said Bohr. Look at them through a wave-measuring apparatus—an apparatus that focuses their property as waves. A wave can be at two places at the same time. So if we allow electrons to pass through a double-slitted screen, they will go through both slits as possibility waves, creating two waves in possibility (fig. 3a). The two waves will now recombine and interfere. By detecting the waves on a fluorescent screen behind the double-slitted screen, we can see the effect of this splitting and interfering. At some places on the fluorescent screen the two waves from the two slits will arrive in identical phase; those are the places where they will augment one another (fig. 3b), enhancing the probability for the electrons to manifest there. In between these bright fringes, there will be places where the two waves will arrive out of phase with one another and cancel each other out (fig. 3c), producing a zero probability and dark fringes. This pattern of alternate bright and dark fringes is called an interference pattern (fig. 3d), and its presence guarantees that we are seeing a wave phenomenon. For if electrons were particles, like marbles, they would arrive only behind the two slits.

However, notice the subtlety. Electron waves are waves of possibility and probability. A single electron always manifests localized in one place like a particle; but by watching a great number of electrons make an interference pattern we are able to draw the conclusion that each electron is a wave, each is able to pass through both slits and interfere with itself.

You may wonder: Perhaps the electrons are passing through one

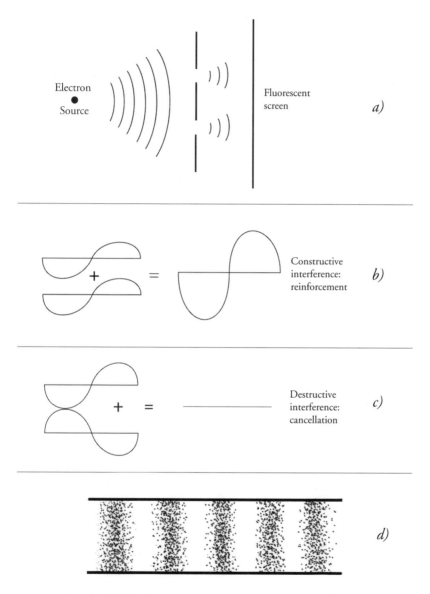

Fig. 3. (a) The double-slit experiment arrangement; (b) electron waves in phase interfere constructively; (c) waves out of phase cancel each other out; (d) the double-slit interference pattern

slit and are deflected at the edge somehow so that they fall occasionally in odd places on the fluorescent screen and give rise to only an apparent interference. Do they pass through only one slit? We can check this out. But guess what? When we try to see which slit an electron *really* passes through, our attempt to see it collapses the electron as a particle at one of the slits, and it appears right where we expect it—behind that slit and nowhere else (fig. 3e). The interference pattern disappears. Niels Bohr explains that now we are observing the electrons with a "particle-measuring apparatus." By our intention of localizing the path of the electron, we succeed in making it into a particle.

Behold! The wave nature and the particle nature of quantum objects are complementary; the wave nature is transcendent and the particle nature is immanent. They are also complementary in an ex-

e)

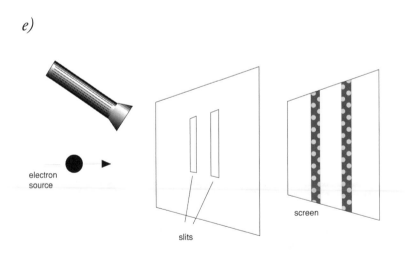

electron source

slits

screen

Fig. 3. (e) When we attempt to see which slit each electron is passing through, the wave-interference pattern disappears.

perimental sense: we can measure only the wave nature or only the particle nature with a given experimental arrangement.

Zen Buddhists dramatize the fundamentally complementary nature of reality. "Does a dog have Buddha nature?" Sometimes a Zen master will say yes; at other times the same Zen master will shake his head and say no.

"Is the electron a wave?" "Yes," says Bohr, "if you are looking through a wave-measuring apparatus." "Is the electron a wave?" "No," says Bohr, "if you look through a particle-measuring apparatus."

Does the dog have Buddha nature? The most astute Zen masters respond by saying, "mu"—neither yes nor no. It depends on how you look. You choose reality by how you look at it. Is reality independent of how you look at it? How can it be? You choose how the electron is going to reveal itself by choosing the experimental arrangement. Is the electron's nature independent of you, as the doctrine of strong objectivity demands? No. It is not that simple.

This is not the only context where consciousness chooses reality. Passing through a double-slit arrangement, the electron has a strong probability of arriving at any of the bright fringes. Over a large number of events, all the bright fringe positions will fill up with arriving electrons. But at which fringe does an individual electron arrive in a particular quantum measurement? Mathematician John von Neumann said that this question has only one sensible answer: consciousness chooses—we choose—where an electron will manifest in a particular event (von Neumann 1955).

Where is the (strong) objectivity in physics, if consciousness is essential in determining how reality manifests? And if consciousness has the causal power to choose material reality, can it be an epiphenomenon of matter? Consider once again the simple hierarchical picture of consciousness that materialists give us: elementary particles make atoms, atoms make molecules, molecules make cells, cells make the brain, the brain makes consciousness—upward causation all the way. The problem with this picture is that all levels of the hierarchy, from elementary particles all the way up to the brain, remain as possibility waves according to quantum mechanics. Upward causation can only produce possibility. Consciousness is needed to collapse possibility into actuality via what, we must admit, is downward causation. Consciousness cannot do that if it itself is material, if it itself is composed of quantum possibility. So not only is objectivity in doubt; material monism is in question if consciousness is nonmaterial, for then *all* things are not within the realm of matter. And epiphenomenalism is doubtful if consciousness is not a product of the brain.

Do We Create Our Own Reality?

WHAT IS THE NATURE of consciousness such that it can resolve the quantum-measurement paradox—the problem of who or what collapses the quantum possibility wave to actuality? As we have seen, positing consciousness as the causal agency for collapse is a paradox in material realism because in that philosophy consciousness itself is an epiphenomenon of the material brain. An epiphenomenon of matter cannot cause a material possibility to become an actuality!

In the late seventies and early eighties, this quantum measurement paradox and the associated question of the nature of consciousness occupied most of my time. The mathematician John von Neumann had suggested that consciousness may be the collapser, and in the early sixties the Nobel laureate physicist Eugene Wigner supported the idea (von Neumann 1955; Wigner 1962; see also London and Bauer 1983). But both von Neumann and Wigner looked upon consciousness as part of the mind, in which case consciousness collapsing the quantum wave function evokes the notion of mind over matter—a separate world of mind acting on the world of matter. And this notion takes us into dualism's trap: what mediates the interaction between the two? And what happens to the law of conservation of energy if such interaction occurs?

Because of my East Indian heritage (I had studied the Upanishads with my father at an early age), I was aware of the tenets of Indian philosophy, according to which both matter and mind are subsumed within Brahman, the all-pervasive ground of being, consciousness. And I was convinced that this was wrong. The source of my conviction was physicist Richard Feynman's assertion, expressed in *The Feynman Lectures in Physics*, that everything—including mind and consciousness—is made of atoms. Somehow, mind and consciousness must be emergent epiphenomena of the material brain, of the atoms making up the brain, and ultimately, of elementary particles. Like most physicists and scientists, I was a true believer in this. There was no room for Brahman—a ground of being other than matter—in my physicist's philosophy.

An epiphenomenal consciousness has no causal efficacy to collapse wave functions. Yet I could not give up the idea that consciousness collapses the quantum wave function. Somehow I knew that this was a key of some sort. This impasse stymied me for quite a while. Meanwhile, I was investigating the nature of consciousness directly; I was meditating and hobnobbing with mystics. A breakthrough came at last through this adventure.

I accompanied a mystic friend, Joel Morwood, to Ojai to hear the famous spiritual teacher Krishnamurti speak. After the talk, Joel and I got into a huge argument about my predicament regarding quantum measurement. I was saying, "I think I understand consciousness, but—"

Joel interrupted me: "Can consciousness be understood?"

"It certainly can," said I, with not a little physicist's arrogance. "I told you how our conscious observation, consciousness, collapses the quantum wave—" I was going to tell him that I knew that this was the key to understanding consciousness, but Joel interrupted me again.

"So is the brain of the observer prior to consciousness, or is consciousness prior to the brain?"

I could see Joel's trap. "I am talking about consciousness as the subject of experiences."

"Consciousness is prior to experiences. It is without an object and without a subject," said Joel.

"Sure, that's vintage mysticism, but in my language you are talking about some nonlocal aspect of consciousness."

But Joel was not to be intimidated by my quantum jargon. "Your scientific blinders keep you from understanding. Underneath, you believe that consciousness can be understood by science, that consciousness emerges in the brain, that it is an epiphenomenon. Comprehend what the mystics are saying. Consciousness is prior and unconditioned. It is all there is. There is nothing but God."

That last sentence somehow triggered a turnabout in my thinking. I suddenly realized that consciousness *is* the ground of all being, what the Upanishadic *rishis*, or seers, had called Brahman. If consciousness is the ground of all being, then matter exists as possibilities within consciousness. And consciousness chooses among the available possibilities by recognizing a particular one for a particular event.

When you look at a gestalt picture of double meaning, such as the famous drawing of a vase that can also be seen as two face profiles (fig. 4), you see only one aspect at a time. But you do nothing to the lines of the drawing when you see the other aspect. The possibility is already there; you are just recognizing it.

To avoid dualism we must turn materialist metaphysics on its head. Matter is not the ground of being, as Feynman asserted. Nor is it the only source of causality in the world. Sure, material interactions among the elementary particles determine all the material possibilities and their probabilities under a given dynamic situation calculable by quantum mechanics—this is upward causation and continuous change. But we have in addition downward causation as consciousness collapses the possibility wave into an actual event. This is discontinuous change.

Our looking changes things. The artist René Magritte saw a beautiful cake displayed in a store window and went inside to buy it. When the shopkeeper proceeded to bring the cake out of the display case, Magritte objected. "I don't want that cake; give me an identical one from your backroom," he demanded. The shopkeeper was surprised. "They are all from the same batch I made this morning," he protested. "You don't understand," said Magritte. "People have been looking at the one in the display case."

My intuition that quantum measurement is the key to understanding consciousness was right. But such understanding requires discontinuous creative leaps that defy conventional wisdom. Making these leaps became my next preoccupation.

Fig. 4. The reversible goblet, introduced by Edgar Rubin in 1925, is still a favorite demonstration of figure/ground reversal. Either a goblet or a pair of silhouetted faces is seen.

We Are That: Self-Reference

Quantum superpositions of possibilities (packets of possibility waves related by phase) occur within consciousness. When consciousness recognizes a particular possibility, it chooses it; the recognized possibility becomes actuality. But that actuality is revealed within an experience, and experience introduces an implicit division of subject and object—a duality. How does this duality arise? Is dualism back again? To avoid dualism, we must answer the question: How does the one undivided consciousness with its possibilities become divided into an experiencing subject and an experienced object?

The *rishi*s of the Upanishads were truly great in both their realization of the truth and in their expression of it. Among the great sentences in the Upanishads, the greatest, the most intriguing, is the statement "you are That"—*tat tvam asi*.

If we are That—the unlimited—then why do we feel so limited? If we are That, the whole, then why do we feel separate from the objects of our experience? How does the one whole become many? As the mystic-philosopher Shankara emphasized, the answer of Vedanta, the monistic idealism sourced in the Upanishads, is that the whole becomes divided through the action of maya, the force of illusion. The unlimited experiences itself as limited, as separate, only because of a misunderstanding. But how does maya work, how does the misunderstanding arise? Here the Upanishads, Shankara, and everyone else are silent.

Can resolving the quantum-measurement paradox with Upanishadic ideas about consciousness solve this puzzle that baffled even Shankara?

Let's look at the problem from the perspective of Western idealist philosophers. George Berkeley created havoc among the realists of his time by proposing the tenets of idealism, the view that ideas are what is real. Since all information about material objects comes through our sensations and our ideas about them, it is impossible to refute idealism. But after much pondering, the realists asked Berkeley the question: If a tree falls in the forest but nobody is there to hear it, is there a sound? Now Berkeley was confounded. After a little thought, though, he came up with a solution: God is still there in the forest! The sound is there because of God's mind.

This, of course, is dualism. This is how the West traditionally thinks of consciousness. God's mind is separate from our mind; God is separate from us. If Berkeley was right, then quantum mechanics and its wonderful technology based on the propagation of waves of possibility could not be true, because "God is always in the quad." Whenever possibilities arose and began to spread, God would observe and collapse them to actualities. The material world would be reduced to a Newtonian deterministic one.

But quantum mechanics is true, and deviation from determinism is ample. Why? The collapse of the quantum wave function requires an embodied sentient being—a human observer, for example. Consciousness collapses the quantum wave function by choosing actuality from the superposition of possibilities, but only in the presence of brain-mind awareness. In this context, think of awareness as the field of experience.

In other words, we must distinguish between consciousness (God, the ground of being, the whole) and awareness (a subject-object split, implying an individual sentient being). When possibility waves move about in the brain without collapse, consciousness is present (it is the ground of being; where would it go?) but not awareness. This condition is what in psychology, following Freud, we call the unconscious—an interesting misnomer. Only with awareness is there collapse.

But there is a paradox here. Awareness is necessary for collapse, we are saying, but awareness implies a subject-object split. How can such a split—itself a manifestation of awareness—arise without a prior collapse?

The answer is that the split occurs through dependent co-arising. The subject (let's call it the quantum self) that chooses and causes the collapse co-arises dependently with the objects of awareness. Yet since this is only an apparent split, there is no ultimate dualism. The unlimited consciousness from which both subject and object arise identifies with the subject "pole" of the experiential duality, thus mistaking itself to be separate from the objects of experience. This mistaken identity is responsible for the subject-object world of our experience. Experience itself could not exist without this "mistake."

So Shankara was right about the world of separation arising from a mistake, from maya. And Buddhist philosophy, with its postulate of dependent co-arising, *paticca samuppada,* is even more clear about the origin of our self-reference, our ability to see ourselves as separate from the objects we see. But how does dependent co-arising happen? Some recent work in artificial intelligence theory about logical paradoxes in language, specifically, about self-referential sentences, gives us a clue (Hofstadter 1980).

Consider the sentence, "I am a liar." A little thought makes it clear that the sentence is talking about itself. In an ordinary sentence, the predicate simply defines the subject. But in this sentence, the subject then redefines the predicate, the predicate redefines the subject, and so on: if I am truly a liar, then I am telling the truth, in which case I am a liar, and so on, ad infinitum. Their hierarchy oscillates from one to the other endlessly. This is called a tangled hierarchy. Once we enter a tangled-hierarchical oscillation, we cannot escape it. The sentence is self-referential, unique among sentences of discourse.

How do self-reference and dependent co-arising take place in the brain? By means of a tangled hierarchy that takes place there. Von Neumann saw an infinite chain in the quantum measurement problem. We can try to measure a quantum possibility wave with a measuring-aid apparatus. But the measuring-aid apparatus itself is a quantum object; it, too, becomes a wave of possibility. We can imagine an infinite number of apparatuses, each "measuring" the previous one in the chain, but all become a jumble of quantum possibility that cannot collapse of itself. The von Neumann chain is infinite, and like the infinitely oscillating liar's sentence, represents a tangled hierarchy. The brain manages to simulate the infinity of the von Neumann chain for quantum measurements within it, and our self-reference arises from these tangled-hierarchical quantum measurements. The details will be further explained in chapter 7 (see also Goswami 1993).

Can we escape self-referential separation from the wholeness of consciousness once we have identified with the subject "pole" of an experience? Can we solve the liar's paradox and escape the self-referential sentence? The self-reference is not real; it is merely an appearance and baffles us only as long as we choose to go along with the appearance. If a door-to-door salesman offers you a double-bind pitch—"I have excellent merchandise for you, cash or charge?"—you know you can slam the door in his face (Oshins and McGoveran 1980). Similarly, at any moment we can escape by jumping out of the system of the sentence.

Likewise, the subject-object split is only appearance, the result of maya, an epiphenomenon; all the causal power of the quantum self resides in consciousness itself. If we don't identify with the subject of the subject-object split, then we can escape maya. This consciousness is what Indian spirituality refers to as *turiya*—consciousness in its suchness. There is no truly equivalent word in English (*gnosis* comes close). The American mystic Franklin Merrell-Wolff has coined the term *introception* to denote consciousness without an object (and so without a subject).

Beyond the darkness of ignorance, of mistakenness, is the clear light of consciousness. In turiya, there is wisdom of pure conscious-ness (*jnanam* in Sanskrit). This wisdom is also absolute truth (*satyam* in Sanskrit) and it is infinite (*anantam* in Sanskrit). Mystics all over the world bear witness to the same truth (see also chapter 7).

Consciousness Is One

If measurement, or collapse, is precipitated by the choice of the ob-server, the question then arises: In the case of two simultaneous measurements by two separate observers, whose choice counts? Sup-pose a traffic light is triggered to change with a quantum device—for example, with the decay of a radioactive atom. You and your friend approach the light from perpendicular directions, and being busy people, both choose green. Whose choice prevails?

This paradox is called the paradox of Wigner's friend because Eugene Wigner, a Nobel laureate, recognized it. Wigner formulated the paradox in a slightly different way. Suppose Wigner sets up a quan-tum experiment with an ambiguous result, but instead of looking at the result himself, sends a friend to look. Will the possibility wave of the quantum experiment collapse when the friend looks? Or will Wigner's friend remain in suspended animation until Wigner asks about the result? In other words, who gets to choose, Wigner or his friend (Wigner 1967)?

In the case of simultaneous measurements, we cannot say that both observers get to choose because that would obviously cause pan-demonium. But what criterion can help us figure out which observer chooses? In the philosophy called solipsism, I am the only conscious observer and everybody else is a figment of my imagination because I see them only through internal images that only I can see. If the world were solipsistic, I or you or any other experimenter would be the only legitimate observer, and the paradox of Wigner's friend would not arise. That is, Wigner's friend would not be conscious to count his choice. So unless we agree to use solipsism as a criterion, there seems to be a paradox. But who will go along with solipsism—even though within conventional Western philosophy solipsism cannot be refuted?

There is, however, another way to resolve the paradox of Wigner's friend. Suppose the consciousness that recognizes, chooses, and collapses the quantum possibility wave is unitive, that behind our apparent individuality and separateness there is one transcendent unity that is consciousness. This monistic idealist resolution has been proposed independently by me, by Australian physicist Ludwig Bass, and by Rutgers physicist Casey Blood (Bass 1971; Blood 1993).

The paradox of Wigner's friend arises because of a giant misunderstanding about consciousness. Wigner assumes that consciousness is individual, that consciousness is something we possess, that we have consciousness like we have a brain. But instead, consciousness has us.

We are entities with brains in which self-referential quantum measurement takes place, making memory. When a stimulus is encountered for the first time, there is no previous memory of it; consciousness chooses freely from the available quantum possibilities permitted by the quantum dynamics in the brain. I call this event primary awareness. Subsequent acts of quantum measurement of similar stimuli will be reflected in the mirror of previous memory, the previous choice. Revisiting a memory reinforces it, and the result of repeated reinforcement is conditioning.

Memory produces an internal stimulus, the brain responds with a quantum superposition of possibilities, and consciousness collapses one of the possibilities to actuality, giving us a secondary-awareness experience. Notice that now the choice among these possibilities is not free but is conditioned in favor of the previous response (Mitchell and Goswami 1992). The probability mathematics of the possibility waves of conditioned quantum systems is modified in this way, a modification I call quantum memory. It is this conditioning that produces the particular confluence of tendencies that shape our personal identity—that and the personal history that goes with our memory. Consciousness, collapsing a conditioned outcome, identifies with the conditioned habits and history to produce the false impression of individuality.

So mystics and spiritual teachers have been right all along. We choose, but not in our ordinary state of ego consciousness; instead, we choose in the nonordinary state of one consciousness. This is what spiritual traditions mean when they say that all is God's will, not individual will. However, this does not mean that when God identifies with an individual, what we call the ego, God has no free will left (see later in this chapter).

The Tale of Two Selves: Unity and Separateness

In one of the Upanishads, we find an exquisite metaphor for our two-self nature: Two birds, united always and known by the same name, cling closely to the same tree. One of them eats the sweet and bitter fruits; the other looks on without eating (Nikhilananda 1964). The one that eats the sweet and bitter fruits of the world is the personal ego; it experiences itself as separate from the world and is sustained by that separateness. The witness is the universal atman, the unity within us, the quantum self, in our terminology. We identify, first of all, with the quantum self, the subject "pole" of primary awareness. Then we identify with the ego, the self of limited choice, the self of our personal history. We acquire not only the apparent separateness that enables experience but also the limited identity of an individual personality.

Our two-self nature (fig. 5) is of great consequence for our spirituality—how spirituality manifests in us and how we proceed on our spiritual journey. American psychologist Abraham Maslow and Italian psychologist Roberto Assagioli have rediscovered via clinical studies the concept of a transpersonal self beyond the behavioral ego (Maslow 1968; Assagioli 1976). This recognition of a two-level self-identity has initiated the field of transpersonal psychology.

Note that the ego and the quantum self are not a dualistic partnership; rather, they are "united always." Both are apparent identifications that consciousness takes on in the process of manifestation in a physical body and in a self-referential quantum brain. In identification with the quantum self there is unity and joy, there is freedom of choice and creativity, there is tangled hierarchy in the relationship between subject and object(s), there is two-way relationship and love. In identification with the ego there is separateness and anxiety, there is conditioning and dogmatism, there is simple hierarchy and solipsistic tyranny.

Yet the spontaneity of the quantum self is without fixity. And without the fixity of the ego, civilization is impossible. The quantum

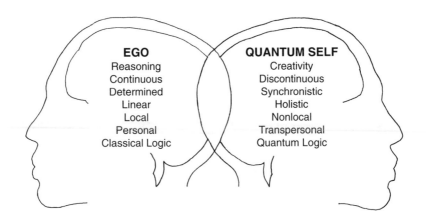

Fig. 5. The ego and the quantum self

self gives us creativity, but the ego is essential to bring the creative insight to manifestation and to augment it with reasoning. This creative process ending in manifestation provides the scaffolding for the next insight, and thus civilization can grow. The Biblical metaphor of Eden and our fall from it captures this dilemma perfectly. Adam and Eve were happy in the unity of identification with the quantum self, but they were not quite human. Chomp! Eve bit into the apple, and the journey of individual separateness, which is also the journey of civilization, began.

Intuiting that something is lacking in individualistic separateness, Christianity has viewed this fall from the perfection of Eden as original "sin." Accordingly, the spiritual journey is to first remember the unity, then to repent for the sin, and finally to return to perfection. In Hinduism, the progressive nature of the journey of separateness is captured in the concept of the four *yugas*, or ages: *satya, treta, dvapara,* and *kali*. Civilization and technology have progressed from the satya yuga to the kali yuga. Spirituality was easy during the satya yuga, but technology has brought many diversions in the present kali yuga; unity is more difficult to remember, and separateness dominates in society. The history of humanity vouches for this.

As civilization promoted separateness everywhere, science and religion also took separate courses. The separate concepts of "sacred" and "profane" also arose. The unity we become aware of as we begin the spiritual journey is experienced in awe; thus it is called sacred, in contrast to profane, worldly stuff. In Christianity, the world represents sin and our fall from grace; in Buddhism, the world is described as *dukka*, unease. Spiritual traditions seem to have a built-in prejudice against the world, not realizing that the separateness is necessary for experience and is part of the divine plan of manifestation. The lack of this understanding has caused much grief.

Modern science has exacerbated the problem by emphasizing separateness and individuality: "selfish" material pursuits make sense, and even the philosophy that there is nothing but matter makes sense. What is forgotten is that without the creativity that our unitive self brings, we could not even discover the very science we are deifying.

To say that the world is sin is to denigrate God, because the world is not outside of God, outside of consciousness; it is the play of consciousness. And to say and believe that we are nothing but matter is to stagnate within the bounds of conditioned sameness. Both approaches are polarizing, and both exclude creativity if one carries them to the extreme. This is why exoteric religions sometimes become moribund; without creativity, the return to wholeness is impossible. This is why scientism, science as religion, is not science; it is against the creative thrust of science. An integration of science and spirituality can happen when we fully understand that neither of these positions is tenable, neither is complete, neither enables creativity.

The creative process has four stages: preparation (learning what is known), incubation (unconscious processing of possibilities), insight (a discontinuous "ah-ha!" experience), and manifestation (expressed as a product). Whereas the first and last are primarily ego-based processes, the middle two—unconscious processing and the ah-ha insight—may be recognized as quantum. Unconscious processing occurs by the proliferation of quantum superpositions of possibility—there is processing but no collapse and no awareness. The discontinuous creative insight is the recognition/collapse of the new; here the quantum self is the main actor. But preparation and manifestation require the ego-identity as well as the quantum self-identity; in fact all the stages of creativity do. Creativity is the encounter of the ego and the quantum self—depicted perfectly by Michelangelo on the ceiling of the Sistine Chapel as God and Adam reaching out to each other (May 1976; Goswami 1996, 1999).

Creativity and Conditioning

Esoteric traditions recognize that the play of consciousness manifests as a struggle between the two forces of creativity and conditioning. Both comprise our nature. We cannot grow up to have an ego identity without creativity. As children, we are naturally creative as we discover language, mathematics, conceptual thinking, physical skills, and so forth. As our learned repertoire grows, so does our ego-identity, until as adults we have sufficient repertoire to function in our society and culture.

We develop an adult ego through alternate stages of creative spurts (quantum leaps of discovery of new contexts) and homeostatic adaptation (learning to use the new context and to assimilate it into our repertoire of contexts). This is what idealist science tells us, and this is what psychologist Jean Piaget found in his studies of child development (Piaget 1977).

Although in the ego-formative developmental stages we all participate in both creative and conditioned actions, as adults the habit patterns that make up our character can come to so dominate our self-identity that we resist any change in them. Those of us with a developed talent retain a small window of creativity in the outer arena of our field of activity; we continue to engage in the act of discovering new contexts of thought in this small area of expertise. Most societies value this outer creativity, at least to some extent. But once the ego is fully formed, once our habit patterns are fully established and we have fully identified with this pattern, is there any freedom from this ego-identity? In other words, can the ego rid itself of the ego?

The ego is a conditioned identity, but the conditioning is not 100 percent complete. The neurophysiologist Benjamin Libet has done a beautiful experiment that demonstrates the extent to which consciousness retains free will even while identifying with the ego (Libet 1985). Western philosophers cite the raising of an arm as an act demonstrating free will. Modern experiments, however, falsify this: If my brain is connected to an electroencephalogram (EEG) machine, it will record predictive electrical activity (a readiness potential) in my brain even before I am aware of freely willing to raise my arm. Where is my free will if somebody can predict my behavior by looking at a machine?

Libet added a nice twist to this. He told the subjects of his experiment to will to raise their hands and then to try to stop the action in the small time window of a few hundred milliseconds between the appearance of the EEG readiness potential and the actual raising of the arm. And the subjects were able to do so. The experiment clearly showed that even identified with our ego, we have the ability to say no to our conditioned habit patterns.

In a similar vein, imagine that you are out driving and come to a T-shaped intersection; which turn are you going to take? If your place of work is to the right, that's where you are going to end up if you are not very aware. However, if you are aware, you are free to choose the direction you desire. We have all seen how our behavior takes the most conditioned course when we are not paying attention, even though several options are evident, but if we are aware, we are free to choose the option we want.

To call this kind of freedom the ego's free will is a matter of semantics. Western culture is action-oriented, and individuality is greatly valued. Therefore it is appropriate to think in terms of the ego having the free will to say no to conditioning, or more generally, having the freedom to choose between conditioned alternatives, thus opening the door to a creative change of character—a process I call inner creativity.

But mystics know that all is God's will, that even saying no to a conditioned habit is the grace of God. (Of course, saying yes to conditioning is also the grace of God.) There is no ego; the ego is not real; it is a false identification. Intuiting this leads to inner creativity. Understanding it fully enables us to jump beyond ignorance and discover our true nature. The work of mystic Ramesh Balsekar contains a good discussion of the question of free will (as an introduction, see Balsekar 1989).

The Correspondence Principle

Quantum physics is esoteric compared to classical Newtonian physics for the simple reason that we can never see quantum objects directly; we need to amplify them with a measuring-aid apparatus (such as a cloud chamber or a Geiger counter) before we can see them. These measuring-aid apparatuses take a small microscopic signal—from a single charged electron, for example—and produce a signal large enough to view in the macro world. The measuring-aid apparatuses themselves are macro-sized. Because of their large mass, they don't quickly spread in possibility, so different observers are able to share the result of a quantum measurement. The measuring-aid apparatuses can also retain long-term memory of the measurement; it takes a long time for them to return to their original state. In other words, for all practical purposes, the behavior of the measuring-aid apparatuses is classical, and we make full use of that fact to "see" a micro quantum object.

A most important aspect of the quantum physics of matter is that in the limit of large masses, quantum behavior tends to give way to classical; for infinite masses (which are impossible to achieve), the behavior becomes exactly classical. This is called the correspondence principle: the new science corresponds to the old science in the domain where the old science is valid.

Notice that a similar correspondence principle operates in the way science within consciousness relates to material-realist science. As our conditioning grows, we become more and more entrenched in the ego, and a deterministic psychology such as behaviorism is able to predict our behavior. As we approach infinite conditioning (admittedly, a situation that never arises), behaviorism holds completely. In chapter 6 we will see that a similar correspondence principle operates in biology.

This is reassuring. The ego and material-realist science go hand in hand. The past three hundred years have produced great advances in material-realist science and have also produced enormous inflation in the state of the ego. And now, as the tide turns to quantum physics and idealist science in the ongoing saga of scientific paradigms, our ego can begin giving way to more inner creativity and spirituality.

Quantum Questions and Answers

THE IDEA for this chapter came
from talking with my friend Hugh Harrison. Hugh became intrigued
with the idea of science within consciousness when he read my book
The Self-Aware Universe (1993)—so intrigued that he signed up for a
reading course with me at the University of Oregon. For many months
he and I spent an hour a week discussing the subtleties of quantum
physics.

Not surprisingly, Hugh's questions were often very basic; for
example, what is an electron source? They reflected how foreign some
of the routine concepts in modern physics are to the nonscientist.
Questions and answers about these concepts form a substantial part
(the first section) of this chapter. If you already are a connoisseur of
the quantum, skip this section.

In connection with developing the new science, I travel a lot giving
talks and workshops, and I love fielding questions from the audience.
These questions are often metaphysical, and also sociopolitical; for
example, how many other scientists support your theory? I decided to

supplement Hugh's kind of questions with this other kind since the reader may have some of the same questions. These sociopolitical questions ultimately go to the heart of one genuine concern that we all share: Given what we have today—a good beginning for a new paradigm in which science and spirituality are integrated—how long is it going to take to free our minds from the familiar materialist perspective and turn to the new paradigm in our thinking?

I have rounded out the chapter with a set of questions and answers on the role of the brain.

Basic Quantum Questions

Q: What is the difference between a regular wave and a wave of possibility?

A: Waves are periodic disturbances that may either travel (a traveling wave) or do their waving in one place (a standing wave). A regular wave—for example, a traveling water wave—does its waving in manifest space and time; you can see the disturbance, the displacement of the water from the level position changing with time, the crest lines progressing, and so forth. In contrast, a quantum wave of possibility cannot be seen in manifestation. Our attempt to see the wave collapses it to a particle, so to speak.

Q: Please give an example of a wave of possibility.

A: Consider an electron that is free to move in space. In a matter of seconds, the wave of that electron can spread all over town just as the water wave expands, but in possibility only. To be sure, the probability is high for the electron to arrive at some places and low for it to appear at some other places. In fact, these probabilities (which the mathematical machinery of quantum mechanics calculates) form a distribution, a bell curve (see fig. 2a in chapter 2).

Q: What is a standing wave?

A: Actually, you are quite familiar with standing waves. The musical notes that you hear from a guitar begin as standing waves; if you watch the string, it vibrates, waving while standing in place (fig. 6).

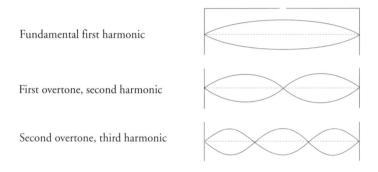

Fundamental first harmonic

First overtone, second harmonic

Second overtone, third harmonic

Fig. 6. Standing waves on a guitar string

Q: Please give an example of a standing wave of possibility.

A: Consider the possibility wave of an electron in the lowest energy state (the ground state) in an hydrogen atom. Since an atom confines the electron, the electron is described by a standing wave of possibility. In the Newtonian physics you were taught in school, the electron is supposed to orbit around the proton. In the new view, you can picture the electron wavelength waving around the orbit once (fig. 7a). But the difference between the classical and quantum pictures is astounding. In the quantum picture, the electron forms a probability distribution;

the orbit just describes the places where the electron is most likely to appear. Again, by making many measurements, we find that the quantum picture agrees with experimental data (fig. 7b).

a)

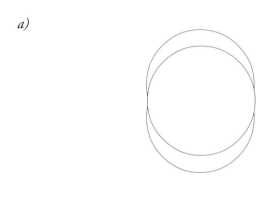

b)

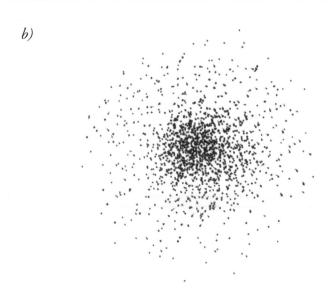

Fig. 7. (a) The standing wave of an electron in the ground state of a hydrogen atom; (b) experiments reveal the electron's probability distribution.

Q: You say a measurement collapses the wave into a particle, and so the quantum object is always found in one place, not spread all over. Then how do you know that there was a wave of possibility before the measurement?

A: When we make a large number of measurements of electrons in identical situations, we find the electrons appearing at all the different places predicted by quantum mechanics following the bell-curve distribution. This is the more general answer to this question: theory checks with experiment, so we trust the theory, which says that the electron is a wave of possibility before we see it.

In some situations we can tell that the electron has a wave nature even without going through the trouble of studying the entire distribution. For example, take the double-slit experiment (see chapter 2). The very fact that electrons appear on the fluorescent plate at places other than directly behind the slits gives away the electron's underlying wave nature.

Q: Speaking of the double-slit experiment, what constitutes an electron source?

A: Electrons are all around us. They are constituents of the atoms that form the bulk of the matter on earth. They are particularly available in metals, where some are free to move around inside the entire metal. To get free electrons from a metal, we shine light upon it, giving us photoelectrons. Burglar alarms run on this principle. You can also free electrons from their metallic bondage by heating the metal. If you have ever seen a thermionic tube, it works on this principle.

Q: Let's go back to the double-slit experiment for a moment. Why can't the electron collapse its own possibility wave?

A: Myriad experiments have verified that the electron's average behavior is completely determined by quantum mechanics. Does a single electron in a single event exhibit free will in its choice of actuality from possibility? In the early days, even Niels Bohr pondered the question of an electron's free will. Hardly any physicist today would go along with that kind of idea. But it is ultimately an experimental question, and it is probably ruled out experimentally (see Herbert 1993).

Q: Why can't we say that the fluorescent plate measures the electrons and by doing so collapses the electron's possibility wave?

A: That would contradict quantum mechanics, according to which even the fluorescent plate must be described as a possibility wave. The collapser must be outside the jurisdiction of quantum mechanics altogether.

Q: I have difficulty accepting that the results of the double-slit experiment on the fluorescent plate remain in the limbo of possibility until I decide to look.

A: Consider one electron at a time. Each electron can appear in one of the bright fringes (with somewhat varying probabilities). The fluorescent plate amplifies the electron signal at each possible position; this is its job. The total wave of possibility now comprises the superposition of each of these possible electrons amplified by the fluorescent plate to a possible signal. But when we look, only one of these possible signals becomes manifest; that's where we spot the electron.

Notice that the measurement automatically collapses all things that are correlated with the event. For example, the lighted spot is part of a whole plate. Notice also that a measurement-aid apparatus has a second job: Because of its bulk, its possibility wave expands rather sluggishly, so several observers can share the results of the same measurement.

Q: Is that why some books call it a classical measurement apparatus?

A: Yes. The near-classical description of the measurement-aid apparatus guarantees a shared reality for all of us.

Q: Why is the electron's wave called a coherent superposition?

A: Waves in general are superpositions of simple waves, which are known as sine waves. When you hear a musical note on a guitar string, you are hearing a superposition of several simple notes (fig. 8). A music synthesizer makes music by making superpositions of simple wave forms.

Note also that when we add waves, we must add them algebraically, taking into account not only the magnitudes of the wave disturbance but also the phases. It's the same with electron possibility waves. The various simple waves in the superposition have phase relationships with one another.

Fig. 8. The superposition of sine waves

Q: I still don't understand. Give me an example of a phase-coherent versus a phase-incoherent situation.

A: Consider the dancers in a chorus line; that's phase coherence (fig. 9a). But watch an ordinary dance floor late at night, especially when people have been drinking: you will know what phase incoherence is like (fig. 9b).

Fig. 9. (a) Phase coherence: coherent laser light is like a chorus line of dancers; (b) phase incoherence: ordinary, incoherent light is like dancers dancing out of step.

Q: Quantum physicists often say that all things in the world are interconnected because of their quantum nature. Is this interconnection what you call consciousness?

A: It is an overstatement to say that all things are interconnected in quantum mechanics. If that were true in any substantial way, we could not do any calculation in quantum mechanics without involving all the objects in the universe. The correct statement is that all things are potentially interconnected. As waves, quantum objects spread in possibility; so if we wait a while, there will be overlap—interconnection. And for macro objects the spreading is very slow, so interconnection in this sense would take a long time.

In science within consciousness, the interconnection occurs via consciousness. Consciousness, via intention, can correlate two objects, two brains, and collapse similar actualities in both. There is now experimental evidence of interconnection that supports this view, thanks to the work of Mexican neurophysiologist Jacobo Grinberg-Zylberbaum and his collaborators.

In this experiment, two subjects become correlated by meditating together with the intention of establishing direct communication. After being instructed to maintain direct communication, they are separated, put in electromagnetically insulated chambers, and wired up to separate electroencephalogram (EEG) machines. When one of them sees a series of light flashes, which produces an evoked potential in his brain's EEG, a transferred potential similar in phase and strength to the evoked potential is found in the other subject's EEG as well (fig. 10a). Control subjects, however, do not show a transferred potential (fig. 10b). The conclusion is straightforward: consciousness collapses similar states of actualities in both brains because the brains are correlated via conscious intention (Grinberg-Zylberbaum et al. 1994).

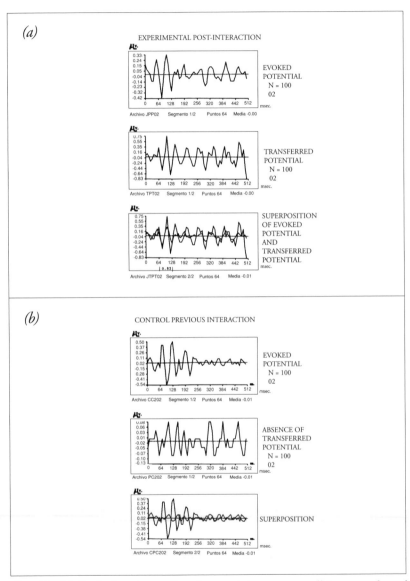

Fig. 10. (a) Evoked and transferred potential compare well in strength and even in phase (bottom) when analyzed by computer; (b) control subjects do not show a transferred potential (note scale of the y-axis when comparing the potentials of the two subjects).

Q: There is that word again, *correlation.* What does that mean?

A: Correlation between two objects means correlation in their phases of movement, the particular condition of their waving. Phase coherence—the example of the chorus line—is an instance of correlation. You can think of correlation also as phase entanglement.

Q: How do uncorrelated electrons behave?

A: Uncorrelated electrons can be regarded as separate and independent. Their possibility waves are not phase-related with any other possibility waves. When you collapse their waves, they are individual collapses that do not affect anything else in the universe. After correlated electrons are collapsed, they become uncorrelated.

Q: How long do electrons remain correlated?

A: There are two ways to affect the relationship of correlated electrons: If the two electrons interact with a third object, their special relationship expands to a correlated relationship involving the three objects. But if you want to wipe out quantum correlated behavior completely, you have to collapse the possibility wave of the correlated electrons by measuring them. Subsequently, the electrons will be uncorrelated.

Metaphysical and Sociopolitical Questions

Q: Your whole approach depends on consciousness. What is consciousness? Can you define it?

A: You have to be careful here. Consciousness is the ground of being; it is the one and only, the absolute. Definitions are possible in terms of other concepts only, but all concepts are secondary to consciousness. This inability to be defined is sometimes expressed in statements such as "The Tao that can be expressed is not the absolute Tao."

But don't despair. The mystics of the world refuse to define consciousness, but they tell us how to investigate it, how to know it in its suchness. It's a little like trying to understand music with words; a wordy definition is quite inadequate, but a teacher can show you the piano and teach you how to play it.

Q: How do you prove experimentally that consciousness transcends matter?

A: If you take your own experience as data, it is easy. Your free will (such as in a creative act or an act involving a moral decision) is downward causation on matter (the brain) and proves the transcendence of consciousness. Experimental proof is also now available, thanks to Grinberg-Zylberbaum's experiment. Only a transcendent, nonlocal consciousness can maintain correlation in two brains that have been separated by distance and collapse similar actualities in them.

Q: Has anyone replicated Grinberg-Zylberbaum's experiment?

A: In England neuropsychiatrist Peter Fenwick has replicated it, as reported in a preprint. Besides, there is now some additional data about interconnectivity that can be properly explained only with a model of transcendent consciousness. It has been discovered that when many people focus on a single event such as a football game or the O. J. Simpson trial, they may become correlated. This correlation produces a measurable anomalous behavior. Researchers simultaneously studied random number generators (based on radioactive decays) and found that their behavior turns positively nonrandom in the presence of such correlation (Radin and Rebman 1996). But what is producing the correlation at a distance and maintaining it through the entire duration of the measurement? At present, there is only one agency known to be capable of this: transcendent, nonlocal consciousness.

Q: I agree that it is important to study consciousness, but do I need quantum mechanics to do it?

A: The physicist Henry Stapp showed in a paper that classical deterministic physics can deal with consciousness only in one of two ways (Stapp 1995). The first is epiphenomenalism—consciousness is a causally impotent epiphenomenon. The second is dualism—matter is governed by the laws of physics, and mind and consciousness belong to a different world. This is, of course, Cartesian thinking, but as Daniel Dennett has pointed out, this dualistic picture lurks as a hidden assumption in the work of many cognitive scientists and artificial-intelligence researchers (Dennett 1991). Dennett's own answer is operationalism, which basically means forget metaphysics, forget the question! This is obviously not satisfactory. Many holistic thinkers, the physicist Paul Davies for example, recognize that consciousness is the missing causal organizing principle in today's science (Davies 1989). But how to go beyond dualism stymies the holist. How to find an explanation of the subject-object split without dualism is now called the "hard" question in fashionable circles of philosophy (Chalmers 1995). Quantum mechanics offers genuine scope, so far the only scope, for answering the hard question—the quantum visionary window.

Q: How are you so sure that recognizing consciousness as the ground of being is the answer to the hard question?

A: Once I recognized consciousness as the ground of all being and saw that one can build a science on that metaphysical basis, I had no need for philosophical speculation. My secret hypothesis is that the spiritual literature of the world contains a great amount of insight and empirical data regarding the nature of consciousness and its manifestation. But it is hard to see the validity of these insights and data until you delve into spirituality yourself. I use the mystical literature of the world along with personal practice to guide my consciousness research. So far, this approach has not failed me.

Q: Is the idealist interpretation of quantum mechanics your own brain child, or are there other scientists who have contributed to it?

A: As I mentioned earlier, the quantum window was opened by none other than the great mathematician John von Neumann. Perhaps that opening was only a crack. I have helped to open the window wide.

There are many physicists who have independently reached some of the same conclusions as mine. Fred Wolf coined the phrase, "we create our own reality." Casey Blood and Ludwig Bass discovered independently the one-consciousness resolution to the paradox of Wigner's friend (Bass 1971; Blood 1993). In his 1986 book, *Quantum Reality*, Nick Herbert recognized von Neumann's interpretation as one of eight viable pictures of reality (Herbert 1986). And in 1993, Herbert published another book, *Elemental Mind*, in which he asserts (although not in as clear terms as one would like) the primacy of consciousness (Herbert 1993). Berkeley physicist Henry Stapp comes perhaps the closest to my work. Still, he hesitates to endorse the mystical position on the nature of consciousness, hanging on to William James's ideas, instead (Stapp 1993).

Q: Why aren't more scientists bothered by the Aspect experiment, which proves quantum nonlocality? Perhaps if they were, they could see the cogency of the idea of transcendent consciousness more clearly.

A: A 1984 issue of *Physics Today* quoted what one physicist told another in the corridors of a physical society meeting: "Anybody who is not bothered by Bell's theorem (the detailed theory behind Aspect's experiment) has to have rocks in his head." So scientists *are* bothered. But as people, we have an infinite capacity to delude ourselves; scientists are no exception. The quantum window is a huge invitation to the real freedom that consciousness offers us. It is also very scary. Once you see consciousness as the ground of all being, it is hard to carry on the often meaningless, materialist research programs that form the bulk of the academic, governmental, and industrial research. Do you see the problem?

Q: Earlier in history, Christian philosophers sought the signature of the divine in the remarkable order we find in living nature. This they attributed to the exquisite design of a grand watchmaker. But their watchmaker turned out to be blind because, as Darwin's theory clearly shows, life evolves as a matter of chance and necessity. Similarly, is it possible that your one consciousness and real freedom can also be explained in terms of blind chance?

A: Don't be so sure that Darwin had the final word on how life evolves. On the contrary, I believe that consciousness plays a crucial role in biological evolution (see chapter 6). The new theory not only rescues evolution theory from recent controversy but also gives us a satisfactory definition of what life is.

Here is the thing. When you look at all the different puzzles and paradoxes of ordinary science and find that idealist science answers them all, at least qualitatively, your perspective changes. However, to see the power of the new consciousness-based science, scientists have to delve into all the anomalies of their current belief systems—not piecemeal but comprehensively, Unfortunately, very few people today are willing to develop the interdisciplinary breadth required for such a task. This is a major hindrance.

Q: It is still hard to believe that all our free will resides in the collapse of the quantum wave function.

A: Ken Wilber recently compiled a fairly inclusive list of the different tracks people are pursuing in consciousness research. Included are cognitive science, neurophysiology, introspectionism, individual psychotherapy, social psychology, clinical psychiatry, developmental psychology, psychosomatic medicine, nonordinary states of consciousness, Eastern and contemplative traditions, quantum consciousness, and subtle-energies research (Wilber 1996a). Some of these tracks—such as cognitive science, neurophysiology, and clinical psychiatry—are based on the old Newtonian paradigm. Others—such as psychosomatic medicine, nonordinary states of consciousness, and subtle-energies research—call for a consciousness-based paradigm. Whichever theory integrates all these disparate views must have a correspondence principle. The quantum approach—positing that the collapse of the quantum wave function is an act of free-willing consciousness—integrates all these disparate approaches precisely because it has a correspondence principle built into the paradigm from the get-go.

Q: You mention anomalies in today's science. The biggest anomaly, of course, is extrasensory perception (ESP). But many scientists say that the data need not be taken seriously since they are not strictly replicable. What is your answer to that criticism?

A: What criteria we use to evaluate data depends on the phenomena we study. So long as the phenomena studied were classical phenomena, the criteria of strong objectivity (reality is independent of the observer) and strict replicability made sense. But with quantum physics, we had to give up strong objectivity in favor of a weak objectivity, which says that reality is independent not of any observer, but only of a specific observer (see also d'Espagnat 1983). In other words, under weak objectivity whatever data we get should on the average be consistent from one observer to another. Well-conducted ESP experiments pass this criterion with flying colors. Importantly, an ordinary quantum experiment, such as detection of a radioactive decay event, is not strictly replicable and also passes the criterion of weak objectivity but not of strong objectivity.

About the Brain

Q: Aren't you implicitly assuming that the brain is a quantum device at the macro level? While quantum uncertainty and the play of possibility prevail at the micro level, at the macro level quantum behavior tends to give way to classical. Macro quantum behavior is present only in special situations like lasers, superconductors, and superfluid.

Furthermore, the brain operates at room temperature, which makes it hard to set up quantum coherence because of thermal noise. Isn't it true that on that basis alone, there is doubt that the brain can display macroscopic quantum behavior? Isn't this a major weak point of the theory?

A: There is a class of theories that propose that the brain is macro quantum and that all the wonderful things about ourselves and consciousness come from the quantum nature of the brain—for example, the quantum self (see, for example, Zohar 1990). The present theory is different—more fundamental and much less conjectural. The present theory asserts only that quantum measurement taking place in the brain is hierarchically tangled and therefore self-referential. Nobody denies that the processing of a stimulus in the brain involves quantum processes at the micro level. The present theory asserts that the amplification of micro to macro, via which the brain presents a superposition of macroscopically distinguishable possibilities for consciousness to choose from, is hierarchically tangled. This is to be compared with the Geiger counter, which also amplifies an incoming signal, but the amplification is not hierarchically tangled. Why is the brain special? This is not that hard to see; the argument is given in chapter 7.

Q: If the brain presents macroscopically distinguishable possibilities to choose from, shouldn't this be verifiable experimentally?

A: Indeed. Such verification may already exist. The psychologist Tony Marcel did an experiment two decades ago that is very hard to explain with computer models of the brain, but when interpreted with the quantum-within-consciousness model, provides solid evidence for quantum superpositions in the brain at the macro level (Marcel 1980).

Here's a quick review of the Marcel experiment: Marcel asked subjects to look at strings of three words, the middle word of which was ambiguous in meaning. He left a time gap between words and measured the recognition time for the last word of the string. The strings were sometimes congruent, such as *hand-palm-wrist*, and sometimes incongruent, such as *tree-palm-wrist*. Clearly, we'd expect that in the congruent case, the priming word *hand* would precipitate the "hand" meaning of the ambiguous word *palm*, and that would facilitate the recognition of *wrist*. The opposite should happen in the incongruent case. So with a 600-millisecond time gap between words, Marcel measured the recognition time to be 499 milliseconds for the congruent case and 547 milliseconds for the incongruent case. Everything seemed to check out.

Unexpected results arose, however, when the middle word was masked by a superimposed pattern. Now measurements no longer distinguished between the congruent and incongruent cases. The recognition time for the final word was virtually identical for both: 511 milliseconds for the congruent case as opposed to 520 milliseconds for the incongruent.

What does pattern masking accomplish? With pattern masking the word is no longer visible for ordinary subject-object-split cognition, but experiments suggest that perception still occurs, though unconsciously. In other words, there is perception, but without awareness. Such phenomena have been an exciting part of psychological research since the seventies, when a cortically blind man was found to be able to avoid obstacles in his path 100 percent of the time but always denied that he saw anything (Humphrey 1972). Such "blind sight" is now explained as unconscious perception through colicullar vision. Similarly, if a picture of a bee is flashed too quickly before a subject's eyes, the subject denies seeing anything discernible, but an association test evokes words like *sting* and *honey* from her, indicating that perception occurred. She sees, but unconsciously. Pattern masking is another way to ensure unconscious perception.

With computer models of the brain it is very difficult—I think logically impossible—to distinguish between conscious and unconscious perception. But you already know the distinction according to the quantum model: in unconscious perception there is no awareness; thus the brain's possibility wave does not collapse. In our example this means that when the word *palm* is masked, both the "hand" meaning and the "tree" meaning are equally accessed in the congruent and the incongruent cases, making the recognition times virtually the same. However, the recognition time is now intermediate between the times for the congruent and incongruent cases, because the middle word takes on the "hand" meaning only half the time.

In summary, the experiment strongly suggests that when the brain sees an ambiguous word like *palm*, the brain becomes a superposition of two macroscopically distinguishable possibilities, one corresponding to the "tree" meaning, the other corresponding to the "hand" meaning (see McCarthy and Goswami [1993] for more on this subject).

Q: Are there other ways to verify whether the brain goes into a superposition of macro quantum possibilities in response to stimuli?

A: Absolutely. The quantum nature of objects can be tested empirically by finding evidence for (1) coherent superpositions of possibilities, which we have just discussed; (2) discontinuity; and (3) nonlocality. As already pointed out, there is now quite an accumulation of data on nonlocality in the brain's behavior, including that of transferred potentials. The data on quantum discontinuity comes from our creativity, which is the subject of part III.

Part II

The New Cosmology

CHAPTER FIVE

Reconciling Scientific and Spiritual Cosmologies

OSMOLOGY is the logos of the cosmos—the theory of how the entire manifest world came about. All religions tell more or less the same story: in essence, God created the world. For a long time, science followed the same story line as far as the creation of the universe was concerned. But difficult questions gradually accumulated. If God is the creator, is he a separate agent? We already know that dualism is not allowed by the laws of science.

In the West, where modern science developed, an unofficial truce was formed and the territories were divided. Theologians invoked story lines with God, angels, and such to support morality, the idea of an afterlife, and similar matters. Scientists sought descriptions of the world of space, time, matter, and motion that did not require God or any other supernatural agency.

But the truce hasn't held very well. First, science kept enlarging the boundaries covered by its stories. According to the Judeo-Christian religions, God created both the world and humanity. Newton and

LaPlace challenged the first doctrine, and as if that wasn't enough, Darwin challenged the second in favor of a theory of evolution that gave no role to God. We humans have evolved from animals, animals from plants, and plants from one-celled prokaryotes, said Darwin; God is superfluous.

But more recently religions have struck back. Big holes have shown up in science's answers to such cosmological questions as: Who created the world? Who created humanity? Scientists have calculated that the universe was created at a finite moment of time in one big bang about fifteen billion years ago. But the problem with the idea of a singular moment of creation is that it represents an actual singularity in the otherwise smooth, mathematical description of the cosmos that Einstein gave us. The laws of physics break down for this singularity. This hole in science's cosmological story line constitutes what theologians could hail as the signature of the divine.

There is a hole in the Darwinian story line, as well. The evidence for evolution is fossils, the remnants of living creatures of past eras. The fossil record suggests that species have a finite beginning and that many species have now become extinct. There is also evidence that some species have undergone significant change since their origin. However, there is no fossil evidence of a continuous evolution from one species to another in the way that Darwin's theory suggests. Instead, the lines of fossil evidence reveal unmistakable gaps between plants and animals, between reptiles and birds, between primates and humans.

These are serious holes in the scientific account, but the theological alternatives seem no more compelling. A new approach is needed to deal with these holes. Taken seriously, this approach will also take us to a reconciliation of antagonistic story lines. In this chapter I take on the case of the cosmological story, deferring the biological story to the next chapter.

The Quantum Cosmos and Quantum Measurement

The creativity of the world is camouflaged to a large extent by determinism; it is not a coincidence that deterministic classical physics was discovered before we had sensory access to the creativity of quantum mechanics. Macroscopic bodies at large, with their huge masses, spread (as packets of possibility waves) so slowly that we tend to see them as moving along predictable trajectories. Only very recently, with laser measurement, have we been able to verify that even macro objects are subject to Heisenberg's uncertainty principle, that their wave packets do spread. Even so, space and time, it seems, are not quantized; no one has found any solid evidence for limits to the division of space and time. Thus, the universe in bulk seems to be classical and hence determined.

The cosmology of the big bang—the theory that the universe was created in an explosion of cosmic proportions—accounts nicely for the observed expansion of the universe. In Einstein's theory of general relativity, the universe is looked upon as a three-dimensional analogue to the expanding surface of a rising loaf of raisin bread. The separation of the raisins becomes greater and greater as the bread expands; similarly, the galaxies move further and further away from one another as the space between them expands. The empirical proof of the expanding universe lies in the measurement of the recession of galaxies. The empirical proof of the big bang is its microwave relic we see today, originally emitted about a million years after the big event. This background microwave radiation bathes us from all directions and is therefore of cosmic origin. Calculations show that its frequency more or less fits the predictions based on a big-bang origin for the universal expansion.

So far so good. But there is a hitch. Consider this story: St. Augustine was preaching one day on how God created heaven and earth.

A fellow in the back asked, "Hey, Augustine, you always tell us how God created heaven and earth. But what was God doing before he created heaven and earth?" Augustine was at a loss, but only for a moment. He retorted, "God was creating hell for people like you who ask such questions!"

But the question remains. Whenever a finite moment of creation is posited, we can always ask, what was before the creation, before the big bang?

A more sophisticated way of worrying about the point of origin of the universe is to notice that in the theory of general relativity the point of origin is a mathematical singularity when the universe was infinitely dense. This means that Einstein's theory is not valid near the point of the singularity. Something else, some other theory, must replace general relativity for those early times.

Physicist Steven Hawking and others have suggested that the early universe was a quantum object—the universe began as a wave function, a superposition of many baby universes of possibility. The assumption of a quantum universe solves the problem of a beginning. The answer is simple: there is no beginning; there is only possibility. The important question then becomes how the possibility becomes actual. The universe of possibilities exists in potentia, but how does it manifest to become physical reality? In part I, I said it is measurement—observation—that collapses the wave function of an electron or any other material object. In monistic idealism, consciousness transcends physical reality. Transcendent consciousness in an observation event collapses the wave function of the universe from outside space and time.

Someone may object that consciousness only manifests in beings like us, which take time to evolve. How can consciousness observe before there is a conscious being around? A valid objection. But nobody has said that the expansion of the possibility wave of the universe and evolution of the cosmos take place only in manifest reality. Monistic idealism proposes that the universe evolves in potentia, as a superposition of possibilities, until a sentient being comes about in one of the possibility branches and, through observation, completes the self-referential loop. Actually, this view solves a knotty problem regarding small probabilities in some of the stages of cosmic evolution, such as the evolution of life. The probability for life to evolve from nonliving matter, though finite, is extremely small. But if the universe is manifest only when consciousness observes itself through the senses of the first sentient being, the problem posed by small probability is no deterrence.

But how can this be? It's hard to believe that the universe waits in potentia until a sentient being evolves on a measly little planet in one of its possibility branches and then observes. Fortunately, there is an experiment that will dissolve our incredulity; it's called the delayed-choice experiment.

The Delayed-Choice Experiment

The physicist John Wheeler first suggested the delayed-choice experiment using a beam splitter (fig. 11), which clearly demonstrates the importance of conscious choice in the shaping of quantum reality. A light beam is split into two beams of equal intensity using a half-silvered mirror M_1; these two beams are then reflected by two full-silvered mirrors (A and B) to a crossing point P. If we choose to detect the particle mode of the photons (the quanta of light), we put detectors or counters past the point of crossing P, as shown in the lower left frame in figure 11. One or the other counter will tick, defining the localized path of the quantum light and showing its particle aspect.

To detect the wave aspect of light, we take advantage of the phenomenon of wave interference. If we put a second half-silvered mirror M_2 at P (lower right frame in figure 11), the two waves created by the beam splitting at M_1 will be forced by M_2 to interfere constructively on one side of P (where the counter will continue to tick) and destructively on the other side (where now the counter never ticks). Notice that when we are detecting the wave mode of the photons, we must agree that each photon is traveling by both routes A and B; otherwise how can there be interference?

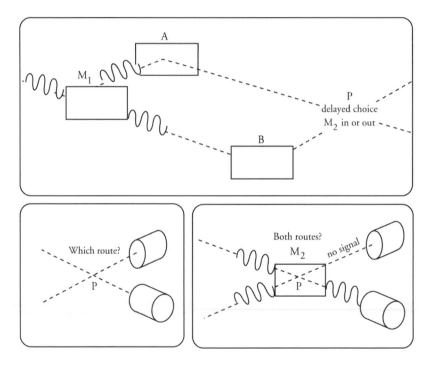

Fig. 11. The delayed-choice experiment

Now the subtlety! In the delayed-choice experiment, the experimenter decides at the very last moment—in the very last nanosecond (10^{-9} second)—whether or not to insert the half-silvered mirror at P, that is, whether or not to measure the wave aspect. In effect, this means that the photons—if you think of them as actualized "real" objects—have already traveled past the point of splitting at M_1. Even so, inserting the mirror M_2 at P always shows the wave aspect of light, and not inserting the mirror always shows its particle aspect. Was each photon moving in one path or two? The photons seem to respond to even our delayed choice instantly—and retroactively! A photon travels one path or both paths exactly in harmony with our choice. This remains a big puzzle until we realize that there is no manifest photon until we see it.

The same principle of delayed choice applies even if the object to be seen is the entire cosmos. There is no manifest cosmos—only possibilities, possible pathways of development—until a sentient being observes the universe. And with that "first" observation the entire pathway in possibility leading to the event manifests retroactively, going backward in time.

The delayed-choice experiment has been verified in the laboratory at a retraction time of a few nanoseconds (billionths of seconds) (Helmuth et al. 1986). At the cosmic scale, delayed choice can be verified at least in principle, albeit not experimentally (Wheeler 1983). There are very distant bright and compact objects in the cosmos called quasars (quasi-stellar radio sources), that are sometimes seen in duplicate. How so? We are seeing the quasar as well as its image, which is formed by the "gravitational lens" of an intervening galaxy. Gravity bends light, as in a lens. Einstein predicted this a long time ago—a prediction that has been verified in earth-based observations. The intervening galaxy can bend the light either right or left, creating two pathways, as in the delayed-choice experiment. Of course, in this case, bringing the two paths together at a point P to create the situation of that experiment is not easy, since in general, the distance traversed by light in the two paths would be widely different. But, in principle, with the facility of moving about in space with rocketships, we can always find the point P.

But now, from the vantage point of P, the arms of the apparatus are billions of light years long (yes! quasars are that far away from us). And so the retroaction time, the time of backward manifestation, is likewise billions of years—a considerable fraction of the age of the universe. In this way, we can and do affect what we suppose has gone before when we think classically; because only we, the conscious observers, can collapse a quantum possibility and create actuality.

The Strong Anthropic Principle

To sum up, we are here because of the universe, and the universe is here because of us. This idea, called the strong anthropic principle, has been popular for some time (Barrow and Tipler 1986).

In a way, we are reversing the history of science. Modern science began with Copernicus, whose model of our planet revolving around the sun can be called anti-anthropic; it robbed us of the Aristotelian notion of the earth—and thus humans on the earth—as the geographical center of the universe. Now we are back again, not as the geographical center of the universe (according to current sophisticated notions of space-time, there is no such center!) but as its spiritual center.

The strong anthropic principle explains many coincidences—why the universe is so finely tuned in very different ways. If the constant of gravity or the electrical charge of the electron were even slightly different, or if the rate of nuclear reaction of three helium nuclei that form the nucleus of carbon were not enhanced because of a resonance match (the same process that has the potential to destroy a bridge if soldiers march on it in unison), the universe would not have produced sentient beings and, in turn, would never have become manifest.

Many physicists feel apologetic for the anthropic principle; it seems to be a thorn in their side because it violates the principle of strong objectivity that they hold so dear. But the monistic idealist knows that the apparent objectivity of the universe at the macro level is a camouflage. The universe is a play of consciousness, and manifest self-reference is the opening curtain on this play.

The Creative Universe and the Origin of Life

The purpose of the universe is to manifest creatively the ideas of consciousness. For this reason, the *rishis* (sages) of the Upanishads addressed Brahman as *kavi*, poet. Manifestation is necessary for consciousness to "see" itself and its ideas. Monistic idealists imagine that these ideas exist as unmanifest archetypes until matter evolves to the point of manifesting them. The famous Platonic archetypes, such as truth, beauty, and justice, are examples; but Plato was not the only one to have this notion. The Hindus have it also. The Hindu concept of *nirguna* Brahman (Brahman without qualities) refers to undivided consciousness. Nirguna Brahman is a great silence; nothing ever happens; only unlimited possibilities exist. But there is also the concept of *saguna* Brahman (Brahman with qualities), referring to archetypes of manifestation.

In the beginning, there are possible themes—archetypal themes such as love, beauty, truth, justice, physical laws, and so on. Later, matter arises in possibility, and with it, the possibility of manifesting the themes in matter. The laws of manifestation are an important part of the theme collective. With the advent of idealist science, the laws of manifestation are becoming clear to us. Matter consists of quantum possibility waves. The themes manifest when these waves of possibility are collapsed to actuality in accordance with the laws of manifestation.

The ultimate possibility is self-consciousness, seeing oneself through manifest eyes as materially separate from the world. "We cannot escape the fact that the world we know is constructed in order (and thus in such a way as to be able) to see itself," notes the mathematician G. Spencer-Brown, "but in order to do so, evidently it must first cut itself up into at least one state which sees, and at least one other state which is seen."

In order for a subject-object split to occur, there must be a distinction between the possibility waves of micro and macro. And indeed, because of the uncertainty principle, submicroscopic matter spreads quickly in possibility; we can never lay down the trajectories of behavior that small conglomerates of submicroscopic matter will follow. But large conglomerates of submicroscopic matter display nearly classical behavior; they spread so slowly in possibility that we can assign future trajectories of behavior to them for all practical purposes (at least in principle).

The world starts its evolution as a triad of possibilities: the unchanging themes, the quantum objects that present creative opportunity by spreading rapidly in possibility, and the near-classical objects that maintain a reference point, a scaffolding, once consciousness has collapsed actuality from possibility.

Whereas the simple possibility forms—atoms and molecules—are stable, the complex conglomerates of them that make up the macromolecules of life are unstable because of their interaction with their environment. They form and break up until, via evolution, a symbiotic quantum system/measuring-aid-apparatus duo evolves that is stable and also self-referential. The first such system, a living cell, can self-organize, self-preserve, self-reproduce, and most importantly, can perceive itself as separate from its environment. The basis of these capacities is conscious choice. Quantum dynamics provides possible courses of action (bifurcations, if you will). Consciousness is the chooser; more recently, in the West, we have used the name *Gaia* for consciousness in this role of self-referentially choosing the self-organization that we call life on earth, although with a slightly different connotation.[1]

The self-referential co-arising of Gaia as the living cell and its environment manifests the possibility of life into actuality for the first time. This manifestation consists of the choice, over all other possible pathways leading only to nonlife, of the one causal pathway that leads to a self-referential quantum measurement in the living cell.

Real time is born the very moment that life manifests in the first living cell, and it retroactively flows back to the origin so that the entire causal pathway subsequently can be studied as the past. The first act of creation of the creative universe is now complete. The creative process then continues, giving us all the wonderful stages via which the evolution of life has developed on earth. I discuss the evolution of life in the next chapter.

Notes

1. The idea of Gaia was revived in modern biology by James Lovelock (1982) and Lynn Margulis (1993).

CHAPTER SIX

Bringing Consciousness into Evolution

SPIRITUAL TRADITIONS hold that
the universe is made of consciousness, created by consciousness (God),
and designed for consciousness, for its purposive, creative play. The
opposite view prevails in science. Not that long ago, the majority of
scientists believed in a rather grim view of the universe: it was created
about fifteen billion years ago from random machinations of matter as
a giant fluctuation and has been running down ever since. Entropy is
the amount of disorder in a system, and according to the entropy law
of physics entropy always increases, or at best stays the same. The universe, like any physical system, must obey the entropy law. Hence the
verdict: the universe is running down from the relative state of order
in which it was created to ever-increasing states of disorder. The universe has evolved for no purpose at all in this scenario. Galaxies, stars,
planets, even life appear on the scene as local fluctuations that are
permitted within the entropy law. But meaning? Nah.

How can we reconcile, or even integrate, an optimistic, subjective view of the creation with a pessimistic, objective one? The subject

is sensitive because of a bit of Western history—the battle waged in the West between science and theology. Many Christian theologians, employing a strict interpretation of the Book of Genesis, have claimed that the universe was created some six thousand years ago. They have also claimed that all biological species were created at once by God in accord with a grand design.

Meanwhile, by the middle of the nineteenth century scientists had good evidence from geological and fossil records that life evolves. Charles Darwin stated the evolutionary view of life with a theory so cogent that it has guided biology ever since. Darwin said that biological change comes about in a two-step process: There are mechanisms that produce mutations in the hereditary material of organisms, resulting in variations in the offspring. Nature then selects among these variations: only the fittest survives. Over a long time scale, a variant that has even a small survival advantage will win out over the existing homeostasis. Thus change—evolution—can occur. When Gregor Mendel discovered genes, the hereditary material in which variation is produced in living things, his work was recognized as a triumph for Darwinism. This and a few other elucidations led to the dogma that is now called neo-Darwinism: life evolves through the dynamic duo of variation and selection; there is no design and no purpose behind life.

In the past few decades, however, both views have been questioned. The no-purpose, no-meaning view of cosmology has been challenged by scientists themselves with the discovery of the anthropic principle—the idea that the universe is created for the purpose of evolving sentient beings (see chapter 5). The many coincidences in the way the universe has been constructed—the fine tuning of the values of the physical constants, such as the electrical charge of the electron; even the special geometry of the universe that keeps it expanding for a long enough time to provide the extended time scale that the evolution of life requires—suggest that maybe the universe has a meaningful destiny after all, a cosmic purpose: to evolve observers, for example, us humans.

Theologians, too, have fought back against the onslaught of neo-Darwinism by pointing out the weaknesses of that theory. Indeed, the Darwinian theory is weak in many aspects. For one thing, it proposes that variations take place at the micro level (the genetic material, the genotype) while selection takes place at the macro level (traits, the phenotype). Usually there is no straightforward connection between the micro and the macro. Most problematically, many coordinated changes at the micro level, many gene mutations, are required to produce a new macro-level trait that is useful for survival. It is hard to imagine how such gigantic changes (sometimes called "hopeful monsters") could come about all at once. It is also hard to see how they could come about gradually; individual genetic changes usually have no survival value and therefore would be selected against. Consider, for example, the evolution of the eye. It must have taken hundreds, maybe thousands, of gene mutations. What good is one mutation— one thousandth of an eye, even one hundredth, or a half?

Darwinian theory is also not very compatible with the law of entropy. The entropy law says that all things should proceed from order to disorder. The law defines an arrow of time; seeing that entropy has increased today compared to yesterday, you can tell that yesterday was the past and that time has moved on. But biological evolution proceeds in the opposite direction: from less order to more order, from the simple to the complex. It, too, defines an arrow of time; seeing that life in the past was simpler than it is today, we can discern the past. However, there is nothing in neo-Darwinian theory to explain the biological arrow of time. Mutations are random, not directional; selection also has no obvious directional preference toward complexity. As the physicist Paul Davies has argued, natural selection selects for fecundity, not for complexity.

And finally, say the adversaries of neo-Darwinism, the fossil data, the crown jewel of the biological case against the theological argument for creation by design, has gaps. There is no clearcut evidence of a continuous evolution from one species to another.

Unfortunately, the theological alternative, creationism, is hobbled by dogma that insists on a literal interpretation of the Book of Genesis: all life was created in one fell swoop only six thousand years ago. How about the fossils? And how about the human beings who seem to have existed before 6000 B.C.? Well, say the creationists, the fossils and the archaeological evidence were created six thousand years ago, too.

Are the creationists right? Certainly their criticisms of neo-Darwinism make a lot of sense. But their view of an emperor/creator God creating all life in a relatively recent past is not tenable in this scientific age, nor necessary to their ultimate concern.

Criticisms and shortcomings notwithstanding, neo-Darwinism has many successes. It is not the whole story but it is certainly part of the story of evolution; there is ample evidence that genetic variations and natural selection do occur. It is the blanket rejection of purposiveness and design that gives evolutionists a credibility problem. And it is neo-Darwinism's inability to explain scientifically how speciation occurs that gives ammunition to its opponents.

Is there a way to resolve the creationist-evolutionist antagonism? There is. We need to shift the arena of battle from Western culture to world culture. The Eastern religions do not believe that God created life six thousand years ago. But they do believe in purposiveness. They do believe that evolution must have come about from the creative play of consciousness. Hindus even maintain that God took incarnations in the animal kingdom in what amounts to evolutionary order—as a fish, an amphibian, a mammal, in forms intermediary between animal and human, and only then as a human. Clearly, they recognized the cogency of evolution.

Science must also shift from a cosmology rooted in classical Newtonian beliefs to one based on quantum physics. In a quantum cosmology, the universe is created as a quantum possibility and consciousness is necessary to convert possibility to actuality; there is no manifest universe until there is self-referential quantum measurement.

The question for quantum cosmology as a science within consciousness is this: When did the first self-referential quantum measurement take place? Here, we could take a stance akin to the Christian theologian—a very anthropomorphic stance—that the first self-referential quantum measurement took place with us human beings. But that would be like the solipsistic solution of the paradox of Wigner's friend; that would deny self-referential consciousness to plants and animals. There is a self, albeit rudimentary, in animals (though exoteric Christianity denies this). There is a distinction between self and environment even in tiny bacteria. Even a bacterium is self-referential and therefore capable of bringing the entire universe from potentia to actuality.

Don't be unnecessarily alarmed by bacteria power! All power—ours as well as a bacterium's—comes from consciousness. The important idea here is that *life* is something that we share with the tiny bacterium; there is no need to make the anthropic principle anthropomorphic. The universe evolves in possibility to make sentience possible. Out of all the quantum possibilities for a variety of universes with a variety of physical constants and space geometries, the one that was collapsed is the one in which sentience arises. Then a quantum measurement took place: a being looked at itself as separate from its environment (though the separateness is mere appearance, what a grand appearance it is!). A distinction was made between life and nonlife, which dependently co-create one another via self-referential quantum measurement.

Are the universe and life created by God? Yes, if you think of God as the creative principle that we call consciousness. The first self-referential quantum measurement is a gigantic quantum leap of creativity. Nor does the creativity of God end there. Life evolves through creativity, developing more and more complexity. Are the creationists right? You bet. God creates all life. The creator is not, however, an emperor God in heaven, but the infinitely creative principle of consciousness. And it has taken three billion years, not a few days, and lots of individual acts of creation to do the job.

Quantum Evolution

The neo-Darwinian theory of evolution denies the purposiveness of evolution and claims that all evolution can be explained as a gradual process involving chance mutation and natural selection. In the words of biologist Ernst Mayr, "All evolution is due to the accumulation of small genetic changes, guided by natural selection."

How does speciation—the separation or splitting off of a new species from an old one—occur under the neo-Darwinian assumption of gradual evolution? As we noted earlier, a single mutation is rarely beneficial and has a low survival value. It takes many gene mutations at the micro level to make a significant change of trait (phenotype) at the macro level. How can the large number of necessary mutations stabilize in the face of competition from the old, stable species?

According to an idea known as allotropic speciation, when a small subgroup of an original population becomes geographically isolated, the geographical "barrier" prevents any further interbreeding between the two groups. The available gene pool of the subgroup becomes severely restricted. Gradual random genetic variations in both groups and natural selection by the two different environments then produce enough genetic divergence between the two groups that interbreeding between them is no longer successful even if they are reunited. Geographical isolation, the relatively small gene pool of the subgroup, and environmental selection together effectively separate the two species.

However, there is a major objection to this wishful scenario. Whereas there is plentiful fossil evidence for evolution via gradualism within a species, there is really no convincing fossil record of gradual evolution from one species to another. We do not find, for example, a graduated series of fossils that show fish traits gradually being replaced by amphibian traits. Instead, fossil records show conspicuous gaps in speciation.

Thus, an alternative view has gained prominence in recent years. Biologist Gaylord Simpson coined the term *quantum evolution*—quantum leaps—to explain why there are scant or no fossil records of the origins of many groups of organisms for whom fossil evidence otherwise depicts periods of normal gradual evolution. In the same vein, the notorious "missing links" in the evolutionary tree between groups may be explained by quantum evolution.

Some paleontologists, notably Niles Eldredge and Steven J. Gould, have made the bold assertion that fossil records manifestly show long periods of species stasis and then the sudden appearance of a new species. Thus the idea arises of a punctuated equilibrium—that evolution is not a gradual, continuous process but instead is punctuated by rapid changes at the points where new species branch off (Eldredge and Gould 1972).

Biologist Verne Grant (1985) has proposed the name *quantum speciation*, a name we will adopt in this chapter, for the phenomenon of speciation through rapid quantum evolution. The more general term, *quantum evolution*, I will reserve for the entire spectrum of rapid macro evolution, including speciation. I will show that the terms *quantum speciation* and *quantum evolution* are highly appropriate for the phenomenon of rapid macro evolution because they refer to a quantum mechanism—a quantum leap of creativity by which the purpose and designs of consciousness enter the biological world.

To summarize, the theory of punctuated equilibrium suggests that there are two different tempos, two different time scales in biological evolution. One tempo is continuous and gradual, accommodating adaptive evolutionary changes over a long time scale, perhaps millions of years, as we find within a species. The other tempo is rapid and abrupt, like a punctuation mark—like a quantum leap. To this I add that it is through the rapid tempo that consciousness guides evolution to ever-increasing complexity, reflecting the creative mode of evolution. Slow evolution between quantum leaps is neo-Darwinian, reflecting the conditioned mode of evolutionary change.

Ever since the theory of punctuated equilibrium was formulated in the seventies, its critics have demanded a mechanism for the rapid change that can lead to speciation. The originators of the idea, Gould and Eldredge, unfortunately were unable to provide such a mechanism; instead, they were only able to assert that "the basic processes —mutation, selection, etc.—may enter into explanations at all levels . . . but they work in different ways on the characteristic material of diverse levels."

I propose that there is creativity in biological evolution, that speciation is literally a creative quantum leap (Goswami 1997a). The fossil gap is indicative of true discontinuity. As with any creative act, the discontinuity is major circumstantial evidence in favor of creativity.

Analogy to Levels of Learning

Ordinary learning typically involves two elements: a trial-and-error component (for instance, a random number generator) and a component that selects (plays the game of trial and error). In the case of Darwinian gradual evolution, genetic mutations comprise the random element, and nature, through its adaptability, acts as the selector. This is what Gregory Bateson called level one learning—learning by trial and error within a fixed context (Bateson 1980). This learning is also akin to conditioning; it conditions the system to respond in the learned way.

We can describe Darwinian evolution using the behavioral language of environmental conditioning in these terms: Natural selection reinforces certain random genetic changes (functioning at the macro, phenotypic level) after they take place, just as good behavior is rewarded in (operant) conditioning; and selection inhibits certain other genetic changes or equivalent phenotype functions, just as bad behavior is punished. The effect of conditioning is to produce a stable individual. Similarly, the effect of natural selection is to produce a stable species.

The analogy with conditioning clearly reveals that Darwinian evolution is not evolution in the usual sense, that is, it is not a way to produce new species. Instead, it is a way to sustain an existing species, maintaining its homeostasis by enhancing its ability to adapt. One of the best-known examples of Darwinian evolution bears out this conclusion. Gypsy moths in England were found to change their color in response to environmental pollution. The brown-colored wing, more compatible with survival in a polluted environment, was already present in the gene pool. Upon reinforcement, that color rapidly took hold in the population. Natural selection thus ensured the stability of the species. This does not, however, exclude the possibility of an occasional "accidental" speciation event by the trial-and-error, neo-Darwinian process—similar to the rarity of writing a creative poem by trial and error!

Bateson also recognized what he called level two learning or creative learning, the ability to see a new context. Creative evolution involves this ability to see a new context, a new function, that may be possible through a series of unrelated random mutations.

Who has this ability to see? Consciousness, of course! We cannot speak of creativity without consciousness. The answer to the question of why the individual random mutations are not individually selected is that mutation is fundamentally a quantum process. As a quantum process, the series of mutations important for a new function at the phenotype level remains in potentia until consciousness, via choice, collapses the entire series.

The view we are taking is that biological speciation is a creative process, sudden and discontinuous, akin to level two learning, while gradualism is a stabilizing process that, akin to level one learning, maintains the species once it has been established. There are good reasons for positing a quantum mechanism for speciation and evolution. Quantum mechanics provides both aspects of rapid evolutionary change that we are looking for: a mechanism for a discontinuous quantum leap in evolution (discontinuity being a fundamental characteristic of quantum movement), and a way to propagate mutated change without selection or adaptation (in the form of the propagation of uncollapsed superpositions of possibilities, the other fundamental characteristic of quantum movement).

Quantum Measurement and Quantum Evolution

As we have seen, the fundamental problem that any theory for a mechanism of quantum evolution must address is that individual mutations seldom have selective advantage; if selection acted on individual mutations, chances are overwhelming that the mutation would be eliminated. However, if a number of mutations somehow escaped individual selection, they might accumulate a selective advantage as a group and then could be favorably selected by natural selection.

A radical new conceptualization is needed to see how a group of mutations with selective advantage as a set might avoid individual natural selection. I suggest that quantum mechanics and ideas of quantum measurement (see chapter 3) can provide such a conceptualization. The misleading assumptions are that every gene mutation of micro evolution must correspond to a manifest phenotypical change (a new trait), and that the only way that change can escape elimination through natural selection is by either geographic isolation or selective neutrality (the new trait is selectively noncompetitive) (Kimura 1983). But quantum mechanics and quantum measurement theory permit a third possibility.

Gene mutations, whether they are point mutations caused by radiation or chromosomal rearrangements (or even inversions) that take place in sections of DNA when it is duplicated or recombined, are quantum phenomena. In the case of a point mutation, a radioactive agent produces a superposition of quantum possibilities, new and old; the probabilities for each of the possibilities are correlated to the probability function of the radioactive decay. In the case of chromosomal reshuffling, a superposition of possibilities results because, as physicist Walter Elsasser has pointed out, many of the relevant quantum possibilities have the same or nearly the same energy—a situation technically called "degeneracy" (Elsasser 1981, 1982).

Because of their allegiance to scientific realism, biologists assume that the superposition of possibilities obtained by either of these mutation mechanisms immediately collapses to one of the outcomes according to the probabilities assigned by quantum dynamics. But this goes against the grain of quantum mechanics. According to the quantum measurement theory discussed in chapter 3, no such collapse takes place until consciousness chooses from among the possibilities offered by the quantum dynamics of the situation.

When does consciousness choose? Clearly, an amplification of the microphysical gene mutations has to take place before choice occurs. This amplification involves phenotypical expression (a new trait existing in potentia). There is no collapse, no choice among the superpositions of possibilities that develop from the cumulative genetic mutations until enough change takes place to merit phenotypical expression in terms of a new trait in accordance with the purposiveness, or grand design, of consciousness. The amplification in potentia is carried out by nucleic acids and proteins of various kinds.

Here, then, is the solution to our problem. A drift away from the homeostatic condition involves mutated genes, which individually are selectively neutral. These are not manifest mutations; they are superpositions of possibilities, passed on as possibilities to subsequent generations. More superpositions of possible mutations accumulate on top of these uncollapsed superpositions, creating a collage of complicated superpositions; the process of amplification, still in potentia, makes new amino acids and new proteins, which then lead to superpositions of many new traits in potentia. Consciousness then chooses, among all the possible paths, the new gestalt that contains the new trait that is compatible with consciousness's purpose. If the new self-organization, the new trait, also prevents interbreeding with the old, we have a new species—quantum speciation.

Notice how, in this scenario, an entire set of mutations at the micro level—enough to (1) find phenotypical macro-expression and (2) make a quantum leap to a new species—becomes manifest. Natural selection still has the final say regarding whether the new form will survive or not. But instead of applying to individual mutations, selection now applies to the entire set of mutations responsible for the quantum leap to a new species. This is sometimes referred to as species selection in the biological literature (Stanley 1979). This solves the usual neo-Darwinian puzzles, namely, how micro evolution connects to macro evolution and how highly novel speciation (such as change of an entire class or phylum) occurs.

The assumption that the self-referential collapse occurs when the time is right for a creative quantum leap makes macro quantum evolution possible, because selection against intermediate stages is eliminated. But how about probabilities? Unfortunately, the probability of collapse remains small regardless of whether collapse occurs in the intermediate stages. This is true of any creative process. What helps in the case of creative biological evolution is the long time available for unconscious processing. Over and above this, there are morphogenetic fields (see chapter 7) that contain the specific species-defining form that consciousness is awaiting. Collapse is triggered when a "resonance" takes place between the archetypal form carried in the morphogenetic field and its manifestation. Biologist Rupert Sheldrake has a similar idea (Sheldrake 1981).

Is it really true that superpositions of quantum possibilities wait uncollapsed before consciousness is ready to collapse them into actuality? In experiments by parapsychologist Helmuth Schmidt, radioactive decay events, which are random, are recorded by counters and computers and are printed out. No one looks at the computer output or the printout, and the printout is sealed. After a few months, an independent observer who has the sealed printout chooses a direction of deviation from the randomness that he or she wants to see. Then psychics, the first to actually look at the computer output, try to psychokinetically influence the randomness of the radioactive decay in the specified direction. They succeed, even though months have elapsed since the original decay. Control experiments verify that if an observer thoroughly examines the printout beforehand, the data cannot be influenced by any psychic maneuver. The conclusion is simple, straightforward, and astounding: quantum events remain in possibility until consciousness looks at and actualizes them.[1]

Classical Correspondence and Neo-Darwinism

Quantum speciation or quantum evolution is an event of creativity for a living species as a whole. The quantum superposition of possibilities clearly plays a crucial role in evolution. There is complete freedom of choice for the collapse of the creative new form so long as the quantum dynamics of mutation have made the necessary possibilities available.

Life and its evolution has a conditioned modality also. Since all biological forms are connected to some first cell through heredity, conditioning operates on the whole tree of life. Hence, we get stasis-like behavior in the intervals between episodes of quantum speciation; this has been noted already. The similarity to behaviorism of normal Darwinian evolution within stasis periods has also been noted already. When a certain variety of gypsy moth undergoes a change of color to adapt to environmental pollution, it is a Darwinian change from one already selected mode to another (adaptation). The required genes were already in the gene pool of the species.

If the organism is already adapted to the environment, the quantum modality is suppressed and stasis dominates. But in the presence of rapid changes in the environment, such as those at the advent of the prehistoric Cambrian period, many existing species that cannot genetically assimilate the changes demanded by the environment become extinct. Still others adapt through preadaptation—drawing upon already selected responses available in the gene pool. A few take the creative leap to a new species, giving us quantum speciation and sometimes even more significant quantum evolution—a big quantum leap to a new family or phylum. With time, as later species develop more adaptive gene pools, the need for creative responses to changes in the environment at the species level decreases. Thus there is less quantum speciation and quantum evolution as time progresses. This is what is found empirically: no new phylum has appeared since the Cambrian revolution.

The living cell is fundamentally a self-referential system, consisting of a quantum system and its measuring-aid apparatuses, that makes available macroscopically distinguishable quantum possibilities for consciousness to choose from. Through millennia of conditioning, however, the quantum behavior of the system is suppressed except for relatively rare quantum speciation events (or the even rarer big changes of quantum evolution). This is the reason that cell biologists usually need not refer to quantum processes to describe the cell; classical deterministic explanations suffice. This suppression of quantum behavior also explains at a fundamental level why, as evolution progresses, there is less and less proliferation of family, order, class, and phylum.

Purposiveness and Directionality in Evolution

Quantum evolution also offers a nice compromise solution to the dilemma of purposiveness in evolution. Gradual, neo-Darwinian evolution is causally driven: what exist now as organism and as environment exert selection pressure and determine the future. Purpose, on the other hand, is usually seen as a final cause that pulls the organism from the future. If purposiveness is interpreted as final cause, the future is already determined in detail; this does not mesh with the idea that antecedent causes such as chance mutation or environmental selection also play a role.

But what if purposiveness is creative? The idea of creativity in evolution opens the door to a new way of looking at purposiveness. If consciousness chooses—creatively, opportunistically, and contingent upon environmental changes—life forms of greater and greater complexity, then there is a directionality in evolution. We indeed find this to be the case. There is no need to say that things are taking place according to some predestined teleology.

This does not mean that evolution cannot proceed toward less complexity occasionally. Consciousness is free to choose from available possible mutations a quantum possibility pattern that leads to less complex species, if this species is part of the design—the archetypal forms of the morphogenetic fields. It is the overall purposiveness toward complexity that gives rise to the biological arrow of time. In the monistic idealist literature, this purposiveness is referred to as the desire of consciousness to see itself in its fullness.

Evidence for the Quantum in Biology

The answer to the old question "who is right, creationists or neo-Darwinists?" seems to be "both and neither." Neo-Darwinism works, but only for the part of biological evolution that maintains species homeostasis in spite of environmental changes. Creationism in the literal Biblical sense cannot be justified, but a good case can be made for the creation of biological order by consciousness via a quantum measurement mechanism.

Is there any independent evidence of the quantum in biology? One spectacular aspect of any quantum mechanism is the possibility of nonlocal correlation—parts of a system that are separated by distance dancing in phase in a coordinated, coherent fashion. Is there evidence of nonlocal correlation in biology, particularly in biological evolution?

The complicated way in which genes contribute to a macroscopic trait seems to be evidence of quantum nonlocality. A macroscopic trait may be associated with many genes, and these genes may lie far apart from each other on the body of the DNA. Clearly, if these genes act in coherence to make a trait, some sort of an action at a distance is involved, but this is not "allowed" in deterministic biology.

There is also a subtle nonlocality at work in any individual complex being. Even if we human beings (in the West, at least) tend to live more in our heads than in our bodies, most of us would agree that being alive is a unitary, not a fragmented, feeling. We don't feel our aliveness in our right big toe and our left ear separately.

A less subtle demonstration of unitary action in spite of physical distance is suggested by what is known as the "binding problem" in neurophysiology. Now that we can take pictures of brain neurons while someone is thinking, we know that our mental experiences involve activity in several areas of the brain at once. Yet we also do not doubt that we have a unity of experience. So the neurophysiologist puzzles: How do disparate processes in different brain areas bind together to give us a unitary experience? This is a clear case of quantum nonlocality.

Quantum nonlocality also shows up spectacularly in biological co-evolution—when two entirely different species must evolve together in order for either to survive. The conventional argument—that each puts selection pressure on the random variations of the other as part of the other's environment—ignores the extremely low probability of even single beneficial mutations, let alone mutually beneficial ones. A more plausible answer is that mutually beneficial mutations are held in limbo until a opportune time when both species are ready to make a sudden change. So again, the change seems to be nonlocal in character.

Further evidence of possible nonlocality is available in the work of biologist Mae Wan Ho, who documents many examples of coordinated acts between biological molecules. The rapidity of these activities that are coordinated over long distances rules out any explanation in terms of classical processes of coherence. They may well be examples of quantum nonlocal correlation (Ho 1994).

Notes

1. Schmidt (1993); note, however, that Schmidt's experiment has not yet been replicated.

How the New Science Champions Sacred Cosmology

THERE IS a beautiful episode in one of the Upanishads. A son tells his father, who is a *rishi*, that he wants to know what is reality, Brahman. His father says, "Meditate and find out." The boy meditates on Brahman and realizes, "Brahman is *anna*, food," of which our physical body is made. He tells this realization to his father, who affirms his discovery but tells him to meditate some more. The son returns to meditation and soon is rewarded with another insight. He goes back to his father and declares, "Brahman is *prana*," the life energy. The wise father says, "You are right, but meditate some more." Further meditation gives the son another insight. "Brahman is *manas*, mind," he now declares to his father, and the father again affirms the insight and sends him back for more meditation. Again the son comes back to declare, "Brahman is *vijnana*," the themes or contexts of all movements. The father likes the boy's response but sends him back to meditate one more time. This time the son discovers the deepest truth, "Brahman is *ananda*, spiritual joy." And now he has no further need to go to his father for confirmation; he knows.

These five bodies of Brahman (consciousness)—*annamaya* (physical), *pranamaya* (vital or emotional), *manomaya* (mental), *vijnanamaya* (theme), and *anandamaya* (blissful)—came to be called *koshas*, sheaths that hide the light of consciousness. This is the doctrine of the *panchakoshas*, the five sheaths, so called by spiritual seekers of truth. I have found the idea of five bodies of consciousness to be a most useful springboard for a modern scientific understanding of cosmology and evolution. Of these five, the bliss body is consciousness as the ground of being and as such has already been the focus of much of our discussion. In this chapter we will concentrate on the other four bodies.

One quick note in passing. Is there anything like the concept of bodies of consciousness in other esoteric traditions? Yes. Jesus said: my father's house has many mansions; he knew that we have more than the one physical body. The clearest analogue to the Upanishadic description of the five bodies, however, is found in the Jewish Kabbala. According to the Kabbala, the divine manifestation of the One (Ein sof) as many takes place in terms of four worlds: Atziloth, the world nearest to pure spirit, the source of creation—the archetypal theme world; Beriah, the mental world; Yetzirah, the feeling or vital world; and Assiah, the densest world, the physical (Seymour 1990; Kamenetz 1994). It makes sense to conceptualize that we have not only a physical body but also bodies corresponding to each of the other worlds.

Is the Mind the Brain?

In the view of Vedanta, not only is consciousness not a product of the mind—it transcends both matter and mind—but the mind is also distinct from the brain. Both concepts are crucial in the development of science within consciousness.

When researchers into artificial intelligence talk about the brain as analogous to a computer, they are only partially correct. Conceptualizing the mind as computer software is valid until we raise the issue of meaning. Computers are symbol-processing machines in which symbols act on symbols. How do we jump from symbol-processing software to meaning?[1] If you think that we can reserve some of the symbols for designating the meaning of other symbols, think again. You would then need symbols for designating the meaning of *those* symbols, ad infinitum.[2] No. Meaning is processed in the mind of the computer programmer, who assigns corresponding meaning to the symbols of his or her programs. So also with the brain, looked upon as a symbol-processing computing machine (albeit quantum); we need a mind to associate meaning with what the brain processes.

Consider also how our brain makes sense of the world outside. A computer can process only its own symbols. So also, the brain as a symbol-processor can process the world only to the extent that the world affects its symbols, which are interpreted in the brain by the same internal logic used for the effect of symbols on symbols. The brain cannot process the world as the world really is.

There are two problems here; one concerning meaning, the other concerning the knower. A computer lacks both. In previous chapters we discussed the knower, nonlocal consciousness. From the standpoint of our nonlocal consciousness, all the material world is within us. We can know the symbolic logic behind every part of the world because we originated it. The material world is bound by the laws that reside in the theme body, *vijnanamaya kosha*—the laws of physics, for example, which we can discover creatively. But to give meaning to the world, we need another body, the mental body within consciousness.

When I see a flower, there are two objects in my awareness. One is the external flower in my external awareness. This external flower I share with anyone else who may be looking at it—it is public. But concomitantly I am aware of the internal flower in my thoughts, giving meaning to what I see. This internal awareness is private. Only I am aware of it. In this way, we directly experience the mind to be different from the brain. You can wire up my brain with EEG machines, open it up through surgery, or explore it by positron tomography to see what is happening inside while I look at the flower. But the instruments will not elucidate my internal awareness of the flower.

This mind, whose objects are internal and private to our awareness, is what gives meaning to the physical objects of external awareness for which the brain provides the sensing apparatus, which is quantum and self-referential. The brain also records a memory, a representation or map of the observation, so the next time it encounters the same object, the same mental state that consciousness used the first time for interpretation will be drawn upon.

Readers familiar with the Upanishads will recognize what I have done here to establish the case for the mind beyond the brain as a *prakriya*, a systematic methodology used extensively in the Upanishads to pierce through the coverings (thus the word *kosha*, sheath) of the grosser bodies to the more subtle ones.

Solving the Problem of Dualism

The mind-body dualism (also understood as the mind-brain dualism) proposed in the seventeenth century by Descartes was properly discredited by the general objections to dualism (see chapter 1). Now, however, we can dispense with these objections. With quantum physics we have discovered that matter is less material that we thought; it is only quantum possibilities in consciousness. We can think of the movements of the mind in those same quantum terms—as quantum possibilities of mental dynamics, or thoughts in possibility. Suppose consciousness collapses not only the quantum possibilities of the brain (matter) but also of the mind, and collapses them simultaneously, to make the actualities of an experience? Note that there is no dualism in this process (see chapter 3).

Is there any evidence that consciousness can simultaneously collapse possibilities in two disparate bodies with no signal contact, no local interaction between them? Yes. This is how mental telepathy works—direct mind-to-mind and brain-to-brain communication between two people without exchanging signals. More objective evidence has come from the work of Grinberg-Zylberbaum and his collaborators. Two subjects are asked to maintain direct nonlocal communication via conscious intention. When one subject is shown a series of light flashes, producing an evoked potential in his brain, the brain of the other registers a transferred potential without seeing any light flash (see chapter 4). Clearly, consciousness is mediating the interaction between the two correlated brains (two disparate bodies) by collapsing similar actualities in both brains.

So also, although there is no direct local interaction between the physical and mental bodies (two disparate bodies), consciousness mediates the interaction between them by collapsing correlated actualities, one in the brain, one in the mind.

The crucial new assumption is that the mind, the separate mental body that we are positing in keeping with the panchakosha model, obeys quantum mechanics. What evidence is there for the quantum nature of the mind?

In fact, we directly experience the quantum nature of thought. Physicist David Bohm has pointed out that an uncertainty principle operates with regard to thoughts (Bohm 1951). If we focus on the content of thought, we lose the direction the thought is following. On the other hand, focusing on the direction of thought leads to loss of its content.

Moreover, in any creative process we make discontinuous leaps of thought without going through conditioned, continuous steps. And, as we have seen, an important signature of the quantum is the discontinuous quantum leap—an electron jumps orbits without going through the intervening space, while emitting a quantum of light (Goswami 1996).

Perhaps the best evidence of the quantum nature of thought, however, is its nonlocality, as demonstrated in telepathy. Nonlocality can never be simulated by Newtonian objects (Feynman 1981).

Normally, we think of both the physical and mental worlds as made of substances, as concrete. Sure, the mental substance is more subtle; we cannot quantify it in the same way as we can the physical, but it is still a substance, or so we think. The quantum picture, however, enables us to think about the physical and the mental worlds differently. We must change our view. Even the physical is not substance in the ordinary sense; as physicist Casey Blood says, physical objects are just mathematical entities. The same is true of mental objects. Both physical and mental worlds remain as superpositions of quantum possibilities until consciousness gives them substantiality by collapsing an actual experience.

Cognition Is Recognition

Cognitive models of perception say that the brain makes a representation of the object that the senses perceive. But how is the brain able to translate the representation back into the object (so that we see the object, not the representation)? And how can it do this in a way that forms a consensus with other brains as to the object's name and form? Can neuronal activity in the neocortex evoke a perception of an object in external space-time?

The representational model does not work unless we regard perception as a matter of recognition, not cognition. Consciousness maps into the physical brain the object's representation with the help of the states of the mental body. A new stimulus, from a physical object seen for the first time (which is only a pattern of disjointed tendencies before collapse), produces an image in the physical brain in the form of macroscopically distinguishable possibilities, but these possible images are devoid of meaning. The self-referential quantum measurement in the brain simultaneously collapses (1) the physical object in our external awareness, which includes space-time; (2) the brain representation; and (3) the mental object in internal awareness. The state of the physical brain chosen in the collapse becomes memory and forms the syntactical symbol of the representation, and the correlated chosen state of the mental body provides the semantics; together they form a meaningful representation of the stimulus. Once a representation is made, the subsequent response of the brain to the (learned) stimulus is a computer-style operation.

As consciousness recognizes and collapses a learned state from the pool of quantum possibilities of the physical brain in response to a learned stimulus, it also recognizes and chooses the correlated mental state. Thus, as representations of the physical world are made in the physical brain in the process of perception, there is a change in the correlated mental body through modification of the probabilities of the experienced mental possibilities. Possibilities do not change; only the probabilities for collapsing them become biased in favor of prior collapse. Imagination is the reciprocal process: we recognize and choose mental states that are represented in the physical brain via a correlated collapse.

Repeated perception thus produces a tendency in the mental body for a certain state to collapse whenever a certain object/stimulus is presented to the brain. In this way, the states of the mental world are individualized to fit a particular history of conditioning. In other words, although potentially we all share the same mind structurally (the mind is an indivisible whole), because we acquire our individual patterns, we can be said to acquire a personal mind, functionally speaking.

Why the Experience of Mental Objects Is Private

Why are the mental aspects of perception—thoughts, concepts, and other mental objects—internal and private while the physical aspects are external and public? This is an unsolvable puzzle for material-realist science. However, our new science of the quantum mind can explain it.

According to the uncertainty principle, we cannot simultaneously measure both the position and momentum of quantum objects with utmost accuracy. Moreover, our measurement of an object affects that object. For perceiving the physical world, we must use the intermediary of a macro body, a macro measurement-aid apparatus, to amplify the quantum possibilities of the micro quantum objects before we can observe them. When we collapse the possibility waves of the quantum object, the possibility wave of the measurement-aid apparatus also collapses to a unique actuality, to a unique reading of some sort of pointer. The possibility wave of the quantum object at once starts spreading rapidly. The possibility waves of the pointer reading, on the other hand, spread extremely sluggishly. For this reason we can share the reading with others. Thus, the price we pay—losing direct contact with the microcosm—gives us something of a bargain: we have a shared reality of physical objects in the macrocosm; everybody simultaneously can see the macro bodies.

Regarding the mental world: As Descartes correctly intuited, mental substance is indivisible; there is no reduction of the mental substance into smaller and smaller bits, no micro out of which the macro is made. The mental world is a whole, or what physicists sometimes call an infinite medium. There are waves—waves of thought—in this infinite medium, which are quantum possibility waves obeying a probability calculus. We directly observe these quantum modes without the intermediary of the macro measurement-aid apparatus, for there is none. But there is a price for the direct experience. The observation, or experience, of a mental mode of movement, a thought, is subject to the uncertainty principle; it disturbs the thought so much so that another observation would not be the same experience of thought. Therefore, thoughts cannot ordinarily be shared by two different observers: thoughts are experienced internally; they are private.

Why Mental Experiences Cannot Be Collapsed without a Physical Body

It also turns out that the mind cannot operate independently; the presence of the brain is needed for consciousness to collapse the possibility wave. That is, the collapse of the possibility wave calls for the particular self-referential dynamics of a tangled hierarchy, which requires the micro-macro distinction that only a material brain can provide. As we discussed earlier, a tangled hierarchy is the infinite oscillation of the causal efficacy between the levels of a hierarchy: the lower level causes the upper, which causes the lower, which causes the upper, ad infinitum, as in the sentence, "I am a liar."

Quantum measurement in the brain is self-referential because there is a tangled hierarchy. There are micro quantum systems in the brain that respond to an external stimulus, such as a photon; the signal from this quantum system is then amplified by other, macro systems in the brain (we can call them measurement-aid apparatuses), but in a tangled-hierarchical manner.

Ordinary quantum measurements, such as the observation of an electron using a Geiger counter, are simple-hierarchical. The micro quantum system that we measure (the electron) and the macro measurement apparatus (the Geiger counter) that we use for amplification to facilitate our seeing are of distinctly different sizes. Which is the quantum system and which is the measurement-aid apparatus is clear. But in a self-referential system, be it a brain or a single living cell, this distinction is blurred, since the supposed quantum system is not as micro as the electron and the supposed amplifying apparatuses are not as macro as the Geiger counter. Instead, as physicist Henry Stapp has emphasized, both are of some intermediate size. In truth, these systems *amplify one another.* Another way of making the distinction between quantum measurements in the Geiger counter and those in the brain is to realize that whereas in the former the coupling between the quantum system and the measuring-aid apparatus is weak, in the latter it is strong.

However, no number of amplifications, even if the interaction is strong, can ever by themselves collapse actuality from a superposition of possibilities. Only consciousness can do this—from a transcendent level. With consciousness you have all the elements of a tangled hierarchy. An excellent example of a tangled hierarchy is the picture "Drawing Hands," in which the Dutch artist M. C. Escher has sketched the left hand drawing the right while the right draws the left. But we know that Escher has drawn them both.

So why can't consciousness collapse the possibility waves of the mental body by itself? Because in the mind there is no differentiation between micro and macro. In effect, there is no question of any amplification. Thus a tangled-hierarchical, quantum-measurement situation is impossible. And without a tangled hierarchy, there is no collapse of the quantum possibilities. But the possibility waves of the mental can collapse in one fell swoop of self-referential quantum measurement when they are correlated with the possibility waves of the brain.

In the view of idealist science, the subjectivity of our experiences, both physical and mental, comes from consciousness. Modern philosophers trained in the Western tradition might find it strange that we are speaking of the mind in an objective fashion, for they have traditionally made the mistake of thinking of consciousness as an aspect of the mind. But see the new possibility that opens up when we correct this mistake: We should now be able to study the mechanics of the mind with mathematics. Some work has already begun in this direction (see, for example, Sirag 1993; Stapp 1994).

The States of Consciousness

As mentioned earlier, the Upanishads "prove" to the reader the ultimate nature of consciousness through a methodology that is called *prakriya* in Sanskrit. Besides the *panchakosha prakriya*—the prakriya of the five sheaths—another well-known Upanishadic prakriya is the one that relates to the states of consciousness. With the help of what we have developed so far, I will reconstruct a modern version of this prakriya.

When most neurophysiologists and neurophilosophers talk about consciousness, they mean waking consciousness. But there are two other states of consciousness that everyone experiences on a regular basis: dream and deep sleep. Who is to say that dreams are not as real as waking awareness? We tend to say they are not because dreams don't seem to have the continuity of experience that waking awareness has. We can talk about and analyze our dreams in the waking awareness, but not the other way around. And yet, if you study your dreams for a prolonged period of time, you will discover a subtle continuity, a progression in your dream life, a progression at the meaning level. So continuity may not be such a big argument against the reality of dreams after all. Australian aborigines are, of course, famous for taking their "dream time" more seriously than waking awareness. Recent studies of lucid dreams have further blurred the distinction of dream and waking states.[3]

The Chinese philosopher Chuang Tzu dreamt that he was a butterfly. When he woke up, he wondered aloud, "Was I dreaming of the butterfly, or is the butterfly now dreaming of me?" He found himself giving as serious a consideration to the dream reality as to waking awareness.

Consciousness is common to both wakefulness and dreaming. Both are states of consciousness, except that dreams are more subtle. And in both there is collapse of the possibility waves—of the brain and of the mind—and there is a subject-object split.

What are the differences between the two? In the dream state there is only internal awareness of thoughts and internal brain images, constructed from the Rorschach of electromagnetic "noise" that is plentiful in the brain. There is no shared external awareness. Dreams, on their own terms, are reflections on the meaning of our internal life, containing experiences that progress with time, give rise to insights, and use what is learned during waking awareness as additional input. Can we doubt that dreaming is an important state of consciousness?

We generally assume that when we are asleep but not dreaming, we are unconscious. Most scientists of the past regarded consciousness as a property of the waking state. But in science within consciousness,

consciousness is the ground of all being. So consciousness must also be present while we sleep. Otherwise, as Vedanta argues, when you wake up how could you say, as many of us do, "I slept happily?" However, in deep sleep we are unconscious in the Freudian sense; there is consciousness, but no awareness, internal or external.

Today there is general agreement that waking, dream, and deep sleep are different states of consciousness, as indicated by the presence of brain waves in all three states. The frequency of the brain waves progressively decreases and the amplitude becomes higher along the continuum from wakefulness to dream to deep sleep. Furthermore, the Upanishads declare that consciousness in its suchness (*svarupa*) exists in all three states but also transcends them as *turiya*. Sometimes turiya is classified as a fourth state.

Some people make the mistake of asserting that since sleep and turiya are operationally indistinguishable, they must be the same thing: consciousness without a subject-object split. The error is revealed by meditation, which leads to a state known as *nirvikalpa samadhi*—a trance-like state, in which there is no subject-object split, that leaves a feeling of unalloyed bliss in its wake. Whereas in deep sleep the happiness that is felt is rather dull (it is called the lazy person's happiness in India), in nirvikalpa samadhi the happiness is dynamic and creative. One way to arrive at nirvikalpa samadhi is to practice creative sleep, sleep yoga (*yoganidra*, in Sanskrit). Turiya, however, transcends even nirvikalpa samadhi (see chapter 14).

The Vital Body

One among the five sheaths, or bodies, posited by Vedanta is the vital body, the *pranamaya kosha*. The vital body, like the mental body, does not have extension; an infinite medium, its modes of movement are called *prana* in Sanskrit (*chi* in Chinese and *ki* in Japanese). In the West the modes of the vital body are called vital energy. The poet William Blake wrote:

> Man has no Body distinct from the Soul!
> for that called Body is a portion of Soul
> discerned by the five Senses,
> the chief inlets of Soul in this age.
> Energy is the only life and is from the Body;
> and reason is the bound or outward
> circumference of energy.
> Energy is eternal delight. (Blake 1981)

The "energy" that Blake experienced as eternal delight is not the energy that physicists talk about, but vital energy or prana.

The contents of the vital body are the living functions that are represented by the various organs of the physical body, just as the contents of the mental body are represented as software in the hardware of the brain. In chapter 6, we saw that quantum leaps in biological evolution, in which consciousness collapses a whole gestalt of genetic possibilities, lead to a new trait and thereby create a new species. But where is the design that consciousness recognizes when it chooses the appropriate gestalt? It is in the morphogenetic fields that are part of the vital world.

Can the modes of movement of the vital body—prana, chi, or ki—be described as the quantum possibility waves of the infinite medium of the vital world? Since both the Indian and Chinese systems talk about pathways or channels for the flow of vital energy, vital energy must be more localizable than its mental counterpart. However, it is interesting that the Indian pathways (called *nadis*) do not exactly match the Chinese pathways (called meridians in English). Moreover, an acupuncturist needs the help of a patient's feeling of chi to locate a given acupuncture point, so the localization of meridians is not firmly fixed. Additionally, the location of the acupuncture point and the direction of the meridian seem to be complementary, like the position and velocity of physical objects; accurate determination of one makes the determination of the other inaccurate. The Chinese system expresses this complementarity by saying that there are yin and yang aspects of chi.

Like thought, the movement of prana displays quantum leaps of creativity. Moreover, vital energy, like thought, is experienced internally (see the discussion in connection with the mental body earlier in this chapter). Both of these facts further confirm the quantum nature of the vital modes. And of course, like thought, the movement of prana also becomes conditioned, camouflaging this quantum nature.

We are quite familiar with the conditioned aspects of pranic flow, although we may not recognize them as such. The feelings in the region of the heart associated with romance, the knot we feel in our stomach when we are nervous, the constriction of the throat when we first sing or speak before an audience, the pressure and heat between our eyebrows when we concentrate are all due to the conditioned movement of prana. These points where we feel the conditioned movements of prana are called in Sanskrit *chakras* and are now being rediscovered by many scientists of the body in both East and West (Motoyama 1971; Joy 1979). The creative movement of prana is signified by the rising of *kundalini shakti* (latent prana) and the "reopening" of the chakras; it breaks up the homeostasis of pranic conditioning and is the source of the creative breakthroughs that kundalini rising often initiates (Krishna 1971).

Scientific research in China indicates that some *chigong* masters (masters of the movement of chi) are able to affect the rate of biochemical reactions in cell cultures in vitro. If they project a peaceful chi, it increases the growth and respiration of the cultured cells; if they project a destructive chi, the biochemical reaction rate of cell cultures is reduced (Sancier 1991). This suggests that the movement of chi is nonlocal, and therefore quantum.

At the Vivekananda Kendra in Bangalore, India, physician and yoga researcher R. Nagarathna works with a spiritual healer, Asha Jain. With one pranic sweep of a subject Jain can make the subject promptly and demonstrably lose her strength; with a reverse sweep her strength is restored.[4] This is a clear demonstration of quantum nonlocality of the experience of prana. I am convinced that the nonlocality of the pranic experience can and does play an important role in healing (see chapter 12).

The Theme Body and Mathematical Platonism

Mathematician Roger Penrose, in his book *The Emperor's New Mind,* invites us to consider Goedel's famous theorem to see the nonalgorithmic nature of discoveries in mathematics. In essence, he gives us what constitutes nothing less than a prakriya to establish the validity of the theme body of consciousness as a body subtler than the vital and mental bodies.

The purport of Goedel's theorem is this: every mathematical system of algorithms used to ascertain mathematical truth, if sufficiently elaborate, is either incomplete or inconsistent; it always contains a proposition that the system cannot prove. Although the mathematician can see the validity of the proposition without a doubt, the algorithmic logic of the system is unable to prove it (Penrose 1989). In other words, when mathematicians discover new mathematical truths, they do not use algorithms or logic; instead, they jump out of the system—they must bring an already existing mathematical truth from a world that transcends the mental world, where proof and logical process operate. This is the theme world, the theme body of consciousness.

Physical laws are mathematical, a fact that puzzles many scientists. But in the same vein as Penrose's proof, if mathematical scientific laws guide the behavior of material objects, they must exist a priori to matter and transcend the material world. This idea is called mathematical Platonism, because Plato realized that the movements of the material world are guided by mathematical symbols belonging to an archetypal world.

The theme body is the repertoire of laws pertaining not only to the physical body but also to the vital and mental bodies. It contains not matter but laws that govern matter, not the morphogenetic fields but the laws that govern the fields, not the content of thought but the contexts that govern thought. Notice how subtle the theme body is—its quantum objects are not thoughts but contexts of thought. Empirical data on creativity suggest that we classify creative acts as two kinds: situational and fundamental. Situational creativity is the exploration of new meaning in already known contexts—this is creativity at the level of the mind. Fundamental creativity is the discovery of new meaning in a new context (Goswami 1996, 1999). It involves the movements from possibility to actuality of not only the mental body but also the theme body.

Involution and Evolution

Vedanta has another concept that two philosophers of recent times, Sri Aurobindo in India and Ken Wilber in the United States, have emphasized (Aurobindo 1955; Wilber 1981). This is the idea that descent, or involution, of consciousness must occur before ascent, or evolution, can take place.

According to this cosmology, the transcendent Godhead (Brahman, or consciousness) in order to know itself projects itself into levels that are grosser and grosser. The first level is what I call the theme body (also called the intellect), the body of the contexts of all subsequent movements—the laws of science, for example. Consciousness limits itself by becoming lawful, by becoming thematic in a certain, fixed way. The next two levels are the mental and the vital, which give content to the themes that will be played out. The grossest level of manifestation is the physical, in which those contents will be mapped (fig. 12).

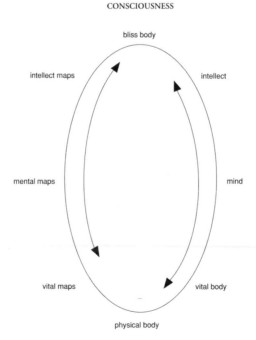

Fig. 12. The involution and evolution of consciousness

As consciousness descends, it also forgets itself and thus binds itself with ignorance. Each level of descent delegates the previous level to the unconscious and corresponds to another level of increasing forgetfulness and decreasing freedom. At the lowest level, the material level, all is unconscious. This journey is called involution because all the higher levels remain potential in matter, ready to unfold.

Once involution is complete, evolution begins. But the picture of the evolution of matter in this cosmology is quite different from that of the materialists. Life is not seen as emerging from matter—from material properties and interactions—alone, for a higher level can never arise from a lower one. Instead, life is understood to exist already in potential and to emerge at the level of complexity of matter where it can be supported. Mind emerges, likewise, at a certain level of complexity of life (the brain) because it was already potential.

These levels are not dualistic. All this separation in consciousness is illusory, a mere appearance. Consciousness forgets itself for the sake of play—it pretends to forget, so to speak.

The cosmology just presented is typical of esoteric religious traditions; in a certain way it makes sense and is very satisfying, yet it lacks details. How does forgetfulness, or maya—its cause—come about? How does what is potential become actual?

Idealist science, as we have already seen, gives a satisfactory answer to the first question: Manifestation occurs via a tangled hierarchy, causing the illusion of separateness, which in turn causes temporary amnesia. That is, at the intellect and mental level of descent, the intellect and the mind's subtle quantum bodies present to consciousness possibility structures that contain thought contexts and thought itself. Consciousness and its mental and contextual possibilities are still an unseparated whole. However, when consciousness self-referentially collapses the possibilities into actuality at a lower (physical) level of descent, this creates apparent separation between subject (thinker) and object (thought), which leads to forgetfulness of the unity. Similarly, at the next level of descent, the vital level, consciousness creates the potential for the (apparent) separation between life and environment—a still grosser separation—and there is the possibility of further forgetfulness. As argued earlier in this chapter, though, no actual collapse or separation of the intellect, mental, and vital bodies takes place until the physical body arrives on the scene.

How does what is potential in matter become actual? At a certain level of complexity of physical matter, tangled hierarchy and quantum measurement enter the play. Now consciousness can supervene and the self-referential collapse of the quantum possibility waves of all four bodies—theme, mental, vital, and physical—occurs. And consciousness remembers the levels of life, mind, and intellect that came before matter. It employs matter, as we employ a computer, to program life (vital functions) in living forms. The evolution of life can now take place (see chapter 6). With evolution, the conglomerate of cells known as the brain comes into the picture so that mind can be programmed and embodied. Eventually, with further development of physical form, even the intellect might be mapped in some future evolution of humanity—this is the vision of Aurobindo.

Notes

1. For a good discussion of this question, see Varela et al. (1991).

2. Banerji (1994) sees this as an example of Goedel's incompleteness theorem.

3. For a review of recent scientific work on lucid dreaming, see Wolf (1994).

4. R. Nagarathna in a private communication.

The Science and Spirit of Reincarnation

I N THE LATE NINETEENTH century the Theosophists under the leadership of Madame Helena Blavatsky were rediscovering ancient Eastern truths for the West. The truth of the perennial ontology—that consciousness is the ground of all being—was clear to them. They also recognized two cosmological principles. One is the principle of repetition for the entire cosmos— the idea that the universe expands from a big bang only to retreat in a big crunch and then expand again, bouncing back and forth in a cyclic fashion (an oscillatory model of the cosmos, in modern terminology). The second principle was the idea of reincarnation—the idea that there was another life before this one and there will be another after death; we have been here before, and we will be reborn many more times.

To the modern mind, reincarnation seems a little absurd. Under relentless pressure from materialist science we identify almost totally with the physical body, so the idea that a part of us survives the death of the physical body is hard to swallow. Even more difficult is to imagine rebirth of that part in a new physical body. The picture of a soul departing from the dying body and entering an aborning fetus seems particularly bothersome because it assumes a soul that exists distinct from the body. We have tried so hard to eradicate dualism from our worldview!

But our monism does not have to be a monism based on matter. If consciousness, instead of matter, is the ground of being, then the first difficulty—accepting that a part of us survives death—is considerably mitigated; for consciousness, if nothing else, survives the death of the physical body.

Then, when we learn that the new science needs to include the vital and mental and intellect bodies to capture the meaning of what happens at the material level of reality and that the physical body is something like a (quantum) computer in which vital and mental functions are programmed into easily usable software, even accepting the idea of something like a soul becomes easy. No, this does not entail dualism. None of our bodies—physical, vital, mental, or intellect—is a solid substance of classical Newtonian vintage; rather, they are quantum possibilities in consciousness. Consciousness simultaneously collapses parallel possibilities of these worlds to make up its moment-to-moment experience.

Of the four bodies, only the physical body is structural and also materially localized; it is called the *gross body* for that reason. Our vital and mental bodies are entirely functional, created by conditioning. We develop propensities for particular confluences of vital and mental functions in the process of map-making in the physical. These habit patterns consist of quantum memory—the conditioning of the quantum probabilities that are associated with the mathematical quantum wave functions of these bodies. This is a good scientific description of a part of us that would survive death: the *subtle body*—the conglomerate of vital, mental, and theme bodies—in which the memory of past propensities (what the Hindus call karma) travels via the modified quantum mathematics of the vital and mental bodies. We can call this conglomerate the quantum monad. (Along with the gross and subtle bodies is a third, the *causal body*, consisting of the bliss body of the panchakosha model, which of course survives death because it is the ground of being. Where would it go?)

Reincarnation is now elevated to a phenomenon worthy of scientific investigation; for the best scientific proof for the existence of a subtle body with its vital and mental components would be evidence of its survival and reincarnation. This is the main agenda of this chapter.[1]

The surviving quantum monad, according to our model, retains the quantum memory of habit patterns and propensities of past lives. And there is ample data to support the idea that propensities indeed survive and reincarnate. However, all the story lines that we accumulate during a lifetime, all our personal history, generally die with our physical body, with the brain; these stories are not carried by the quantum monads. Even so, there are data showing that some people, children especially, are able to remember past-life story lines, often in amazing detail. What is the explanation of such reincarnational memory? Quantum nonlocality across time and space would account for it.

I believe that all reincarnations of a given quantum monad are connected nonlocally across time and space, correlated by virtue of conscious intention. Shortly before the moment of death, as we enter a state that Tibetan Buddhists refer to as the *bardo* (transition), our ego-identities relax considerably; and as we fall into the quantum self, we become privy to a nonlocal window of memories—past, present, and future. As we die, we may share a nonlocal relationship with our aborning next incarnation, so that all our remembered stories become part of its stories, joining its childhood memories. These memories may be recalled later under hypnosis. And in a few cases, children may spontaneously recall these stories of their past lives.

How does the quantum monad know where to be reborn? If different physical incarnations are correlated via quantum nonlocality and conscious intention, it would be our intention (for example, at the time of death) that carries our quantum monad from one incarnated body to another. There is a Sanskrit word, *sutratman* (literally, the thread of the atman) that describes this aspect of the quantum monad perfectly. The thread is quantum nonlocality and conscious intention.

I am often asked the question: Assuming that souls exist, why are there so many more people today than in earlier times? Doesn't this violate conservation of the number of souls? This issue may be a serious argument against dualistic assertions of individual and eternal souls, as found in the Sankhya philosophy of India and implicit in the assumptions of popular Christianity. However, in the nondual model of consciousness that I have adapted, there is no problem. The individuality of the soul, the quantum monad, is an epiphenomenon of experience; it is illusory. There is no need to think of the number of individual souls at any given time as a constant.

Evidence of Survival and Reincarnation

There are three kinds of evidence in favor of the theory of the survival and reincarnation of the subtle body:

- Experiences related to the altered state of consciousness at death. Deathbed visions, near-death experiences, and life-review experiences fall into this category. This data supports the idea of a window of quantum nonlocality that connects the death and rebirth of the quantum monad.

- Reincarnation data. This includes past-life recall, details of which have been verified and have passed scientific scrutiny; past-life recall via hypnosis, LSD, holotropic breathing, and other techniques; readings of others' past lives by psychics, such as Edgar Cayce; and people with unusual talents or psychopathologies that cannot be explained as due to conditioning experiences of this life alone. This data supports the idea of a nonlocal connection between incarnations, as well as the propagation of quantum memory of propensities via the quantum monad.

- Data on discarnate beings. Not only mediumship and channeling but also the phenomenon of angels fall in this category. This data directly supports the idea of the surviving quantum monad between incarnations.

Deathbed Visions and Near-Death Experiences

One class of evidence comes from the threshold of death, the dying experience. Experiences of visions communicated psychically to relatives and friends by people who are dying have been recorded since 1889, when Henry Sidgwick and his collaborators began a five-year compilation of a Census of Hallucinations under the auspices of the British Society for Psychical Research. Sidgwick discovered that a substantial number of reported hallucinations concerned people who were dying at a considerable distance from the hallucinating subject and occurred within twelve hours of the death. More recent data is even more suggestive. In the study of the psychologists Osis and Haraldsson, the subject does not experience the hallucinations of a dying person who is suffering; instead, the communication more closely represents ordinary ESP with a well person (Osis and Haraldsson 1977). But if a dying person can communicate the peace and harmony of a healthy person, wouldn't he or she be experiencing an altered state of consciousness that transcends the pain and suffering of dying?

More well-known, of course, are near-death experiences (NDE), in which the subject survives and recalls his or her own experience. In

NDEs we find confirmation of some of the religious beliefs of many cultures; the experiencer often describes going through a tunnel into another world, often led by a well-known spiritual figure of his or her tradition or by a dead relative (Moody 1976; Ring 1980; Sabom 1982).

In both deathbed visions and near-death experiences, the subject seems to transcend the dying situation, which after all is often painful and confusing (Nuland 1993). The subject seems to experience a "joyful" realm of consciousness different from the physical realm of ordinary experience. There is evidence that even Alzheimer patients recover lucidity when dying (Kenneth Ring, private communication).

In my opinion, both deathbed vision and NDEs corroborate the theoretical picture proposed in the preceding section. The joy or peace communicated telepathically in deathbed visions suggests that the death experience is a deep encounter with nonlocal consciousness and its various archetypes. In the telepathic communication of a hallucinatory experience, the identification with the suffering, dying body is clearly still strong. But the subsequent release from that identification allows an unadulterated communication of the joy of quantum-self consciousness, which is beyond the ego-identity.

That near-death experiences are encounters with nonlocal consciousness and its archetypes is borne out by direct data. A new dimension of NDE research shows that an NDE can lead to a profound transformation in how the NDE survivor lives (Ring 1992). For example, many of them no longer experience the fear of death that haunts most of humanity. They often exhibit marked love and selflessness, suggesting that a creative transformation manifests from the insight gained in the encounter with the quantum self.

What is the explanation of the specific imagery described by near-death subjects? The images seen—spiritual figures, close relatives such as parents or siblings—are clearly archetypal. We may learn something by comparing the subjects' experiences with dreams, since the state they are experiencing is similar to the dream state: their identification with the body is lessened and the ego is not busy monitoring and controlling.

In what Jungian psychologists call a "big" dream we experience archetypal images. In agreement with recent neurophysiological ideas, I think that we construct these images—whether in a "big" dream or an NDE—out of the Rorschach of random electromagnetic signals that are always present in the brain. We use these signals to map the mental imagination that is behind the dream. This brain noise is quantum in nature, however—not deterministic, as neurophysiologists assume—and consciousness collapses suitable patterns as it recognizes them. The key to the NDE is the lessening or even release of the ego-identity. This allows the subjects to remember archetypal images that they have forgotten.

Recently there has been much debate about whether the experience of light reported in the NDE is simply a physiological phenomenon. In my view, it is. But what the materialists miss is that the near-death subjects take what is available in the brain physiologically and map new meaning with its help, much as in a creative experience. In other words, consciousness, and not the brain, orders the neurological events into a unique experience.

Many near-death subjects report that their entire lives, or significant portions of them, flash before their eyes. This also fits with our model. As the dying person has a life-review experience, the aborning child of the next incarnation shares it, and it becomes part of the childhood reincarnational memory of the next incarnation.

Finally, many NDE subjects also report being out of their physical bodies (out-of-body experience, or OBE), literally identifying themselves with a discarnate body. This is direct verification of the existence of a quantum monad beyond the physical body.

Reincarnational Data

The evidence for reincarnational memory obtains mainly from the accounts of children who remember their past lives in verifiable details. Psychiatrist Ian Stevenson has accumulated a database of some 2,000 such verified reincarnational memories. In some cases, he actually took the children to the locations that they remembered from past lives to verify their stories. Though they had never been to these places, the children recognized the locales and were able to identify the houses in which they had lived. Sometimes they even recognized members of their previous family. In one case, the child remembered where some money had been hidden, and indeed, money was found there. Details of this data can be found in Stevenson's books and articles (Stevenson 1974, 1977, 1987). One of Stevenson's associates, Satwant Pasricha, has also collected considerable data (Pasricha 1990).

One way to verify our current model—that reincarnational memorization takes place at a very early age through nonlocal communication with the dying self of the previous life—would be to see if adults are able to remember past-life experiences when they are regressed to their childhood.

Growing up in India, it is not unusual to hear of a child who remembers his or her past-life experiences. Parents and siblings are quite sympathetic with this phenomenon. The same is true in Tibet. "It is common for small children who are reincarnations to remember objects and people from their previous lives," says the Dalai Lama. "Some can even recite scriptures, although they have not yet been taught them." But in Western cultures, reincarnational memory recall is considered weird, so children who experience it quickly learn to suppress it. However, the suppressed memories can be recalled under hypnosis. Although hypnotic regressions have received a bad reputation because too many subjects remember being Cleopatra or Napoleon in their past lives, there are good data of hypnotic past-life recall as well

(Wamback 1979). In fact, psychiatrist Stan Grof has elicited past-life recall in many adult subjects using a variety of techniques: primal therapy, rebirthing, LSD, and holotropic breathing (Grof 1992).

There are also data of transmigration of special propensities and phobias; in our model we can explain these data as tendencies carried via the quantum monad from one incarnation to the next. What gives rise to phobias, the avoidance of certain responses, or, in terms of our model, the refusal to collapse certain quantum possibilities into actuality because of trauma? Stevenson has correlated certain phobias with past-life memories. In psychoanalytic theory, phobias are connected with traumatic childhood experiences. But there are cases of phobias in which no relevant childhood trauma occurred. In the same vein, there is neither a genetic nor an environmental explanation of gender confusion, such as cross-dressing. These are cases of conditioning flowing from a past life into this life. In such a case, regression to a past life should be of therapeutic benefit. Indeed, there is evidence that reincarnational memory recall under hypnosis has been therapeutically useful (Netherton 1978; Goldberg 1982; Lucas 1993).

Stevenson has also correlated special talents with reincarnational memory. How is a Mozart able to play piano so well at the age of three, or a Ramanujan able to add an infinite mathematical series with no exceptional mathematical training in his background? The usual answers of genetic or environmental conditioning seem quite inadequate. Genes are instructions to make proteins; there are no special-talent genes for people to inherit. And environmental conditioning can be checked in each case of a child prodigy. Indeed, there are a substantial number of cases, such as Ramanujan's, in which an appropriate environmental conditioning to explain the special talent is conspicuously absent. This strongly suggests that the talent is due to past-life conditioning.

Even the conditioning of the vital body can be transmitted. Consider the following case investigated by Stevenson: The subject, an East Indian man, clearly remembered that in his previous life he had been a

British officer who served in World War I and was killed in battle by a bullet through his throat. The man was able to give Stevenson many details—later verified by Stevenson—of the Scottish town of his previous incarnation, details quite inaccessible to him in his present life. Most interestingly, Stevenson found that the man had a pair of birthmarks on his throat that exactly resembled the bullet wounds he described from his past life. This suggests that a memory of the vital body was transmitted via the quantum monad from one incarnation to the next.

"I find myself thinking increasingly of some intermediate 'nonphysical body' which acts as the carrier of these attributes from one life to another," says Stevenson. I agree. The subtle body in the form of the quantum monad is the carrier of the attributes of one life to another.

Data on Discarnate Entities

We have been speaking of data that involve experiences of people in the manifest reality. But there is other, very controversial data of survival after death in which a living person (usually a medium or a channeler in a trance state) claims to communicate with and speak for a person who has been dead for some time and apparently inhabits a realm beyond time and space. This suggests not only the survival of consciousness after death but also the existence of a quantum monad without a physical body.

How does a medium communicate with a discarnate quantum monad? Consciousness cannot collapse possibility waves in an isolated quantum monad (see chapter 7), but if the discarnate quantum monad becomes correlated with a physical living being (the medium), collapse can happen. Channelers are those people who have a particular talent and an openness to act in that capacity. Via the purity of their intention they can establish nonlocal correlation with a discarnate quantum monad with whom they have never had any previous connection. It is well-known that while channeling, the channeler's behavior, manner of speaking, and even thinking undergoes amazing changes. This is because the subtle body of the medium is temporarily replaced by the discarnate quantum monad whose habit patterns the medium takes on.

I myself have observed channeler JZ Knight, who channels a spiritual teacher named Ramtha. When she channels Ramtha, Knight transforms into an authoritative male spiritual teacher, and she takes on masculine mannerisms. In her own nature, Knight is neither dominating in conversation, nor does she have much spiritual expertise. Philosopher Robert Almeder made the same observation of the medium Mrs. Willett. While she was channeling, Mrs. Willett displayed considerable philosophical savvy that was not her own, demonstrating that she was "borrowing" propensities for philosophical argumentation. These propensities must have come from discarnate quantum monads who retained the propensities of their past lives (Almeder 1992).

There is now evidence based on brain wave data that mediums, when they are channeling, go into an altered state of consciousness. Parapsychologists Gilda Moura and Norman Don have been working in Brazil with a channeled entity, allegedly a German surgeon named Dr. Frisk. They have found that while the possession is occurring (during which the channeler can perform complex surgery), the brain waves of the channeler suddenly jump in frequency to the unusually high beta frequency of over forty hertz (Moura and Don 1996). Similarly, JZ Knight has been tested while channeling for eight different psychophysiological indicators, and they yield markedly different results from her normal range of physiological responses (Wickramsekhara et al. 1997).

The phenomenon of automatic writing can also be explained in terms of channeling. Creative ideas and spiritual truths are available to everyone, but accessing them requires a prepared mind. How was the prophet Muhammad able to write the Koran though he was practically illiterate? The archangel Gabriel—a quantum monad—lent Muhammad a mind, so to speak. The experience also transformed Muhammad. A spectacular recent case of automatic writing is *A Course in Miracles*, which was channeled through a couple of psychologists, one of whom was not even particularly sympathetic to what was being channeled.

Angels and Bodhisattvas

In all cultures there are concepts of beings corresponding to what in Christianity are called angels. *Devas* are the angels of Hinduism. Often angels or devas belong to the transcendent archetypal realm of the theme body, which Plato called the realm of ideas. These are the formless angels. They are the contexts to which we give form in our creative acts. But in the literature and even in modern times, there are also angels experienced by people as helpers (such as Gabriel, who helped Muhammad). In terms of our model, such an angel could be a discarnate quantum monad whose involvement in the birth-rebirth cycle is over.

Mahayana Buddhism speaks of *bodhisattvas*—liberated beings who after death take rebirth in *sambhogakaya* form (possibility form, in scientific terminology); this is a metaphor for saying that they no longer identify with physical bodies. Their quantum monads no longer need to transmigrate propensities and unfinished tasks from one life to another because they have finished their karmic obligations. Thus their discarnate quantum monads become available to all of us, and their minds and vital bodies serve all who desire help. Buddhism also recognizes archetypal, formless bodhisattvas, for example, Avalokiteshvara, the archetype of wisdom.

Similarly, in Hinduism, there is the concept of *arupadevas* and *rupadevas*. Arupadevas are purely archetypal, formless contexts. Rupadevas represent the discarnate quantum monads of liberated people.

The service or joyful play of helpful angels, rupadevas, and bodhisattvas comes to us not only through spectacular cases of automatic writing such as the Koran and *A Course in Miracles* but also as inspiration and guidance in our most difficult moments. The intention of bodhisattvas and angels to serve us is omnipresent. When our intention matches theirs, we become correlated with them; then they act through us and live through us.

When the sage Ramana Maharshi was dying, his disciples kept pleading with him not to go. Ramana finally chided them, "Where would I go?" Indeed, a discarnate quantum monad such as Ramana's would live, forever if necessary, in the rupadeva realm, guiding whomsoever wants his guidance. Note also that the rupadeva realm is not necessarily somewhere apart from the physical realm we know. Transcendent realms are paradoxically "within all this" and "outside all this."

Notes

1. Note that Wolf (1996) has constructed a model of survival after death even within the materialist paradigm. However, there are many assumptions in this theory that may not be viable; for example, his model of survival is valid only if the universe ends up in a big crunch.

CHAPTER NINE

Cosmology Questions and Answers

THE EVOLUTION of the cosmos is a creative play of consciousness for the purpose of revealing itself to itself in manifestation. Materialists were premature to declare that cosmology—and even biological evolution—is nothing but blind chance. However, religions were also mistaken to see deterministic purpose, not creative purpose, in cosmology and evolution.

In order to creatively reveal itself to itself, consciousness goes through a series of steps, each more limiting than the previous one: the theme or intellect body, the body of laws and contexts; the mental body, the body of meaning and thought; the vital body, the body of life; and finally, the physical body, the body that maps representations of the vital and the mental. Through the quantum visionary window, we are able to see how consciousness mediates the interaction of the physical, vital, and mental realms and how this does not involve dualism.

The insight this spiritual cosmology brings to evolution is truly astounding. Life, mind, and consciousness no longer need be looked upon in terms of exotic and impossible theories of emergent epiphenomena of matter, as they must if reality were materially based. Instead, evolution is an evolution of representation, or map-making, of what is already in consciousness. This is satisfying; this we can understand. We already do this with our computers.

In the new cosmology we see the true enormity of our own evolution. We are not separate from our ecosystem. A reincarnational viewpoint enables us to see the spectacular vista of the range of our past lives. We have reincarnated as single cells, as plants, and as animals—albeit with "group souls," or species consciousness—and now as humans. Consciousness learns about itself in the course of the vast journey through all these incarnations; each one of us has traversed space and time in this manner many times over. This journeying quantum monad gives an intermediate perspective of our being that is complementary to our very local ego and the totally nonlocal and impersonal quantum self.

So gradually, a new science that will replace the current materialist science, a science within consciousness, is coming to the fore. In this chapter, I field hypothetical questions regarding this paradigm shift.

Simplicity

Q: You certainly have woven a fantasy science with not one but four worlds of consciousness. What about Occam's razor, the value of succinctness?

A: Einstein used to say, "Everything should be made as simple as possible, but not simpler." In keeping with their limited picture of humans as conditioned beings, behavioral psychologists replace humans with rats in their research; that *does* simplify things. Similarly, in biology, the idea that all life comes from genes is very simplified: all organisms, humans included, are nothing but gene machines, and genetic determinists can study biology in their laboratories without ever studying an organism.

But these simple pictures leave out the most important thing of all: consciousness. Such attempts to reduce everything in biology and psychology to genetic and behavioral determinism—akin to classical physics—have done little more than create an enormously prejudiced and thus unscientific attitude toward all aspects of biology and psychology that do not fit this reductionist view.

Q: So you are saying that the study of life and mind cannot be reduced to the study of the physical body alone; we must consider the vital, mental, and intellect bodies as well?

A: Exactly. In the old days, we could point to the phenomenon of mourning—people cry when their dear ones die—to suggest that we are something more than our physical body; otherwise, why cry when the deceased's physical body is still there? Now we have to go through more sophisticated arguments, but the truth remains the same.

Concerns about Dualism

Q: In *The Self-Aware Universe* you presented the mind as part of the brain. Aren't you taking a step backwards toward dualism by proposing that the mind and the brain are separate?

A: *The Self-Aware Universe* was the beginning of constructing a consciousness-based paradigm. It was never intended to be the final word about the paradigm. After that book was published, I gradually began to see the problem with thinking that the mind is the brain: it does not address the question of meaning. Consider a TV set. Physically, the images on the screen are a play of electrons—no doubt about that. But looking at the picture as a play of electrons tells you nothing about the stories of the characters in the soap opera being broadcast. It is your mind that projects the story—the meaning—onto the images that the movements of the electrons create. The mind enables consciousness to see meaning, which the brain cannot process. There is no way of getting around this meaning problem without proposing a distinction between mind and brain.

Q: A staunch Darwinist would say that the perception of meaning is a result of evolution; it arises because it has survival value.

A: A little logic shows otherwise. Ultimately, a material brain is a symbol-processing machine. Even a quantum-mechanical brain processes symbols, albeit in possibility. There is no room there for meaning, for semantics.

The Vital Body

Q: I may accept the argument that the mind is not the brain, but what about the vital body? Didn't biologists long ago discard that idea as extra baggage? What use do you propose for it?

A: For one thing, the vital body processes the functions of what we call life. Take survival, for example. Darwin made survival the pivotal point of his theory, and nobody denies that survival is central to living. But what physical reason is there for the survival instinct in biological beings? The fact is, molecular behavior can be explained completely without the concept of survival, without demanding an additional property called "wanting to survive," and yet living beings, which are molecular aggregates, do want to survive.

Q: Okay. But of what practical use is the vital body?

A: You can see its usefulness in a creative situation. Ordinarily, our physical body functions admirably with its conditioned representations of the vital functions. But when one of these representations or the vital movement that is associated with it, goes awry—a situation we call disease—we need the creativity of the vital body.

When the representations work, when the maps are good, the vital correlates play in tandem—automatically and perfectly. Consciousness simultaneously collapses both sets of possibilities to assure us of that functioning that we call health. But when the maps become faulty or the vital body modes—prana or chi—become unbalanced, the physical representations no longer evoke the proper vital mode and vice versa, and we feel a lack of wholeness, a dis-ease.

Chinese and Indian healing sciences emphasize the role of the vital body. The reinstatement of the vital body in idealist science thus integrates Eastern medicine, which emphasizes the vital, and Western medicine, which emphasizes the physical (see chapter 13).

Q: What is the use of the vital body for healthy people?

A: Consider the emotions. It is easy to see that emotions have a vital component in addition to physical and mental components. When we are in love, there are unmistakable physical signs and there are also thoughts that we readily perceive. But in addition, there are unmistakable feelings, especially in the heart area, that can be categorized neither as physical nor as mental. So prominent is this vital-body feeling that in all cultures love is associated with the heart. But what has the physical heart got to do with love besides beating a little bit faster?

There are spiritual practices in many traditions that are said to lead to mastery over the emotions. If you study them closely, you will find that these practices—Asian martial arts and Hindu kundalini practices, for example—are all concerned with the creativity of the vital body for healthy people.

Q: Would you call ordinary creativity the creativity of the mental body?

A: Yes, indeed. And mental creativity can also be a leap to the intellect. Creativity is the discovery of either new meaning (creativity of the mental body) or a new context of thinking (creative jump to the intellect body). For example, the laws of physics reside in the theme realm, and they already operate in the movements of the physical universe. Discovering these laws gives them a meaning in the mental realm that enables us to predict and control the manifestation of these laws in our affairs.

Miracles

Q: If even the vital body can be creative, is there also such a thing as the creativity of the physical body? Can the physical universe be subject to creativity beyond normal lawfulness?

A: Why not? An integration of science and spirituality that does not deal with the creativity of the physical would not be complete. In other words, we must agree in the new science that it may be possible to reach such heights of creativity that miracles are possible. In mental creativity, creatives transcend ordinary mental thoughts to new themes or contexts of the intellect body that include new physical laws. In physical creativity, creatives quantum leap to the intellect body and bend the physical laws to their creative will—momentarily at least. Of course, this implies achieving unusual control of the intellect body, of supramental movements.

The surprising thing is that spiritual traditions are unanimous about the existence of supramental creativity, irrespective of time, space, or culture. Look at the great chain of being as envisioned by an ancient philosopher of the West, Plotinus, and by a modern philosopher of the East, Sri Aurobindo (fig. 13). They are virtually the same vision, and they both recognize being that is beyond mind.

PLOTINUS	AUROBINDO
Absolute One (Godhead)	Sacchitananda/Supermind (Godhead)
Nous (Intuitive Mind)	Intuitive Mind/Overmind
Soul/World-Soul (psychic)	Illumined World-Mind
Creative Reason (vision-logic)	Higher-mind/Network-mind
Logical Faculty	Logical mind
Concepts and Opinions	Concrete mind
Images	Lower mind
Pleasure/Pain (emotions)	Vital-emotional; Impulse
Perception	Perception
Sensation	Sensation
Vegetative life function	Vegetative
Matter	Matter (physical)

Fig. 13. The great chain of being according to Plotinus and Sri Aurobindo

Q: Is there any controlled experiment that supports the occurrence of miracles?

A: It is safe to say that we are still tadpoles in our explorations of consciousness. The recent scientific prejudice in favor of materialism has not helped. We have to progress far in our explorations of consciousness, individually and collectively, before we can stabilize miracle-making enough to do controlled experiments.

Q: Is this why you talk about transformative practices such as meditation, whereas most philosophers of consciousness omit this subject?

A: Exactly. The best part of science within consciousness is that everyone can be an explorer, everyone *is* an explorer. But you don't have to reinvent the wheel all the time.

In part III we will delve into spiritual practices designed for the creative explorations of first the mind, and then the vital body, that can open us to wider being—to identities that increasingly reach beyond the ego-identity to the supramental intellect and bliss bodies. This will give you the proper perspective for thinking about miracles.

Psychosocial Questions

Q: Most new age scientists who talk about the integration of science and spirituality don't sound as radical as you. They don't talk about transformation, let alone miracles, as you do. Why don't they?

A: Because most of these scientists, sometimes unwittingly, still look at spirituality within a materialist metaphysics, and this limits them. How can you talk about creativity of the mental and vital bodies and even of the physical body when you believe matter and material laws to be the only causal forces in the universe?

These scientists certainly have to be commended for their support of spirituality and for creating a supportive environment for further dialogue. But within materialism, spirituality is an emergent phenomenon. Thus spiritual experiences are seen as interesting adventures, but they are given no causal efficacy and no ultimate meaning. In other words, these scientists, limited by their materialist belief system, ignore the transformative aspect of their experiences.

This is why the late philosopher Willis Harman emphasized commitment to personal transformation as a prerequisite for the scientist of consciousness (see, for example, Harman and De Quincey 1994). Without that commitment, it is difficult to reach the creative understanding of how consciousness, not matter, is the ground of being.

Q: Are there any scientists, then, who support spiritual cosmology as science?

A: Yes. In 1999, I lectured in several international conferences on consciousness. In all these conferences scientist after scientist reported a shift of their thinking from a material base to a consciousness base. In one conference, after some debate we signed a joint communiqué declaring that the time has come to recognize that a metaphysics that recognizes the primacy of consciousness is a more effective way of doing science. At still another conference I found that everyone assembled already took the new view for granted and had proceeded to apply it to all human fields of endeavor.

Q: Materialists will say that scientists who hold this view are trying to sell mysticism on the basis of their beliefs, and that's not science.

A: I am afraid they say that because they do not know what meditation is, what mysticism is. Mysticism is not a belief system; it is a transformative system based on "see for oneself." Meditation enables us to see through our conditioning, our belief systems, and helps us to transcend them and come to new, creative conclusions on the basis of our own experience.

Q: In the same vein, are there biologists who have proposed ideas similar to yours?

A: At the time he was working out his model, Rupert Sheldrake did not have the benefit of the complete new paradigm that the quantum window gives us; yet by the sheer power of intuition he was able to go beyond biological determinism to propose morphogenetic fields and morphic resonance as nonmaterial and nonlocal mechanisms for the making of biological forms. With the new science, we can give proper theoretical backing to Sheldrake's ideas (Goswami 1997b).

Q: I concede that if your ideas of biological evolution and morphogenesis take hold, then a major step will have been taken for a reconciliation between Christianity and modern science, because you have incorporated a creative role for God (consciousness) in biological evolution without negating Darwinism. But I am puzzled that you insist on the idea of reincarnation as part of the spiritual cosmology. Isn't reincarnation primarily an Eastern concept?

A: Yes, if you consider that all the major religions, Christianity included, originated in the East! But seriously, the Kabbala, which according to many thinkers provides the mystical basis of Judaism and hence of all Judeo-Christian religions, accepts the validity of reincarnation in its concept of *gilgul*—being on the (karmic) wheel. And recently, philosophers have argued that the Christian concept of purgatory is completely consistent with reincarnation (MacGreggor 1992). Finally, it is fairly well agreed now that the rejection of reincarnation by the Christian church, which happened as late as the fifth century, was primarily a political matter (Bache 1990).

Science and the Great Chain of Being

Q: What does the spiritual cosmology do for us that the materialist cosmology is unable to do? That is the real issue, isn't it? Which cosmology is more useful?

A: Indeed. But you must be careful not to restrict the spiritual cosmology's use to a smaller domain than it merits. The materialist cosmology is quite adequate for the conditioned aspects of the cosmos. Only when we open ourselves to questions of creative quantum leaps of evolution do we begin to suspect the inadequacy of the materialist view.

The hierarchy of being in the manifest world of evolution is sometimes called the great chain of being. In the West we often refer to this as the body-mind-spirit trio, but there is a sometimes-forgotten subtlety here. The Hebrew word from which the concept of "spirit" in this trio came means animation (through breath, for example). So, in this context spirit means what we call the vital body. The great chain of being is the chain from the physical to the vital to the mental to the intellect. Quantum leaps are involved in going from one level of being to another, as well as within each level.

Q: Are you saying that materialists do not treat the entire great chain of being, but only the conditioned part of it?

A: Exactly. Materialist physics is conditioned physics—classical physics. Materialist biology (molecular biology and neo-Darwinism) is the study of homeostatic aspects of life and conditioned aspects of evolution—adaptation. Materialist psychology (behaviorism and cognitive science) is the study of the conditioned programs of the mind, for which representations already exist in the brain. In contrast, idealist science deals with the whole quad of physical, vital, and mental bodies in both their conditioned and creative aspects (fig. 14).

CONVENTIONAL SCIENCE (Physical reality is primary)		IDEALIST SCIENCE (Consciousness is primary)
————	*Spirit*	Science of the supermind
————	*Soul*	Science of the quantum monad
Psychology (behaviorism/cognitive science)	*Mind*	Science of the mapping of the intellect and the mental body
Biology (neo-Darwinism/molecular biology)	*Body*	Science of the mapping of the vital body
Physics/Chemistry (Newtonian-Einsteinian/quantum mechanics)	*Matter*	Quantum Measurement Theory with consciousness as the causal agent

Fig. 14. The great chain of being as viewed by conventional science and idealist science

Q: Why do you exclude quantum physics from materialist physics? Certainly quantum physics is emphasized in all physics curricula today.

A: Yes, but only in a statistically deterministic way. In other words, quantum physics is used for calculations in physics. Physicists ignore the question of individual quantum measurement, the window through which consciousness in its purposiveness and creativity enters the manifest world of the living. When quantum physics is properly interpreted, it belongs in idealist science.

Q: You introduce consciousness first as the ground of being and then as the subject manifested through self-reference in the living cell and the brain. In contrast, many anthropologists define consciousness entirely in its social aspect, the society of brains. Can you deny that there is a social aspect of consciousness? Everyone knows about the boy who was nurtured by a wolf in his first few formative years. When he entered human society, he could not adjust; his consciousness was not developed enough. Why couldn't a quantum monad of developed human propensities take reincarnation in his body?

A: There are subtle laws of correlation that govern reincarnation. We have yet to discover many of the mysteries of the laws of karma, I am afraid.

But idealist science does not ignore the social aspect of consciousness. Remember, it agrees with behaviorism in the limit of infinite conditioning, which includes social conditioning. The new science just says that there is more to our being than physics and conditioning.

Actually, the new science can include aspects of social interaction that are ignored in behaviorism. Ken Wilber calls this the collective, intersubjective, interior aspect of consciousness—ethics, for example (see chapter 12) (Wilber 1997).

Q: So you are saying that with this new science you can integrate all aspects of consciousness within one cosmology and develop a science for the entire great chain of being—a science that not only deals with the conditioned homeostasis of these beings, but also with evolution, which requires quantum leaps. This is certainly a worthy step.

A: I am glad that you see it. This finally puts science in the same class as the humanities and the arts, as a great vehicle with which to investigate ourselves. Now that we include the physical body, the vital body, the mind, and the intellect—all four levels of being—in our science, we can also look at the methodology for integration of these beings, which is what yoga is about and where the value of mysticism ultimately lies. This is the subject of part III.

Part III

Creativity in Science and Spirituality

Inner Creativity

W HAT IS CREATIVITY? To define it as the discovery of something new is only a partial definition. Write a new love story—is that creative? Only if the story reveals new meaning in the well-known context of love. Find a new equation of physics—is that creative? Only if the equation opens a new context for further investigation. Creativity, then, is the discovery of something new in a new context (fundamental creativity) or the discovery of new meaning in an old context (situational creativity).

Discovering new meaning in an old context is a familiar concept. An example will illustrate what it means to discover a new context. Given nine dots arranged in three rows of three (fig. 15a), what is the minimum number of straight lines you can use to connect all the dots together without raising your pen? If your answer is five, you are trapped in the context of assuming that you have to stay within the space de-fined by the matrix of the array while connecting the dots; but in fact the instructions have not set that limit. The answer is four, as you see if you allow yourself to jump contexts (fig. 15b).

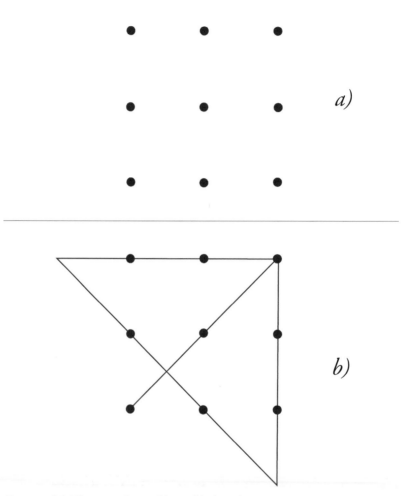

Fig. 15. (a) The nine-dot problem; (b) the solution.

All creativity occurs through a process of four stages: (1) preparation—reading the "good books," the existing material in the field; (2) incubation, or unconscious processing—allowing the unconscious to process thoughts without collapsing them, that is, allowing thoughts to spread in possibility, become ambiguous, and thus give us many more options from which to choose; (3) insight, or the "ah-ha!" experience—this is the discontinuous quantum leap in thought, the collapse to a creative solution, a consistent gestalt, from the ambiguity created by unconscious processing; and (4) manifestation—expressing the new insight in the lived life (Wallas 1926).

These stages are not linear, and they all involve the encounter between the ego and the quantum self.[1] We alternately strive and relax, encountering the quantum self until it chooses to respond. Then comes the grace of insight. And finally, there is expression in a product. In outer creativity, the product is art, music, a new law of science. In the arts we try to express new meaning in the contexts of love, justice, and other archetypal themes. In science, we look for physical laws, new contexts that the dynamics of our various bodies obey. The product of inner creativity is more subtle: self-renewal, a happier and more whole way of being, the transformation of the contexts in which we live and discover such that we can be permanently happy. Expressing the meaning of love in a story requires outer creativity, but becoming loving in one's own life is inner creativity (Goswami 1996).

Science as Outer Creativity, Religion as Inner Creativity

Science is a search for truth and so is religion. Is truth the same in science and religion? What is truth and how do we search for truth?

What are scientific truths but the laws of science that govern the movement of matter, mind, and vital body? A paradox in material-realism is that if matter is ultimate truth, that is, if everything is made of matter, it makes no sense for the laws of physics to govern matter, or for mathematics to apply to physics. But in science within consciousness, having laws of science makes sense. For its purposive play in manifestation, consciousness descends through a series of worlds, the first among which is the vijnana world of themes, which includes the laws that set the context of movement for what come later—the mental, vital, and physical bodies. The endeavor of science consists of the search for these laws. The laws are already in consciousness; a scientist attempts to discover them and express them in the language of mathematics or thought. The process of discovery requires creativity.

Spiritual truths are different; they are truths about our fundamental being, about consciousness itself. Their discovery enables us to live happily, without conflict.

So science is outer creativity—discovery of the objective contexts of movement with which consciousness creates the manifest world. Spirituality is inner creativity, the discovery of deeper and deeper levels of our being beyond ego. The commonality is that in both kinds of creativity we rise beyond thought, beyond continuity. In both, we recognize the limits of rational thought. In science, rational thought enables us to explore only what is already known. In spiritual seeking, rational thought always ends in conflict, even in paradox, its limit exposed. To discover and explore new laws of living, we have to jump beyond thought into insight.

Insight is reached by a quantum leap, a discontinuous transition. The cartoon "The Physics Teacher" by Sidney Harris demonstrates this perfectly. Einstein, baggy pants and all, stands before a blackboard, poised to discover a law of relativity. He has written "$E = ma^2$" and crossed it out; below that he has written "$E = mb^2$" and crossed that out too. The caption says, "the creative moment," and we laugh, recognizing that creative insights are not products of rational arguments or algorithmic steps.

Ordinarily, we acknowledge three modes of knowing: perception, conception, and emotion. We see something with our sensory apparatus, and we know. We conceive via our intellect and thoughts, and we gain abstract knowledge. We emote or feel, and again we know. Creative insight is attracting our attention to a fourth way of knowing—knowing by transcendent being.

Here again is a difference between science and religion. In outer creativity, science, the creative brings back the insight, a new context, and expresses it in thought, a new law. So we sometimes say that outer creativity is a quantum leap of thought from old contexts into new contexts, or at least, new meaning. In inner creativity, insight is the goal. So when we "return," we are inspired to change our pattern of living to one more conducive to insight. Insight is joy; so as life becomes more and more conducive to insight, we become happier.

Insight occurs when our ego is out of the way. Insight happens in outer creativity when we are partially free in our quantum modality to see the gestalt of quantum thought possibilities that unconscious processing offers us, possibilities that contain the answer to our inquiry. In inner creativity, transcending the ego-identity of ordinary consciousness *is* the insight.

The states of the quantum mind are universally available to all of us. We all comprise the universal information highway. Metaphorically, we are all part of a universal hologram; we each retain the information of the whole. But in our ego, we lose this access. It is in the encounter with the quantum self that we regain access, to discover the knowledge required for outer creativity.

For inner creativity, also, the encounter is the key. The quantum-self experience is happening moment to moment, if only we are open to it. We don't have to be stuck in our adult ego-identity forever. Even turiya, consciousness in its suchness, is not away from us. Turiya is present always; it is timeless, or beyond time. It cannot be otherwise.

The Inner Journey: Beyond Ego

Let us reiterate the distinction between primary- and secondary-aware-ness experiences. Primary-awareness experiences occur at the first collapse of the quantum possibility waves in the brain-mind complex that arise in response to a stimulus. The "split" of the one conscious-ness into subject and object occurs at this level, but the subject is still universal; the emphasis is on the verb *experience*, not on the experiencer or on what is experienced. This universal self—the quantum self—is the transpersonal self of transpersonal psychology; it is also the atman of Vedanta philosophy, the no-self of Buddhism, and the Holy Spirit of Christianity. But experiences (quantum measurements in the brain-mind) cause memory. Secondary-awareness experiences via reflection in the mirror of memory in an individual brain-mind complex give a sense of personal identity, the ego (see chapter 3). The ability to reflect arises as part of the secondary-awareness process. The obscuration of the tangled hierarchy of the primary process is fundamental to the simple-hierarchical identification of ourselves with the ego—"I" (*ahamkara* in Sanskrit).

As children growing up, we creatively discover many new con-texts of living; we are all inner creatives. As these contexts accumulate, however, we become more and more conditioned to operate on the basis of our learned repertoire. Finally, as adults, we become quite en-trenched in the conditioned-ego modality for most of our acts. Thus habituated, we depend more on outer stimuli to bring us happiness; we seem to lose the key to happiness within our selves.

Mulla Nasruddin is frantically looking for something under a street light. A passer-by asks, "What are you looking for, Mulla?"

"I lost my key; I am looking for my key," the mulla mumbles.

The passer-by starts looking for the key also. Time passes. "Mulla, where did you lose your key?" he asks.

"In my house," says the mulla.

"Then why are we looking here, you fool?!" the man shouts in exasperation.

"There is more light here," the mulla calmly points out.

There is more "light" in the outer world of sensory stimuli, so we look for happiness there. But the true source of all happiness is inside, with the quantum self, and beyond, in turiya—consciousness in its suchness.

Can we understand this journey beyond ego, the spiritual journey, the most precious journey of all humanity, in terms of our new science within consciousness? Elucidating the process of ego development is fine, but does the new science enable us to see why methods such as meditation and samadhi—methods that enable us to jump out of the ego-identity and that traditionally constitute our spiritual journey—are used in the spiritual traditions? We will see that these methods contribute to the fulfillment of our human potential—they are part of the creative process of further self-development, augmenting our creative outer accomplishments.

There is a major difference between the exoteric and esoteric branches of religion. The higher purpose of exoteric religions is to love and serve God, so these traditions teach ethical and moral principles. The goal of esoteric religions is to *become* God; they teach how to become one who can truly live the ethics taught in exoteric traditions. Exoteric religions use guilt (in the West) and shame (in the East) to bring people to ethics, with only limited success. Prayer, which is part of all exoteric religions, works better, but it is often used in an egocentric way that contributes little toward spiritual transformation. In contrast, all esoteric traditions focus on methods for transformation. In other words, esoteric religions emphasize inner creativity.

The truth is, it is very difficult to commit to a value that derives from somebody else's experience. Yet exotericism relies heavily on such injunctions: be good because Jesus said so. Esotericism demands inner creativity, employing methods that lead one to discover the basis of an ethical principle in practice. In this transformative approach ethical action becomes the natural and obvious way one wishes to live.

Inner Creativity: The Beginning

Inner creativity most commonly begins with a burning question arising from a general dissatisfaction with inner conflict in the ego-identity—what Buddha called *dukka*, sorrow. In the myth of the Holy Grail, when Percival arrives at the Grail Castle, his intuition is to ask the king, who is maimed, "What's wrong with you?" But he had previously been told that an aspiring knight does not ask questions, so he avoids the possible conflict. And no movement occurs. If you don't ask your question, the door to creative transformation remains shut, barring the road to happiness and rejuvenation. Percival stayed patiently with his conflicts for six years and then eventually returned to the Grail King and asked his question. As a result, the kingdom was revitalized.

The crippled Grail King is a metaphor for the ego-dominated psyche. Only by asking appropriate questions and addressing our conflicts do we transform and move from ego-bondage to identification with the creative quantum self.

Inner creativity may also begin with the intuition that there is more to the self than the ego. This leads to an intense desire to know the self, whose nature is consciousness itself, fueling the inquiry "Who am I?"—the hallmark question of the great East Indian mystic Ramana Maharshi.

Or the journey of inner creativity may begin with another deep inquiry: How can I love? When I am ego-centered, I live in a web of solipsism—only my own consciousness is real; others exist only in relation to me. From this ego-centered identity, we can love at best only patronizingly, from the superior level in a relationship that is hierarchical. But this is not love, and it leads only to isolation. We eventually begin to wonder why we feel lonely, why we do not feel loved, and why, in truth, we cannot give unconditional love to another.

Inner creativity can also begin with a spontaneous experience of the joy of oneness with the whole universe, an experience that in India is called *samadhi*. In modern transpersonal psychology it is called peak experience; sometimes it is called the experience of nuance in the literature on creativity (Briggs 1990). We want to discover the source of our unblemished joy in such experiences; we become sensitive to an inner connection with the universe—the "united verse" where we belong, which is our home. And we want to come home.

After the beginning, what next? The Bhagavad Gita discusses four spiritual paths for the journey beyond ego. These paths are *karma yoga*, the yoga of action; *bhakti yoga*, the yoga of devotion; *jnana yoga*, the yoga of knowledge; and *raja yoga*, the "yoga of the king," the path of meditation and samadhis. All traditions emphasize one or more of these paths. For instance, Zen Buddhism emphasizes the jnana path, the Sufis the bhakti path, and Christianity the bhakti and karma paths.

Can these paths be described in the terms of our new science? Yes. Overcoming the ego can be understood as overcoming two obstacles: conditioning and simple hierarchy. Jnana yoga, the path of searching for truth through knowledge gained from mental creativity, overcomes conditioned habits of thinking. Raja yoga uses meditation to transcend conditioned habits of cognizing. Bhakti yoga employs the practice of tangled hierarchy in personal relationship to go beyond the simple hierarchy and the limited boundary of the ego. Karma yoga centers on realizing in the midst of action that the cause of all action comes from a transcendent level (the inviolate level of tangled hierarchy); we are not the doer. Then we can give up the limiting identification with the ego.

From another perspective, the four paths are designed to investigate reality via the three aspects of consciousness: truth, cognition, and limitlessness. The jnana path investigates reality via the truth aspect, the meditation path through cognition, and the paths of devotion and action via the aspect of limitlessness.

Can one arrive at enlightenment using paths? The mystic Krishnamurti used to say, "Truth is a pathless land." So of what use are paths? There is no paradox here when we realize that these well-heralded paths are not recipes; they are not laid out in concrete, they lead nowhere. Spiritual insight is a discontinuous leap to deeper being; the paths set the context for this leap.

The Path of Knowledge

Jnana yoga is the science of the self, obtaining knowledge of the self via creative insights. Simply reading the new science or the sacred texts is not enough. That is just preparation. You must complete the process of inner creativity by going through the alternating steps of preparation and unconscious processing, the encounter between the ego and the quantum self, the insight, and finally, manifestation.

In other words, thought can never lead to self-knowledge, although we use it with gusto in the path of knowledge. We always end up frustrated; nevertheless, thought is still useful. We may use rational thought to negate what we think the self may be, to determine what self-knowledge may entail. We may engage in subtler and subtler thoughts. We may try solving paradoxical puzzles, like Zen koans: "What was your name before you were born?" We may read or listen to a discourse on the self by a master, trying not to add in our own ideas.

In between striving with thoughts, we do nothing, we meditate, we process unconsciously. On occasions we have flow experiences—joyfully contemplating the self for a prolonged period, at least partly through a thought process that is subtler than reasoning. But the joy of getting somewhere unfortunately does not last. There are also difficult episodes, "dark nights of the soul," when we feel that the practice is going nowhere. Then one day a teacher says something and we hear it, directly, without the intermediary of thought. Or a line from a good book jumps out at us and we understand directly, inside, in an about-turn of our ordinary patterns of thought. That is insight. Explains Ramana Maharshi:

> Sadhanas [practices] are needed . . . for putting an end to obstacles. Finally, there comes a stage when a person feels helpless notwithstanding the sadhanas. He is unable to pursue the much cherished sadhana also. It's then that . . . the [quantum/atman] self reveals itself. (Ramana 1978)

There is a difference between intellectual understanding and the certainty of insight. Intellectual understanding is satisfying, but only temporarily. If you try to talk to a friend about your understanding, you may find that you need your notes. In contrast, the understanding reached via insight is permanent and certain. It will be present in the very way you live because it has transformed your entire conceptual gestalt.

The day after his general theory of relativity was experimentally verified in 1919, Einstein was asked by a journalist, "But Dr. Einstein, how would you have felt if the theory turned out to be wrong?" Einstein replied, "I'd have felt sorry for the dear God. My theory is correct." Insights arrived at through jnana yoga are held with that same certainty.

Out of all the four paths, the knowledge or wisdom path resembles outer creativity the most. There is a major difference, however, in how the insight manifests. I will give you an example from my own experience.

I began my scientific career as a theoretical nuclear physicist, pondering the quantum structure of atomic nuclei. When I came to the United States for post-doctoral studies, I was fortunate to find a very great physicist to be my mentor. I would make models for the solutions to a problem I was working on and would become very excited about their prospects. He would say, "Let's sleep on it. Talk to me tomorrow." He knew about unconscious processing, you see. And when we talked, he would usually find a flaw in my model, and that was that; back to the drawing board. One day, I really thought I had a very good solution, but he found flaws in that one also, and I became very demoralized. I went to our basement cafeteria (called the Snake Pit, which suited my mood perfectly on this occasion), sat with a cup of tea, and started feeling sorry for myself. I even thought of giving up. Then suddenly the solution hit me, and I knew it was right. I ran upstairs to my mentor, who confirmed my solution. I spent the entire afternoon in joy. In about three months, after some more calculations, all pretty algorithmic, we wrote a paper on the solution reached that day. This was not a gigantic, Einsteinian quantum leap in scientific creativity, but it illustrates the process just the same.

Now contrast this with my experience of inner creativity. I had become interested in von Neumann's theory of quantum measurement, which is the idea that consciousness collapses the quantum possibility wave, so I began investigating the nature of consciousness. I read voraciously—Ram Dass, Krishnamurti, Rajneesh, Franklin Merrell-Wolff, the Upanishads, lots of Zen. I also meditated in between and hobnobbed with mystics. After several years, I found I was absolutely stuck. I was a materialist with the firm belief that consciousness is a phenomenon of the brain—because "what else could it be?" Yet I had a strong intuition that von Neumann was right, that consciousness collapses quantum possibility into actuality. But if consciousness is a brain phenomenon, it is itself a possibility. I was caught in this paradox. Then one day while talking to a mystic friend, my mind opened. He said, "There is nothing but God," as mystics usually say. But this time I heard it; I heard it directly—not in thought, not with another idea. And it was intensely joyful. I also was certain in my knowledge; I never had another doubt about the primacy of consciousness.

I didn't write a paper on quantum measurement theory immediately (though eventually I did). My first inspiration was to try to transform my being, to stabilize the joy I felt. This urge for transformation is natural with inner creativity; it is the manifestation of the creative insight.

After his "ah-ha!" insight in an Indian jail, the philosopher-sage Sri Aurobindo spent long years in silence. Hui Neng, the sixth patriarch of Chan Buddhism, remained a humble cook for twelve years after his enlightenment, until circumstances catapulted him into public life.

The Path of Meditation and Samadhi

The path of meditation, raja yoga, is based on Patanjali's *Yoga Sutra*, which teaches psychic control (Taimni 1961). *Yogah chittavritti-nirodhah*, wrote Patanjali: "Yoga is the control of the outgoing tendencies (attachment to objects, for example) of the mind." Control here does not necessarily imply active control and certainly does not mean the forced removal of thoughts and other objects of internal awareness. Not paying attention to thoughts as they arise—passive control—works wonders. According to Patanjali, full psychic control requires eight steps of self-discipline that include hatha yoga postures and breathing practices, withdrawal of the sense organs from the outside world, meditation, and samadhi.

What is meditation? When we are identified with our ego, we are always grabbing for something to keep us busy. It can be an external stimulus that captures our attention. Or it can be a thought, a fantasy. But the result is the same: conditioned action. Meditation is a way to intervene in our conditioned patterns. We direct our attention to a word or phrase (a mantra) repeated silently or to an external stimulus such as the flame of a candle.

Why does meditation—such a simple procedure—work? We have seen that the uncertainty principle applies to thoughts and the complementarity of their content, or feature (akin to the position of material objects), and their direction (akin to an object's velocity). In meditation we pay attention to the feature, thus losing control over the direction of thought. When we are completely focused on the feature and have managed to lose the direction entirely, we have become centered in the present. This present-centeredness keeps us from following our future- or past-oriented, outgoing conditioned tendencies.

It is important to recognize that although this kind of meditation helps us to arrive at insight, it alone is not enough. Buddhist sage Hui Neng saw a monk meditating. Immediately, he picked up two stones and began vigorously rubbing them together. Initially, the monk tried to ignore the sound. But after a while he gave up, opened his eyes, and asked, "Why are you making such noise?" Hui Neng said, "I am making a polished mirror." The monk retorted incredulously, "You can't make a mirror out of those stones!" Hui Neng said gravely, "You can't arrive at enlightenment by meditating."

Hui Neng is right. The form of meditation the monk was doing, called concentration meditation, is striving. It is work. In order to complete the creative process, we need to supplement it with relaxation. Another form of meditation, awareness meditation, that can help us with that. In awareness meditation, we become aware of our thoughts without latching on to any one thought. Notice the complementary nature of awareness meditation and concentration meditation in terms of the uncertainty principle once again. In awareness meditation we pay attention to the direction of thought, sacrificing the content of any particular thought. Letting the thoughts parade in our mind's field, we just witness their passing without "jumping aboard the train" to engage in their meaning. When we become a perfect witness, the content becomes completely uncertain, and the attachment to thought falls away.

So, as with outer creativity, inner creativity also boils down to practice. As mentioned before, the spiritual aspirant must alternately delve into unconscious processing, which is a form of nondoing, and strive for insight, which is doing. As Frank Sinatra crooned, "do-be-do-be-do."

How does meditation help with this? Striving for creative insight is aided by the present-centeredness that concentration meditation slowly builds, even when we are not actively meditating. And awareness meditation helps us with being, or nondoing. A verse in the Bhagavad Gita suggests that there can be inaction in action and action in inaction. The nondoing practice of awareness meditation (inaction) shows us that there is still conditioned action even when we are not doing anything. When we become fully centered in nondoing, thus escaping conditioning, we become free to act creatively.

Working regularly with both awareness and concentration meditations opens us to the flow experience, which Patanjali calls *dhyana*, one-flowingness (*ekatanata* in Sanskrit). We become able to hold our attention for prolonged periods; thoughts arise, but they gyrate harmlessly about the center of our attention, and peace and calmness pervade our disposition.

Patanjali also gives detailed descriptions of samadhi—insight discovered in meditation, which is the doorway leading beyond the ego to the awakening of buddhi. There are two types of samadhi. The first, *savikalpa*, takes one closer and closer to the primary-awareness experience of the quantum self, but the subject-object split always remains, though it becomes more and more implicit. Many mystical experiences—*satori* in Zen, "seeing the inner light" for the Quakers, the Buddhist experience of no-self, the peak experience of transpersonal psychology—fall into this category. In the relatively rare second type of samadhi, called *nirvikalpa*, the subject-object separation disappears entirely. Patanjali names many different samadhis of varying levels of bliss within each of these two categories.

Using the insights of the quantum picture developed in this book, we can explicate further the cognitive processes that take place as one delves into the realm of secondary-awareness collapse events—a realm that psychologists call preconscious. In any ordinary ego experience, the many preceding secondary-awareness collapse events (reflection in the mirror of memory) wipe out all discontinuity. So the ego experience is continuous. As one penetrates the preconscious through meditation and the practice of flow, one may suddenly fall into a secondary-collapse event in which there is some reflection of memory, but the quantum self also shines. This is savikalpa samadhi, and its signature is spontaneity, bliss, and the oneness of the quantum self. After further effort, again spontaneously, one may fall into states of secondary awareness that are closer and closer to the primary awareness experience—these are increasingly higher states of savikalpa, accompanied by increased levels of bliss. In addition, there is the possibility of falling into the gap between secondary-awareness collapses, into unconscious processing, which is nirvikalpa samadhi.

Of special importance is the state of primary awareness collapse itself, in which the quantum self shines fully and the knower, known, and field of knowledge converge. In this state there is no reflection from past memory, so it is experienced as dynamic, forever new, and yet timeless, because without memory there is no time. In this state, the wisdom that the tradition calls turiya takes place, the ultimate ineffable wisdom of consciousness in its suchness. Turiya is not an experience because there is no subject-object split. But because wisdom comes in the primary-awareness collapse event, the wise refer to it as the "Fourth."

How is nirvikalpa samadhi different from deep, dreamless sleep? To understand this, let's delve again into the difference between waking, dreaming, and dreamless sleep. In the waking state, the subject-object split is present and there is both external and internal awareness. While dreaming, there is only internal awareness, no external awareness, but the subject-object split continues. In deep sleep, there is no subject-object awareness, internal or external. Is there consciousness in deep sleep, although no awareness? Yes, there is consciousness. A person waking from deep sleep will readily say, "I slept happily," suggesting consciousness.

The unconscious processing in deep sleep and the consciousness that accompanies it are conditioned by the probability biasing of the quantum possibilities from the personal body-mind complex. So there is happiness in sleep, but the "I" that sleeps doesn't change. In nirvikalpa samadhi, this probability-biased unconscious processing—processing that is conditioned by past *samskaras* (learned propensities)—gives way more and more to pure and unbiased freedom. Thus nirvikalpa samadhi is called *ritambhara* in Sanskrit—so full of truth that truth gushes from it—and it is transformative. The "I" that wakes up from nirvikalpa samadhi is never the same "I" that entered it.

Hindu investigators even quantify the difference between samadhi and deep sleep in terms of the levels of bliss experienced. According to Hindu treatises, the bliss level of nirvikalpa samadhi is many orders of magnitude greater than that of ordinary deep sleep. Measuring bliss levels is not as intractable as it seems; for example, one measure is the time duration that the bliss lingers. With deep sleep this is only a few minutes. But the bliss of a samadhi, even savikalpa samadhi, can last for days.

I once did japa (the internal repetition of a mantra) for seven days and was rewarded with an event of awareness of oneness with the universal self (savikalpa samadhi); this was my nuance, my entry point to the journey of inner creativity. The actual experience lasted only for a split second. But the bliss that followed lingered, full force, for two entire days, gradually fading over the following few days. Philosopher Franklin Merrell-Wolff writes that when he had his first mystical realization (a savikalpa samadhi also, but deeper than what I experienced), the bliss lasted for more than ninety days (Merrell-Wolff 1995). Ramana Maharshi arrived at turiya at age sixteen; the bliss of that event was available to him throughout his life.

Yoga is psychic control, control of the outgoing tendencies of the mind, said Patanjali. Another definition is "Yoga is the calming of the mind." But you cannot control the mind or calm it by striving; a better strategy is to alternate willing and surrendering until you become an unattached witness. When the mind does become empty, you transcend the ordinary mind of discourse, becoming sensitive to the primary creative reality of the quantum self. Or better yet, you fall into nirvikalpa samadhi, transcending subject-object awareness altogether. Then your spiritual life blooms.

It happens when you least strive for it, when you least expect it, as in the story of Subhuti, a disciple of Buddha. Subhuti was meditating under a tree when flowers began to be showered on him and voices sang, "We are praising you for your discourse on emptiness of mind." "But I haven't spoken," said a surprised Subhuti. "You haven't spoken, and we haven't heard; this is true emptiness," answered the voices. And the flowers continued to fall.

The Paths of Devotion and Action

Most people in the West are born into the Christian tradition and thus grow up with some familiarity with the Christian spiritual practice, which is devotion to God and doing God's bidding through ethical actions. In devotional practice, we set up a personal relationship with God, as if God is separate from us. In lay Christianity, at least, this is the hierarchical relationship in which God is master and the devotee is servant. This perception of God's relationship with people as dualistic conflicts with the individualism that is pervasive in Western society and with science, where dualism is "disproven." This variance forever sets up a cognitive dissonance in the hearts and minds of many intelligent and sincere people.

Thus it is extremely important to understand, in a scientific way, what the method of devotion, or bhakti, is trying to accomplish. Ordinarily, we are dominated by selfish thoughts and emotions (survival instincts), which become the little cocoon that we call our ego. In bhakti yoga, ego boundaries are transcended through the creative discovery of love, a nonlocal experience of unity in spite of apparent separateness—not only love of God, but also love of other people, as in "love thy neighbor." But there is a subtlety here.

Does love exist in a simple hierarchical relationship? If you have been in one, you know the answer. No. Simple hierarchy sets up conditions that are antithetical to love: you give me sex and I will support you, and so on. True love is unconditional and tangled-hierarchical; both partners must be on equal footing in their causal interchange. But the ego is simple-hierarchical, the head honcho in all its relationships. Thus it is impossible to love unconditionally while we identify with our ego. Bhakti yoga, the practice of unconditional love and devotion, is an affront to the ego.

An outstanding case of bhakti yoga practice is found in the life of Yashoda, the adoptive mother of the child Krishna, who is God incarnate in Hinduism. Can you imagine Yashoda's relationship with Krishna? Krishna is her child who needs her care. But she also knows that Krishna is God, who reigns over everyone, including herself. To love and care for your child and also treat him or her as if he or she is God is a practice of tangled hierarchy in relationship. In India, until recently, children were regarded as God, giving their parents an opportunity to practice bhakti yoga in its fullest expression.

The way devotion to God is taught in conventional Christian churches, however, is clearly simple-hierarchical; it does not—it cannot—lead to a shift of identity beyond ego. How does one set up a tangled hierarchy with God? You not only chant and pray and worship God as your Master, you also make demands on God as Servant. This is what Jewish philosopher Martin Buber meant by an I-Thou relationship with God (Buber 1970). Meister Eckhart developed the same within the Christian tradition, but an ordinary Christian would probably shy away from this; the conditioning of being always the servant of God is too strong.

Exacerbating the problem, churches teach only the practice of prayer and devotion. But practice alone is not enough; it must be incorporated within the entire process of inner creativity. Unconditional love, tangled-hierarchical love, has to be discovered. A discontinuous creative insight into love is crucial; then only can love manifest in one's life.

In prayer we talk to God and expect to be heard; in meditation we listen for what God says to us. With both there is the possibility of tangled hierarchy. And as prayer progresses, from the initial self-centered prayer for that Cadillac or that dream house, to praying for your child's well-being, to praying for the well-being of everyone, to praying for the ability to surrender to God's will, and finally to silence, prayer becomes identical with deep meditation. Then tangled hierarchy has arrived.

Today, in the West at least, perhaps it is better to practice bhakti yoga with one's wife, husband, or lover. The women's lib movement has created a supportive environment for both men and women to practice devotion to one another in a tangled hierarchical manner. First you practice, in both striving and relaxed ways; after a while, the relationship becomes a flow, an uninterrupted experience of love and caring. But this does not last. Invariably, there are down-swings, and you want to give up. Then suddenly, insight comes and you realize what tangled hierarchy is like. Finally, tangled hierarchy manifests in your relationship effortlessly and love manifests with it.

Karma yoga is the yoga of right, or ethical, action. How does right action lead us beyond the ego? Ego-centered actions always serve the ego itself, whereas ethics demand that we optimize other people's interests as well as our own when we act. Karma yoga enables us to see that both kind of actions are important. "If I am not for myself, who am I? If I am only for myself, what am I?" said Rabbi Hillel.

Karma yoga also helps us understand that we, as our ego, are not the doer of our actions—we are simply participating in a maze of conditioned actions. The exception occurs when we are creative. The practice of karma yoga is to partake in creative actions as God's agent. This means deferring our limited will to God's will. But in exoteric Christianity, confusion arises because God is looked upon as separate from us—a dualistic dynamic is created.

So the path of devotion and the path of action are subtle in the way they work with dualism. In the paths of knowledge and meditation, we watch the dualistic nature of thought in order to transcend thought. In bhakti and karma yoga, we use the dualistic dynamics of relationship to transcend dualism.

Chaitanya, a great Hindu mystic of the fifteenth century, was once asked: Is God separate from us as taught in bhakti yoga, or is God (consciousness) nondual as taught in jnana yoga? Chaitanya's answer is famous: God is both separate from us and nondual. How so? The realization that God is both dual and nondual is beyond thinking, said Chaitanya.[2] We have to realize it directly, via insight. In chapter 11 we will explore bhakti yoga, karma yoga, and ethics further.

Which Path is Yours?

The quintessential question for each person is: which path is yours? The famous physicist Wolfgang Pauli seemed distraught as he waited for his luggage at an airport. Another physicist tried to reassure Pauli, "Don't worry. All the luggage will arrive at carousel two, where we are standing." Pauli responded in irritation, "Who is worried about all the luggage? I just want my luggage." So also, which path is your path?

Your choice of path depends on your nature. The four yogas correspond nicely with Carl Jung's classification of humans into four groups. If you are a thinking-oriented person, jnana yoga is the path for you. For feeling-oriented people, bhakti yoga will be the major focus. Sensory-oriented people may find karma yoga to be most appropriate. For those who are intuitive and inwardly directed, raja yoga, the path of meditation and samadhis, may make the most sense. But it is valuable to try them all before you know which is right for you. And different paths may be more helpful at different stages of development. The idea that different paths are right for different people and possibly at different times for the same person is valuable in a world where, even today, most people enter the path determined by their birth—their parents' religion.

The Paths and the Great Traditions

Most of humanity's great spiritual traditions include all the paths in one form or another, even while each may emphasize only one path. In Christianity, Catholicism emphasizes karma yoga through ritual actions called sacraments. A Catholic practices consecrating every action. In contrast, Protestantism emphasizes bhakti, surrendering to love as grace, which according to Protestantism is not achievable by ritual actions. Love and self-forgiveness form the core practices of contemplative traditions in Protestant Christianity. But exceptions abound. Saint Francis of Assisi propounded the practice of love through love of nature. An anonymous Christian mystic of the twelfth century, in a highly evocative book called *The Cloud of Unknowing*, described practices that can easily be identified as mantra meditation.

Buddhism does not have a concept of God. Thus meditation and jnana paths dominate the tradition. Zen Buddhism is famous for its koans, riddles that act as "fingers pointing to the moon" (of enlightenment). The koans are used to trigger creative quantum leaps beyond the ego-identity. The koan will puzzle you until you creatively leap to insight; then the answer will come. Nevertheless, although there is no God, in exoteric Buddhism the Buddha himself is worshipped with love and devotion. In Soto Zen, the emphasis is not only on just sitting (*zazen*) but also on serving humanity—clearly resonant with karma yoga.

Confucianism and, to some extent, Taoism emphasize karma yoga, ethical actions. The point in Taoism is a little subtle; Taoism emphasizes the importance of nondoing and this can easily be misinterpreted. But what it really tells us is to act from the center—which the poet T. S. Eliot called "the still point."

In Judaism, jnana yoga is emphasized in the form of study of the Kabbala. Moses discovered the Ten Commandments, a milestone for ethical action in the West. Therefore, karma yoga is no stranger to Judaism; in fact, it is the mainstay of spiritual practice for Jews. Worth noting is how the name *Israel* originated. Jacob, one of the founders of Judaism, wrestled with God one whole night until he received God's blessing and a new name: "No longer shall your name be called Jacob, but Israel, because you have striven with God and with men, and you have prevailed" (Genesis 32:28). This striving with God is, of course, the same as encountering the quantum self. And although God's name is unutterable in Judaism, discouraging a one-to-one bhakti relationship, Buber transformed the Jacobian struggle with God to a bhakti-oriented, I-Thou relationship.

Sufism, the esoteric tradition of Islam, is an almost unadulterated bhakti path. And yet, one of its great exponents was Ibn 'Arabi, a great *jnani* (one who is established in wisdom through the path of knowledge) by any standard.

At the opposite extreme from Sufism, Hinduism stands out as the one tradition in which every path finds prominence, defining a particular sect or sects. The esoteric tradition favored by the swamis of the Shankaracharya Order is the jnana path of Vedanta. The bhakti path is followed by the Vaishnavites (followers of Vishnu, the sustaining aspect of divinity) and Shaivites (followers of Shiva, the destroying and renewing aspects of divinity). The karma path is emphasized for householders, in general. And raja yoga is supplemented by *tantra*, a practice oriented toward creativity of the body (see chapter 13) for the avantgarde adventurers into consciousness.

The point is that you have a choice of paths irrespective of the tradition you belong to by birth. And there is no need for you to change your religion in order to follow a path that is not the dominant path of your religion. As Carlos Castaneda's guru, Don Juan, said, choose the path of your heart, because that is the path that will transform you.

Notes

1. The encounter between ego and quantum self in creativity has been emphasized by May (1976) and Goswami (1999).

2. This philosophy is called *achintya bhedabheda tattva* in Sanskrit.

CHAPTER ELEVEN

The Science of Ritual and Ethics

I FIRST HEARD the term *practical Vedanta*—a term originally used by Swami Vivekananda—from Professor Satyanarayan Sastry (friends call him Sastriji), a retired professor of chemistry who lives in Bangalore and has studied Vedanta for many years. Sastriji was giving a series of lectures on Vedanta at the Vivekananda Kendra Yoga Research Foundation near Bangalore. He introduced the term in the course of differentiating the purposes of the *karmakanda* (the part of the Vedas that deals with ritual actions) and the *jnanakanda* (Vedanta, the part of the Vedas that deals with knowledge).

The point he made was this: The karmakanda details a lot of ritual actions that, if one has already studied the jnanakanda, may seem somewhat shallow and superfluous, even silly. When one has already encountered the exalted idea of Brahman and is intuiting the unity of one's self with Brahman, why spend a whole day pouring *ghee* (clarified butter) into the fire of some *yajna* (sacrificial ritual)? Contemplation, yes. Meditation, most definitely. But sacrificial ritual does not make much sense.

We think this, however, only because we are not getting the message of Vedanta, or rather, we are not thinking about what immediately obscures the Vedantic truth "I am the limitless Brahman." The fact is, identified with my ego, I am always rushing about boosting my ego-identity with the idea of being the doer of things. I am heeding local signals around me in order to take care of things and identifying with the contracted consciousness that focuses on such tasks.

The ritual actions of the karmakanda are designed to break up these habit patterns of doing. If you examine the rituals carefully, you see that every ritual is designed to do two things. First, it slows us down. All rituals are loaded with details; they are not for impatient, time-conscious, busy people. Or to put it another way, if impatient people engage in ritual action, they have to slow down. Second, the ritual shifts our consciousness away from immediate local signals, allowing it to expand.

What do the slowing down and the expansion of consciousness accomplish? They help the identity shift more readily from the ego to the quantum self. Identified with the ego, we barely retain the free will to say no to conditioning (see chapter 3). With slowing down, the gap between thought and action increases, and a freer exercise of the choice of the quantum self is possible. The reward—the bliss of the quantum-self consciousness—is immediate; this is why people become attached to regular performance of a spiritual ritual—in the evening, for example.

Patanjali, author of the *Yoga Sutra*, sees yoga as psychic discipline and control. Sastriji doesn't disagree, but he augments Patanjali's definition with the idea that yoga is also slowing down. There is a famous saying in Sanskrit: *kartum akartum anyatha kartum yogah*, which means that yoga is the choice to do, not to do, or to do something else. Slowing down allows you greater freedom to choose.

Sastriji points out that many modern rituals unconsciously have the same purpose. Consider the coffee break, for example. What is the coffee break doing if not slowing you down from the busyness of thinking and work? And your response is an immediate "aah." There is an expansion of consciousness (though a small one) from the small cocoon of the ego to the bliss of the atman. We ordinarily mistake the object of enjoyment, the coffee, as the source of happiness. No. The happiness reached through sensory enjoyment (*bhogasukha* in Sanskrit) has its origin in the happiness of identity with Brahman (*Brahmasukha* in Sanskrit). "Whoever finds joy finds it by touching Brahman," said Shankara.

In the terms of science within consciousness, slowing down is the key to going beyond identification with the end product of the secondary-awareness processes of collapse, which is the ego. Conversely, when our actions originate in the preconscious awareness, closer to the quantum self, time seems to slow down for us. Ask any athlete. A cricket fieldsman can make a spectacular catch because he sees the ball moving rather slowly; time has slowed down for him.

The karmakanda, the book of ritual actions, which at first glance seems meaningless, is actually designed to complement the jnanakanda, the book of Vedic wisdom. Of course, the rituals of the karmakanda are now outdated and need to be adapted for modern times. But rituals are valuable aids to spirituality. It is rituals that make Catholicism more attractive than Protestantism for many people. Hinduism and Tibetan Buddhism attract Westerners for the same reason. The expanded consciousness afforded by rituals enables us to recognize and collapse nonlocal states of experience never manifested before. We identify naturally with a larger self than our ordinary identity. Happiness is the quantum self!

Action and the Fruit of the Action

One of the keys to karma yoga—action as a path to inner creativity—is the distinction between the right to act and the right to the fruit of the action. Our right to act does not entitle us to the fruit of the action, says the Bhagavad Gita. What is the Gita trying to convey? Is it scientific to expect that we in our egoism can relinquish the fruit of the action? Won't all our motivation disappear if we stop expecting the fruit of our action?

The point is subtle. The Gita says to give up your right to the fruit of action, not necessarily your expectation of the fruit. To be human, to identify with the ego, is to expect—this is our conditioning. Expectation is how we plan for the future, and some future planning is essential for any but the most trivial acts. But to think that our expectations will always be realized is to make the ego omniscient and omnipotent. This is unscientific.

Actions are either conditioned acts or acts of creation. In the former, the fruit depends on the conditioned interplay of the components of a very complex system, and prediction of the outcome is highly uncertain. In the latter, the freedom of choice that precipitates a creative act belongs to the unitive consciousness—God, or the quantum self—not to any individual human ego. To accept that we have the right to act and the right to expect our action to bring results, but no right to the fruit of the action, brings us to accept the limitedness of our ego-identity, to realize our alienation from God when we are identified with the ego. This acceptance is an opening toward a more inclusive, less limited modality. Ramana Maharshi used to say: Put your luggage down; the train is already moving. That is, once you are on the train you needn't carry your luggage any more; the train is carrying it for you. We don't need to worry about things beyond our control.

With the Gita's counsel in mind, then, we can act even though our expectation may not be met. Opening ourselves to possible failure is an important part of creativity. One failure need not stop us from acting again. We learn from our failures.

We have a right to action, but no right to the fruit of the action. As we learn to act with acceptance of this truth, we also begin to see that we are not the doer. The doer is either the past conditioning of many interacting parts in a complicated system or the unitive consciousness in its freedom of choice. Sure, the action involves my body-mind-ego; I make the causal connection. But that's all I am—a causal vehicle for unitive consciousness to carry out its will.

Now we are ready for the next stage, when our expectations involve not only ourselves but others, not as extensions of our ego but as recipients of our love.

Ethics and Science

Ethical actions are those taken with consideration and compassion for others. The Golden Rule of ethics appears in all religions. For example:

- HINDUISM: This is the sum of duty; do naught unto others which if done to thee will cause thee pain.

- ZOROASTRIANISM: That nature alone is good which refrains from doing unto another whatsoever is not good for itself.

- TAOISM: Regard your neighbor's gain as your own gain, and your neighbor's loss as your own loss.

- BUDDHISM: Hurt not others in ways you would find hurtful.

- CONFUCIANISM: Do not unto others what you would not have them do unto you.

- JAINISM: In happiness and suffering, in joy and grief, we should regard all creatures as we regard our own self.

- JUDAISM: Whatever you hatest thyself, that do not do to another.

- CHRISTIANITY: All things whatsoever ye would that men should do to you, do ye ever so to them.

- ISLAM: No one of you is a believer until he desires for his brother that which he desires for himself.

- SIKHISM: As thou deemest thyself, so deem others. (Iyer 1983, 36)

In the light of materialist science, the question of ethics is puzzling. The only basic value that materialists can come up with is the necessity of survival. Genes want to perpetuate themselves. Acting altruistically may be beneficial to a "gene machine" (such as ourselves) because to the extent that we share genes with the person we help, we are also helping our own genes to survive and propagate. In this view, our ethical responsibility moves concentrically—from our parents or children to our siblings, then to cousins, then to people of our own clan with whom we intermarry, and so forth. But the study of altruistic people does not agree with this narrow view (Ray 1996).

If biology cannot settle the issue, can philosophy? There are two notable philosophies of ethics: the philosophy of utilitarianism, developed by Bentham and Mill, and the philosophy of Immanuel Kant. Utilitarianism is particularly consonant with the spirit of materialism; ethics becomes a convenience to ensure the greatest good for the greatest number. Speaking as a proponent of idealism, Kant suggested that we follow the ways of ethics because of a categorical imperative, conscience. Is there any scientific basis for this categorical imperative? What does idealist science have to say about this?

If consciousness collapses quantum possibility into actuality and we are that consciousness, then certainly it would seem that we choose and are responsible for our actions. Alas, it is not that simple. To the extent that we are identified with our ego, we do not exercise freedom of choice. Our actions are reactive, defensive, and conditioned. We are unable to choose and, therefore, unable to bear responsibility.

Given that most people's identities are defined by and limited to the conditioned ego, the materialist ethic of the greatest good for the greatest number serves to protect the innocent from conditioned criminal behavior. True idealist ethics holds only when we begin to feel conscience or a Kantian imperative to follow ethics. Then the Golden Rule makes complete sense: I will not hurt another because the other is me. When we undertake the spiritual journey beyond ego, ethics becomes an important tool, a creative path to follow on our way (Goswami 1993).

Ethics and Love in Spiritual Practice

What is the role of ethical action in spiritual practice? Why should consideration and compassion for others help us shift beyond the ego's bondage and limitation?

Selfish or unethical actions, which are conditioned, invariably produce the doubt: Am I doing the right thing? The voice of conscience (*viveka* in Sanskrit) tears us apart. The more conflict there is between our actions and our conscience, the more constricted our consciousness becomes. Compassionate action, on the other hand, expands our consciousness and immediately produces the happiness that comes with expansion.

Moreover, since the ego operates in a simple hierarchy, when we are identified with our ego we look at the world hierarchically, with ourselves at the top of the hierarchy. All causal narrative begins with me; all causal importance is attributed to me. I can love you but only if you are "mine" in some way: my spouse, my child, my lover or friend, my countryman. The ego's world is solipsistic; only "I" am real, all else is my extension.

In contrast, the quantum self is tangled-hierarchical in relationship with the objects of its awareness. The subject and object are split but co-dependent. There is experience but no personal self that experiences. There is only the verb—the subject and the object are implicit.

Our action is truly ethical when it is moved spontaneously by unconditional love and compassion; when only the verb—only loving, free of hierarchy—defines the action. Acting from this place, we fall into the tangled hierarchy of the quantum self, abandoning the simple hierarchy of the limited ego. So ethical action, like ritual, is a vehicle for spiritual growth.

From another standpoint, seldom is an act good or evil in itself; its moral value depends on the context, which is often somewhat ambiguous. For this reason, ethics is not a matter of following a moral rule absolutely in all circumstances. That is fanaticism. Moral decisions confront us with choice and responsibility in a way that demands a creative response. If we enter the creative process, when we take the quantum leap the ethical choice arises spontaneously from insight, not from deliberation, which is limited and often self-serving.

Our internal state is more difficult to look at than we acknowledge; it is much easier to preach to others. For instance, the path of peace activism seems easy at the outset, but it is often betrayed because of the activist's own inner violence. The American mystic known as Peace Pilgrim suffered many ups and downs before peace became truly stabilized in her actions (Peace Pilgrim 1982).

In terms of the Hindu concept of yugas, there is a reason for emphasizing unselfish altruism in these times. Three yugas (eras) have preceded the current one, the kali yuga. In the earlier yugas we were much less identified with our egos, the distractions were less compelling, the separateness less intense, and the return journey to unity less arduous. Who now has the time for a rigorous practice of meditation, Patanjali-style? This is why the wise say: In the kali yuga go directly for God's grace. Love someone unconditionally, serve somebody, and remember God. "My religion is kindness," says the Dalai Lama. Make loving kindness your religion. In the kali yuga, that is enough.

We seem to know this intuitively. With the present materialism and distracting technology in the West, we may think that altruism should be at an all-time low. But a recent survey shows that it is on an upswing. More than twenty percent of Americans engage in altruism (Ray 1996).

The Reincarnational Context

Unlike physical laws, ethical laws are not inviolable. However, this does not entitle us to live unethically, even if we are not spiritually inclined. According to the law of karma, every action done intentionally has both immediate and long-term effects. In the context of the scheme of reincarnation, this means that loving another moves us forward spiritually, while harming another sets up karmic reverberations that may take lifetimes to resolve. Understood in these terms, we are wise to avoid the negative results of harming another. Otherwise, we pay for it in another life.

Why do bad things happen to good people? Religions without a reincarnational doctrine constantly struggle with this question. One answer is to simply acknowledge the role of conditioned forces acting on the multiple parts of a complex system. But one can, with some legitimacy, counter that such conditioning is itself part of God's design. And so the question remains.

According to the theories of reincarnation and karma, bad things that happen to people who are ethical and creative provide opportunities to recover from negative propensities acquired in past lives; that is, they are opportunities to burn up past karma. The arrows released in ignorance from your bow must fly their course, for good or ill. It is God's design that the conditioning not only of this life but of past lives influences our actions. The universe is a school, of sorts; we learn to know ourselves in order to gain our most creative destiny. To learn is to take responsibility for our mistakes and then correct our mistakes, even those accrued in past lives.

Supramental Ethics

Ethics and morality are conceived in the West in a rather straight-arrow, linear fashion. Neither creativity nor the karma involved in ethics is taken into account, and thus fundamentalists committed to rigid dogmas become the pallbearers of a dead ethics in Western culture. In the spiritual traditions of India, interestingly, ethics is conceived of as dynamic. (India, on the other hand, lacks the "greatest good for the greatest number" of Western social ethics, which explains why there is so much corruption and callousness in Indian society.) But the literature of ethics in India is confusing, even from a dynamic, creative point of view. Take the case of Krishna, for example. He is an *avatara*, an incarnation of God, born with full knowledge of who he is. But the great epic the Mahabharata describes Krishna acting many times in ways that would be considered unethical for ordinary mortals.

For example, when the evil prince Duryodhana has the upper hand in a fight, using clubs, with the Pandava hero Bhima, Krishna reminds Bhima of his vow to break the thighs of Duryodhana, even though hitting the opponent below the navel is illegal. And Bhima breaks the thighs of his unsuspecting opponent and wins. (Why did Bhima take this vow? To make a very long story short, the Pandava king Yudhishthira lost the Pandava brothers' common wife, Draupadi, to slavery to Duryodhana in a dice game. And Duryodhana lecherously invited Draupadi to sit on his thighs.)

Or take the case of the great renunciate sage Parasara, who saw the beautiful Matsyagandha, daughter of a fisherman, and became so struck with carnal desire that he had to have her. Vyasa, the author of Mahabharata, was born out of their union. But what kind of renunciate is he who cannot discipline his sexuality?

Karma and creativity cannot explain such dilly-dallying with ethical principles. What is the explanation, then? The Indian tradition recognizes an exalted level of being in which ethics itself is transcended. Krishna and Parasara danced to a higher law than the laws of ethics. This higher law Aurobindo has called supramental, beyond the mind.

Lower animals do not have ethics; they are utterly controlled by their instincts, which have been conditioned in them for millions of years. For humans self-discipline is possible. The mind can overrule instinct to some extent. Hence, ethics is important for inner creativity. But with liberation, which is a shift of identity from the ego to the quantum self, there is total freedom. This does not mean that the liberated become unethical or immoral; rather, in their union with truth they transcend even the laws of ethics and morality. They see beyond the laws to the reality that the laws reflect.

CHAPTER TWELVE

The Spiritual Journey

THE BEGINNING of the journey
beyond ego is as varied as the ego-characters of people. But the trans-
formational effect is the same—the shift from an ego-identity toward
an identification with the quantum self. I call this shift the awakening
of buddhi. *Buddhi* is a Sanskrit word meaning intelligence. Etymo-
logically, intelli*gence* comes from the root word *intelligo*, which means
"to select among." Indeed, with the awakening of buddhi we are able
to discriminate among our choices; we begin to become aware of the
quantum self and to take responsibility for the choices we make, or it
makes. In our ego level of being, the process of selection from among
the possibilities that the quantum mind presents to consciousness is
entirely preconscious.

As the center of the self shifts beyond ego and buddhi awakens,
action is increasingly initiated from the quantum self. This action's
signature is spontaneity, which creates the sense of wonder that the
poet Walt Whitman celebrated in these lines:

To me every hour of the light and dark is a miracle,
Every cubic inch of space is a miracle,
Every square yard of the earth is spread with the same,
Every foot of the interior swarms with the same. (Whitman 1969)

The buddhi level of being brings a welcome freedom from compulsive self-preoccupation. You may sometimes feel this freedom—for instance, when you spontaneously burst into singing in the shower. But can you imagine feeling that kind of freedom throughout the day?

Ken Wilber became famous for his idea of a spectrum of consciousness, an idea that has come under some criticism of late. But in the present model we recognize several bands within the buddhi level of identity and thus find some support for Wilber's idea.[1] These bands are not hierarchical, mind you, because as the identity shifts away from the ego, hierarchies also dissolve in the growth of profound humility. Instead, these bands are development stages. The first may be called the creative/psychic/mystic band; people of this band have discovered the potency of the quantum self, heightened awareness, and quantum leaps. They thrive on creative endeavors in arts, music, even science; they have frequent parapsychological experiences; some develop mystical powers of healing. In summary, they continue to explore outer creativity and reap rewards in these domains; the buddhi level of their being is not yet stabilized. The shift of their identity beyond ego is only transient.

The next band can be called the transpersonal, since the psychosocial context of living no longer enchants. In this band people discover the nonlocality and tangled hierarchy of relationship, and their creativity tends to be employed in love and service to others.

To the extent that I identify with the quantum nonlocal self, I "real"-ize the consciousness of others in relationship with me in terms of tangled hierarchy. I no longer fall prey to the solipsism associated with the local and simple-hierarchical ego. Through my tangled-hierarchical relationships I appreciate the "otherness" of others—their individuality, unique perspectives, and unique problems—at the same time experiencing that we share the same consciousness. This experience of otherness is crucial before this band of self-identity can be lived. Stabilization in buddhi has begun.

Jung has shown us an additional subtlety concerning the discovery of otherness. Jung used the designation *collective unconscious* to expand the concept of consciousness in the absence of subject-object awareness (Jung 1971). Borrowing the word *unconscious* from Freud, he was also attributing the Freudian idea of repression to the collective unconscious. What do we collectively repress? In service to the requirement of our manifestation in individual form, we repress our universality. This sets up the drive of inner creativity, the urge to know ourselves. We also repress aspects of our sexuality. Males are apt to repress "female" experiences, and females their "male" experiences. According to Jung, we must bring this archetypal repression to awareness, integrating both attributes in order to be whole. Thus a man must recognize his drive to make conscious and integrate his anima (the unconscious, repressed female within), and a woman must integrate her animus, her missing inner male. This is the most difficult part of the discovery of otherness, and the most sweet.

In the third band, which can be called the spiritual band, one surrenders even the last vestige of individual ego, the idea of creatively serving the world. People of this band act in the wholeness of the quantum self; they experience the seamlessness of consciousness, recognizing apparent individuality as a purely functional aspect of manifestation. Life is firmly anchored in appropriate action—creative or not. Buddhi has stabilized.

We now can explicate a difference between the inner creativity of religion and the outer creativity of science. When outer creativity is manifested, the ego is the central player. So the ego boost inherent in regarding a product as an accomplishment does no harm to the product. But in inner creativity, any such inflation of the ego is a detriment to the process, delaying or distorting the manifestation of the wisdom of the insight.

While in outer creativity manifestation is mostly at the level of the ego, inner creativity involves a surrender of ego. Instead of being the decision-maker, the ego becomes a mere function. The ego is necessary as a function to carry out worldly chores, but the distinction of "I" from others is merely an operational convenience. It's a little like the healing process for a patient with multiple-personality disorder— a fragmentation of the ego into many selves with separate identities. As integration proceeds, the function of each of the fragments is incorporated, making separate identities no longer necessary. So also in the relationship of the quantum self and the ego. As a person becomes stabilized in buddhi, one's identification shifts gradually from the ego to the quantum self. With this shift come both a growing humility and an increasing freedom of choice and creativity in action. The dancer more and more becomes the dance.

Obstructions

A common experience for most everyone who has ever followed a spiritual path is a gratifying success initially, as if a new well of joy or relaxation or subtle happiness has opened. Alas! Sooner than we know it, the well seems to dry up. What happens?

The major obstruction on the spiritual journey is the tendency to habituate. After we have meditated for a while it becomes ritualized and no longer engages us. The same thing happens with jnana practice. We solve our first few koans with gusto, and then we hit a snag. Or the meaning of spiritual treatises seems trite. So also, we discover the joy of altruism, only to find that we are not loving to our immediate family. Or we entirely lose enthusiasm for acting in the service of others.

When habituation obstructs us, it is time to remember that other paths are available, that all the methods support one another. You can have a wonderful jnana insight into the nature of your self, but you must manifest it in your life in the context of your relationships. When your jnana practice dries up and your books cease to be meaningful and exciting, it is time to cultivate your ability to love. In other words, seek wisdom, but seek it lovingly.

Similarly, bhakti without jnana may degenerate into dualistic, conditioned habit patterns. Bhakti sets up a dynamic I-Thou relationship with the inner self. The goal is to penetrate the falsity of the ego's simple-hierarchical relationship with others. But if your practice sinks into dualistic role playing, it sabotages the yoga and calcifies into conditioning. The remedy is to develop a deep conceptual understanding of the nature of maya—the tangled-hierarchical nature of our experiences—to strive for insights into your quantum-self nature; this is jnana yoga's strength.

Are you getting the point? Bhakti afficionados are often experience junkies who tend to belittle conceptual exploration. But if you don't have adequate conceptual contexts for your experiences, how will you ever clothe your experiences with understanding? Your progress will surely be stultified. Once you have a grip on the concepts and insights that lead you forward, you can return to the role of God's devotee. Firmly established in the wisdom of the unity, you can play your role without confusion.

Another obstruction that commonly confuses us on the spiritual path is the deep genetic conditioning of sexuality. How can we manifest true tangled hierarchy in relation to the opposite sex without gaining some understanding and control of our minds and bodies with raja yoga, Patanjali style? The instinctual force of sexuality can easily lead to rationalizing the desire to possess the other as a love object. The frequency of reports of sexual scandals involving spiritual gurus testifies to the power of this drive. The method of tantra, creativity of the vital-physical body, defines a whole new path for dealing with sexuality (see chapter 13).

And, as I see it, when all the other yogic journeys stagnate, there is always the support of karma yoga, appropriate action. Nothing can steady your faltering better. But karma yoga is difficult to sustain without the reciprocal support of bhakti or meditation or jnana.

The preceding are obstructions that arise from our tendency to condition even our deconditioning practices. Additional obstructions are due to childhood conditioning, which contributes to what Jung called the shadow. Past-life conditioning also has important consequences for our spiritual journey, though it is not necessarily all obstructive. And ultimately, as Ramana Maharshi points out, even our practice becomes an obstruction.

Dharma and Svadharma

A verse in the Bhagavad Gita admonishes us to follow our *svadharma*, our own *dharma*; it is preferable to die following our own dharma, says the verse, than to follow the dharma of another.

What is dharma? According to Hinduism, there are four goals of human life: *dharma*, right action or ethical duties; *artha*, money or security; *kama*, desire; and *moksha*, liberation. People often wonder why dharma comes first, even before the egoic pursuits of security and desire. However, dharma is not only ethical duties; it is the creative destiny I chose even before I was born. Thus, in order to live our lives according to the purpose of the universe, our pursuits of security and desire must be guided by dharma.

A story from ancient India illustrates the importance of dharma. One day, a pretty woman approached a wealthy, capable, and right-minded king and asked for refuge. As was his custom, the king granted her shelter in his palace. But the woman was evil and continued to practice her evil ways even under the king's protection.

First, the head security man complained. "O noble king, this woman to whom you have granted refuge is Alakshmi, evil incarnate. I've been watching her for days. Please throw her out, or I will have to leave." The king was sad because he knew the man was telling the truth. Yet he did not turn the woman out, and so he let the security man go.

One by one, the king's servants, relatives, and eventually even the queen, in tears, similarly left. The palace became a place of gloom. And finally, one night the king saw a grand old man with a golden aura leaving the palace.

"Who are you, and why are you leaving?" the king inquired. "I am Dharma," came the reply. "I am leaving because I do not like to be near evil, Alakshmi."

"O Dharma, you are leaving unjustifiably," exclaimed the king. "Undeniably the woman is Alakshmi. And yet, how could I refuse her shelter? It is my dharma to safeguard any person who wants my protection. I rule over both good subjects and bad. I cannot discriminate and still remain within my own dharma."

The god of justice saw his mistake and turned his footsteps back to the palace. And with his return, gradually all the others came back. Finally, Alakshmi came to the king and said, "Since you chose Dharma over me, I have to go." Now the king gladly let her go.

There are such stories in every culture. The knights of King Arthur's Round Table, for instance, lived for their dharma—their honor, character, and above all else, their duty.

An important task as an individual quantum monad (*jiva* in

Sanskrit) is to discover your svadharma—your destiny, your bliss—and follow it! Your character is more important than your particular story line. You learn to honor your character, your duties. Often this means sacrificing the egoic demands of selfish melodrama. So be it.

Living as an Evolving Quantum Monad

As a person of destiny, in addition to your svadharma you also know your ultimate duty: to serve the creative purposiveness of the universe as long as you are tied to the wheel of *samsara*. Knowing this, creativity becomes your steadfast mode of living.

In bhakti practice, you want to develop your character further and enlarge the contexts of service that you now live. In karma yoga practice, you work to enlarge the contexts of your duties. Both these tasks involve jnana and meditation practice as well. Through jnana yoga, you discover the contexts of inner transformation, learning first-hand that you are more than your ego. You meditate to obtain a greater awareness of your karmic patterns. Knowing these patterns helps you to free yourself and to avoid creating new karmic involvements.

Indian psychology recognizes three *gunas* (qualities) that can be interpreted, in modern Western terms, as unconscious drives. *Tamas* is the guna of sluggishness and inertia and can easily be understood as the unconscious drive of behavioral conditioning—remaining as you are. The *rajas* guna is expressed as fickleness and restlessness and is akin to the Freudian concept of the libido. Rajas is the contribution of the vital body's programs, expressed through the genes, to our patterns of thought and behavior. It is rajas that drives us to acquire material prosperity and power for the sake of survival and security. The third guna, *sattva*, literally meaning illumination, is the crown jewel among our drives; it is the drive toward creativity. In Jungian terms, sattva is the collective unconscious's drive to make the unconscious conscious. The dominance or absence of sattva must be attributed to karmic inheritance. Knowing your gunas, particularly sattva, is part of knowing your reincarnational patterns. If your sattva is tainted by too much tamas and rajas, purifying it is a good idea.

Once your identity is firmly established in the fluidity of the buddhi level of being, you will find that following your destiny, maintaining your dharma, and even purifying your sattva have become easy and straightforward. Now you can be creative without creating new karma. You can serve the purposiveness of the universe through outer creativity from a more inclusive level of being. You can examine your life for missing themes and concentrate on discovering them. This involves working with what Carl Jung called repressed archetypes —archetypes such as the hero, the anima, the trickster, and so forth that have thus far not found expression in our lives (Jung 1971).

Working with Archetypes

The anima is the archetypal image in the male mind that is comprised of qualities, such as nurturance, that represent femininity. Similarly, the animus is the archetypal image in the female mind of what is masculine. A human being, male or female, embodies all human characteristics. However, genetic and social conditioning exert considerable pressure to exhibit only, or primarily, those traits that correspond to one's gender. These pressures, accordingly, weight the probabilities of the possibility waves against expression of gender-inappropriate behavior and lead to its repression.

Such conditioned behavior, fortunately, is not destiny. In order to fully realize our human potential, it is desirable for each of us to acknowledge and incorporate the strengths of the opposite gender.

(Notice that our weaknesses, such evils as selfishness, greed, hate, jealousy, and the like, are not gender specific.) Working with the anima or the animus integrates our man-woman polarity, an integration that is alluded to in the famous Hindu depiction of *ardhanarishvara*, God as half male, half female. At this stage you consciously work toward identifying with your individual quantum monad, your jiva—a process that ends in individuation (a term coined by Jung), the fulfillment of your monadic contextual responsibilities. This is a creative task.

Receptivity, for example, is a core "feminine" quality that is commonly repressed in males. An incident in the life of Mira Bai, an Indian mystic, suggests one benefit that comes to males who cultivate this trait. Mira, a fervent devotee of Krishna, traveled to his birthplace, Vrindavan, a spiritual mecca of India, and sought the guidance of a certain guru there. However, when she wrote to him for acceptance as a student, he rejected her because she was a woman. Not to be deterred, she wrote back with the challenge, "How is it that being a woman disqualifies me from your presence? I thought Krishna was the only man in Vrindavan." The guru immediately wrote back inviting her to join him. He saw that Mira recognized the importance of receptivity in approaching the quantum self; it is essential for insight in inner creativity. Bringing receptivity into awareness is a great advantage in a man's spiritual journey.

Similarly, a woman needs her animus awakened to enhance the "masculine" qualities of preparation, perseverence (will), and production—the three "p"s essential to the creative process. The heroine of the movie *Wolf* drifts without will through life until she meets the movie's hero. Impotent before the powers of competitive business, he had allowed himself to be vanquished by the villain until he rediscovered his personal power after being bitten by a werewolf. Courting the werewolf herself, the heroine embraces her animus and rediscovers her own power in a climactic battle with the villain.

A good way to meet your own anima or animus is from within a committed relationship, which inevitably confronts us with the gender tension between male and female. Learning within a context of love to validate the anima/animus qualities we project on the other can lead us toward wholeness. In the unique I-thou encounter at play here, "thou" is your own anima/animus, embodied in your partner. Your dreams during this encounter can provide significant guidance as you integrate these important archetypes.

The hero is a compelling archetype in the creative attempt to purify sattva. Every creative act, large or small, can be seen as the culmination of a hero's journey; the hero steps into the unknown on a quest, gains insight, and returns with a new product: the quintessential creative process. The hero archetype attracts all of us. Zeus, in the *Iliad*, pulls all things to himself with a golden cord; the *gopis* (dairy maids) drop everything to be with Krishna when they hear the sound of his flute. And the sound of the flute or the pull of the golden cord, once felt, propels you irreversibly on the creative inner journey. To integrate the hero, you must surrender the ego and do the bidding of the archetype as you perceive it in moments of intuition or insight.

You can see the challenges to a modern hero's journey in the movie *The Accidental Tourist*. As in *Wolf*, the hero, Macon Leary, has been vanquished, this time by a painful personal loss. He is emotionally dead, having insulated himself from possible further loss by turning his back on creative possibility. He has abandoned the hero's journey. His wife leaves him, after which he meets Muriel Pritchard, whose warmth and Kali-like (Kali is the Indian goddess of purification) energy initiate a guarded thaw in his frozen emotional landscape. He finds he cannot go back to the bleakness of his marriage. Frantically looking for a taxi to the airport, he finally drops the suitcase he has been lugging—and with it, symbolically, the emotional pain he has been clutching. Finally in a taxi, he sees Muriel on the sidewalk. Macon's smile radiates life and hope; he has reconnected with his anima and now can resume his hero's journey.

All great creatives make their hero's journey from within the process of their creative act. The inner creative whose hero archetype has been integrated is the hero personified at all times; without much effort she or he lives on the razor's edge even in ordinary awareness, even off the stage of creativity. In India people regard such a person as an *avatara* of the archetype in play. For example, they see Shankara as an avatara of Shiva, the master yogi, so steadfast and integrated was Shankara's yoga.

Working with the Shadow Archetype

Spiritual people are sometimes considered "mad." But do they really have something in common with schizophrenics? Primary-awareness processes and the flow encounter of the ego with the quantum self are thought to define much of the waking awareness of inner creatives. So the reverse question can be raised: Are schizophrenics in the sway of the quantum modality? Are they frustrated or short-circuited creatives? In my view, no; psychopathology is related to the repression dynamic of the personal unconscious—the ego underfunctions because of repressed mental and emotional states—whereas inner creativity involves the universal quantum self that transcends the ego.

But the strange associations that mental patients sometimes make seem to be similar to those of creative and spiritual people. Carl Jung cited a mental patient suffering from paranoid dementia who thought of the world—in a way not unlike the great philosopher Schopenhauer —as his picture book. To thicken the plot, many inner creatives (the East Indian saint Ramakrishna is a prime example) have referred to themselves as "mad."

I suggest that getting lost in the play of what Jung called the shadow archetype accounts for the craziness of the mystics. The apparent fragmentation of the psyche in creatives is between the ego and the quantum self. (In schizophrenia, on the other hand, the conditioned psyche splinters into multiple ego structures, a fragmentation that originates in the personal unconscious.) When inner creatives seek a new center from which to act, one that is weighted more heavily toward the quantum self, they may find a barrier. This barrier is the shadow—material, both collective and personal, that has been repressed to satisfy the demands of social form and early conditioning. Bringing the "light" of awareness to the shadow avoids fragmentation, facilitating wholeness.

Jung considered shadow cleansing to be a major challenge in Western spirituality because of the cultural tendency to suppress childhood emotions. In general, Easterners are less emotionally suppressed (East Indians, for example, are a very emotionally expressive people), and their shadow is different. On the other hand, Easterners are more conditioned than Westerners to obey and revere authority and elders. Accordingly, their suppression is concentrated in the mental arena, and this is the shadow that needs to be brought to light for them.

The conditioned ego normally mounts a strong defense, richly fueled by personal repressions, against shadow cleansing and the effort to integrate the archetypes of creative freedom. In the story of Orpheus we find this struggle mythologized beautifully. The music of Orpheus charms even animals. When death takes his beloved Eurydice, his anima, Orpheus enters Hades in search of her. He finds her and wins permission to lead her back to light and life, but on one condition: he must not look back while she follows him out of Hades. Unfortunately, Orpheus succumbs to his anxiety, and unable to bear creative uncertainty, he looks back. Death reclaims Eurydice, who is now truly lost to Orpheus.

Replaying the Orpheus myth, some mystics may go crazy or

commit suicide. But more of them successfully meet the challenge of the shadow, transforming the myth and sometimes writing about it. This gave us Dante's *Divina Comedia*. Dante's Beatrice, his retrieved anima, actually leads him to fulfillment.

Thus shadow cleansing is not really cleansing; it is integrating. Working with your shadow cleanses your ego, increasing your openness to the quantum self. Then the ego, functioning appropriately in a strong and aware fashion, is an asset in handling the anxiety that accompanies the creative encounter with the quantum self. Only a strong ego can remain open to transformation until the moment of surrender to the quantum-self modality.

Cleansing the ego enables the mystic to move into ever deeper realms of inner creativity. Ramakrishna was "crazy" in his devotion to Kali. The naked, dark goddess of Hindu mythology, Kali is the cleansing goddess.

The Question of Gurus

There is a lasting myth in some spiritual traditions that to be truly initiated into a path of inner creativity, we must have a guru, an enlightened teacher. But the quantum self, the atman, is the guru, as some of these traditions explicitly acknowledge, and it is not separate from us. If we are sinking into quicksand, we cannot pull ourselves up by our own bootstraps; a law of Newton prevents us. But it is possible to bootstrap ourselves out of the quicksand of ego-identity, because the ego-identity is not real. The ego's simple hierarchy and its solipsistic perspective is a covering of ignorance over the clear consciousness that is the atman. To expect another, guru or not, to do our creative work for us is to perpetuate the ignorance.

Nevertheless, the traditions make a valid point. Investigation into consciousness is difficult because "what we are looking for is what is looking." Liberation, the ultimate goal of esoteric spiritual paths, is always present. Even the covering is ultimately an illusion, so there is nothing to dis-cover. Therefore, Truth, turiya, is an impossible proposition to prove. Only a guru can help you break through this logical logjam. A story illustrates this point. One day, ten school children who are just learning to count go swimming. The teacher has told them to keep count of each other lest someone gets lost, so after the swim, one of them starts counting. One, two, three . . . nine—he counts all the kids and panics. Where is the tenth? The others count too, with the same result. Then an adult appears, who sees the problem immediately and solves it for them—you didn't count yourself; you yourself are the tenth.

Gurus are our reminders. Unfortunately, they become our excuses. For example, in Christianity, Jesus is used as the excuse for avoiding the creative exploration implied in the message "Jesus saves." Yes, Jesus saves, but you have to surrender to him, and that takes inner creativity. Inner creativity requires that we lift ourselves beyond the simple hierarchy of the ego-identity to the tangled hierarchy of the quantum self. We cannot reach a relationship based in a tangled hierarchy through the simple hierarchy that some power-based guru-disciple relationships demand. If perchance we encounter one of those wise individuals who understands and engages in tangled-hierarchical relationships, then only have we found our guru. In India, such a guru is called a *sadguru*.

The following story illustrates what a sadguru is not. Among the disciples of certain guru, one of them excelled in devotion. So great was his devotion that one day he was able to walk on water while uttering his guru's name. The guru began to tell others about this as a reflection of his own greatness. One day, a skeptic challenged him, "If your name is so great, why don't you show me that you too can walk on water while uttering your own name?" Lost in his pride, the guru felt up to the challenge and tried to walk on the river. And not knowing how to swim, he drowned.

Why is a guru, even a sadguru, needed? Gurus let us glimpse, via the interconnectedness that quantum nonlocality and nonlocal consciousness allow us, what a happy being dwelling in wholeness is like. This is a phenomenon much similar to electromagnetic induction—iron becomes magnetic in the vicinity of a real magnet. Gurus also give us direction; they cannot give us the moon but they can point to it. Most importantly, gurus give us inspiration to carry on our intuition-launched investigation toward spiritual insight.

There is also the adage: when the disciple is ready the guru comes. In my life I have found repeated evidence of this. Whenever I needed a teacher, one was there. In the seventies when I began my spiritual journey, I read Ram Dass and Krishnamurti voraciously; they were all the teachers I needed at that time. Then when books failed me, unexpected help came. In the summer of 1984, I found myself six thousand feet up in the Eastern Sierras at the ashram of an American mystic, the philosopher Franklin Merrell-Wolff. Ninety-seven years old, his sense of humor was intact, but he was no longer able to sustain great intellectual discussions. So we just sat together in his garden as he intermittently dozed. I still fondly refer to the month I spent with him in this way as "Shangri-la." Franklin was the living confirmation I needed as to the relevance of spiritual investigation.

Again a little rudderless in 1991, I was invited to give a talk at a conference in Bangalore, India. The travel to India was to be at my own expense, so I was hesitant, but the man on the telephone who invited me was very forceful. He said, "You must come." So I went. There I met the Vedanta teacher Satyanarayan Sastry, who surprised me by asking, "How are you when you are by yourself?" That question catapulted me to the next stage of my *sadhana* (practice), because the more I pondered the question, the more I had to admit to myself that when alone, if I was not working I was restless and bored. Rarely was I alone and at peace.

However, the full meaning of this adage—when the disciple is ready, the teacher will come—can be appreciated only in a reincarnational framework. After many lifetimes, when we are finally ready for the inward journey to liberation, the teacher comes; we don't really have to look. Thus there is no need to lose heart if the sadguru has not come to you in this life and your wanting to want God has taken you to many false or limited gurus. The time is not right yet. Remember! It's a school, and there is no backtracking. One can learn even from false gurus, to whom bad karma can accrue. But there is no such thing as a false disciple.

Notes

1. The idea of bands or levels of a spectrum of consciousness was first discussed in modern psychology in Wilber (1977).

CHAPTER THIRTEEN

Vital Body Creativity and the Meaning of Tantra

SUCH LUMINARIES as Sri Aurobindo and Teilhard de Chardin have suggested that consciousness in manifestation evolves with time as more and more of its themes are better and better manifested. Whether there is overall progress in the evolution of manifest consciousness can be debated. However, we can readily identify periods in history when gigantic leaps in human creativity produced gigantic leaps in the outer manifestations of the self and, thereby, in society. In this vein we can ask, What is the future of human creativity? When will the next giant leap come, and what will its form be? I believe the next major step will involve the creativity of the body.

Our self-identity evolves creatively toward an identity with the quantum self. In chapters 10 and 11, we surveyed practices that help to shift our identity to the buddhi—to stages beyond ego in which the quantum-self and classical-self identities are more integrated. But in actuality, these practices mostly purify the self from tendencies toward tamas; without the tyranny of so much ego-mind driving it, the self can spontaneously fall into sattva.

However, when rajas is also strong, this seldom happens. Transcendence of the tendencies toward rajas is rarely dealt with directly. Rajas is connected with the vital software in the physical body and with the brain-body connection, with our immune and endocrine systems, and so forth. Sigmund Freud spoke of the importance for creative people of sublimating sexuality. Transcendence of rajas is the same issue—the sublimation (transcendence, rather) of sexuality is deeply connected with the creativity of the body, as we will see in this chapter.

Let's begin with a discussion of health and healing from the perspective of creativity. I believe that disease, both physical and mental, is a sign of how far we are from a creative approach to the correlated vital-physical body. "Mr. Duffy lived a short distance from his body," wrote novelist James Joyce. We have all become like Mr. Duffy, living with all our vital energies centered in the brain-mind most of the time, as if separate from the feelings in the rest of our vital-physical body.

Before going further with this idea, let me acknowledge that current medical practices do not view the body's lack of creativity as the major cause, or even one of the causes, of illness. Most psychologists and medical practitioners have missed the import of the paradigm shift that is taking place in physics.[1] When we look upon the brain-mind and the body in the context of idealist science, however, talking about creativity of the body makes sense.

Quantum Healing

The organizing role in the life of a cell, as well as the pivotal role in our self-consciousness that arises in connection with the brain-mind complex, is played by consciousness. In other words, the self-referential tangled hierarchy that closes a quantum measurement was completed on this planet with the manifestation of the first living cell (see chapter 5). This self-reference splits one undivided consciousness into subject and object, into life and its environment. The subsequent evolution of life on this planet is a process of consciousness bringing to bear ever more complex mappings of the vital-body life functions onto the physical body. Eventually, the brain evolves and the mind is mapped.

But it is always consciousness that lives life and underlies mentation, including the contexts of thinking, and in the process identifies with both life and mind. Our mental, vital, and physical bodies not only are interdependent through various (physical) bodily systems but ultimately are interconnected through consciousness.

This view of the life of a cell as a manifest identification of consciousness gives us an entirely new model for the mind-body connection—different from the current dualistic medical model that treats the body separately from the mind, disregards the vital body entirely, and regards consciousness as an epiphenomenon. The new model leads to a new approach to disease and cure that is based on the idea of creativity of the body at the mental and vital levels. I submit that there is plenty of evidence for the body's creativity, and therefore its role in healing is a very fertile subject for investigation. It is reassuring that such an investigation has already begun.

A new medicine is surfacing in response to medicine's own paradigmatic crisis. The new medicine is fundamentally a mind-body medicine—the mind (via consciousness) exerts causative effects on the physical body that can lead to disease and likewise to healing. Techniques of biofeedback and hypnosis have enriched the ideas of mind-body medicine. The new field of psychoneuroimmunology clearly recognizes the mind-body connection and acknowledges (though often dualistically, but the dualism can easily be avoided, as we shall see) the effect of consciousness in healing.

Furthermore, emotional thought, in contrast to rational thought, is being recognized as causative in the "mind as slayer/mind as healer" effect. Our negative emotions, such as fear, lust, and anger, are connected to conditioned maps of movements of the vital body that we call instinct. This acknowledgment has also fueled new interest in alternative systems of healing, such as Chinese medicine and the ayurvedic system of India.

Mind-body healing, of course, has been practiced as spiritual healing since antiquity, but the new trend in medicine is to incorporate these practices into the mainstream. An example is the scientific research being conducted in yogic healing in India and holistic health elsewhere (Nagendra 1993; Weil 1995).

The well-known phenomenon of the placebo effect is another example of mind-body healing. Patients who were given simple sugar pills and were told that they were being given medicine showed a higher rate of cure than patients in a control group who were given the same sugar pills and were not told they were medicine. The physician Deepak Chopra, in his ground-breaking book *Quantum Healing*, has suggested that the mind-body healing in many placebo-like cases occurs via the interaction of mind and brain through a "quantum mechanical body," and is mediated by "bliss," that is, consciousness (Chopra 1990). Chopra's idea can be put on a firm footing when we realize that consciousness mediates mind-body healing through the quantum nature of the mental and physical bodies.

How does a thought initiate the brain processes required to make a neurochemical that communicates to the immune or endocrine system, which takes the appropriate healing action? From the point of view of the psychophysical parallelism developed in chapter 7, consciousness simultaneously recognizes and chooses in the patient the healing thought (from among all the possibilities that his or her mind offers) along with the brain state that leads to the production of the required neurochemical.

Idealist science enables us to formulate an even more general theory of mind-body healing when we remember that along with the mental and the physical bodies, we also have a vital body. If the movements of the vital body—prana or chi or ki—through pathways called nadis or meridians, are quantum movements (see chapter 7), then we can posit that consciousness collapses the possibilities of all three bodies—physical, vital, and mental—simultaneously into actual events for its experience. The collapse is self-referential; the subject-object split implicit in the experience is only appearance. This avoids dualism in all its forms (the dualisms of consciousness-matter, mind-brain, subject-object, vital-physical bodies). This bio-psycho-physical parallelism enables us to understand Eastern medicine and also to integrate Eastern medicine with the medicine of the West.

Healing and the Creative Process

Gradually, a new hypothesis is arising in the field of mind-body healing—that in many cases of illness our body already has access to the requisite wisdom and mechanism for cure; we just have to discover and activate it. To me, this sounds like a program of creativity for the patient. Suppose we take the view that the known cases of remission by the placebo effect are actually spontaneous cases of creativity of the body—discovery and manifestation.[2]

Can we make self-healing into a deliberate program of creativity?

Suppose that instead of passively believing that they are getting some sort of medicine, patients actively operated under the intuition (which becomes a burning question) that their body already has the mechanism for cure, which they need only discover and manifest. The first step in such a creative approach is preparation. Patients would be encouraged to research their diseases (with active guidance from their physicians). At the next stage they and their doctors would try various techniques—visualization, reprogramming, hypnosis, new experimental drugs, to name only a few. This is the stage of creativity in which unlearned stimuli generate uncollapsed coherent superpositions and their unconscious processing (see chapter 3). These techniques are to be used not solely with the idea of cure but also with the idea that they may eventually trigger the creative insight leading the body to access and activate its own mechanism of correction.

A spontaneous remission, in this way of looking at things, corresponds to a creative insight at the body level. In support of this perspective, there is much data about patients who report a spontaneous remission as an "ah-ha!" experience.

The physician Richard Moss tells of a cancer patient who attended one of his workshops. During the workshop, she was somewhat defiant and was not responding to Moss's various attempts to energize her. But at some point Moss broke through her resistance, and she responded by participating in a spontaneous dance that led to a tremendous "ah-ha!" experience, curing her cancer (Moss 1981, 1984).

The final stage of manifestation is also important in the creativity model of healing. After remission occurs, the patient has to bring to manifestation some of the lifestyle changes that were intuited during the creative insight.

In his documented case of self-healing, the late *Saturday Review* editor Norman Cousins intuitively followed, more or less, the stages of the creative process just outlined (Cousins 1989). Some of the reported successes in treating cancer patients may well be the result of such intuitive use of the stages of creative process (Simonton et al. 1978).

An important point: creative self-healing is an idea that can be medically tested. We can study three groups of patients: the conventional placebo group, the creative-healing group, and the control group.

A study by cardiologist Randolf Byrd (1988) already indicates the quantum nature of healing, in this case, the healing of a patient through the efforts of another person. As in all creative acts, one of the telling characteristics of creative healing must be nonlocality.[3] Thus, analogous to brainstorming, one should be able to get better results by involving others in one's creative self-healing. Byrd did a study involving 393 patients in San Francisco General Hospital's cardiac care unit on the effect of prayer carried out at a distance by several home-prayer groups. The 393 subjects were divided into two groups: 192 patients who were prayed for by four to seven different people, and a control group of 201 who did not receive the benefit of any prayer at all. Neither the physician nor the patients knew who belonged to which group. Byrd found the effect of prayer, even when nonlocal, strikingly positive. For example, the prayed-for patients were five times less likely to require antibiotics and three times less prone to develop fluid in the lungs (pulmonary edema)—both statistically significant results.

The new medicine makes much more sense when we add the concept of a quantum vital body. This allows us to bridge the gap between Western and Eastern medicines. Western medicine is based on strict materialism: Life is chemistry; disease is chemistry gone awry, something to be fixed by administering chemicals from outside the system. In contrast, Eastern medicine is aware that the vital body carries the originals (the morphogenetic fields) of which the physical body's organs are representations. The Eastern view acknowledges disease as faulty chemistry in the physical representations of the vital body, to be sure, but recognizes that the fault could stem from the originals in the vital body.

Disease means that a software representation for a certain vital function has gone awry, necessitating a new, creative pathway. Mind-body healing occurs when consciousness creatively collapses new possibilities in the quantum mind, which prompts the brain—and through the brain-body connection, the vital-physical body—to create a new map, a new pathway for the affected vital function.

Both ayurvedic and Chinese medicine go even further in asserting that one is born with certain propensities of the vital body from past incarnations. These propensities are often unbalanced and give rise to defects that often result in malfunctioning physical-body maps or representations. In order to correct this kind of disease, one needs to correct the vital body imbalance. Mind-body creativity alone will not be sufficient.

The difficulty with the creative approach to the vital body is that most modern people, East or West, lack familiarity with vital energy. We even seldom attend to emotions directly through the vital-physical body connection; we are too centered in our brain-mind complex. This, of course, is largely responsible for the "mind as slayer" phenomenon in the first place. In order to heal, we may try to engage the "mind as healer," but it requires mental creativity to move away from the negative emotions that "mind as slayer" created in the first place. Learning to access our emotions through our vital-physical body allows us to make an end-run around negative conditioned thinking. Once we have the same access to our vital energy as we have to our thoughts, we can concentrate directly on the creativity of the body through the creativity of the vital body.

But the problem is more complicated than first meets the eye. Previously we spoke of conscious identity at the cellular level of our body. Each of our cells is alive, carrying out the living functions that necessitate the collapse of correlated physical and vital bodies. Consciousness (none other than ourselves) does this regularly, and yet our identification with the brain-mind so overwhelms us that we are not aware of our cellular self at all. Even if we ignore our self-identity at the cellular level, there are other conglomerates of body cells besides the brain—for example, the immune and endocrine systems—that perform body functions almost as important as those of the brain-mind. Conscious self-identification with these conglomerates should be important in healing.

So, when we say access to the vital body, which vital body do we mean? There are conditioned patterns of the vital body associated not only with the brain-mind but also with many other important parts of the body. Our vital body is fragmented, much like the mind of a person with multiple personality disorder. Therefore, the creativity of the vital body requires the integration of our various vital "personalities."

In this way it is becoming clear that we must regain an experiential, conscious relationship with our vital body personalities, or vital egos, in order to be truly effective in healing; in addition to mind-body healing, we must engage in vital-physical body healing. Many techniques for this were developed in the East long ago, and they are actually the same for healing sick people and developing radiant health in well people. So before we go into techniques, let's discuss the subject of creativity of the vital-physical body for a well person.

Creativity of the Body in a Well Person

The concept of the creativity of the correlated vital-physical body is important in discussing the self-healing of disease. But how does it apply to a physically healthy person? For that matter, what is health? Health is a dynamic balance of the ego and quantum-self modalities in the affairs of the physical, vital, and mental bodies. Freedom from pain in the physical body, the main focus of Western medicine, is important, but so is freedom from the tyranny of instinct and emotions and freedom from self-imposed boundaries of the thinking ego.

In modern cultures, especially among intellectuals, there is tendency to ignore the vital-physical body. Mulla Nasruddin was taking a pundit across the river in his boat. The pundit was giving Nasruddin an earful about the importance of learning proper grammar and how the mulla was wasting half his life by not studying grammar. A little later, the mulla interrupted the pundit and asked, "Do you know how to swim?" When the pundit replied no, the mulla said, "In that case, my friend, your whole life is going to be wasted. The boat is sinking."

How do we approach the creativity of the vital-physical body for a healthy person? Through exercise: organized sports, martial arts, hatha yoga, and the like.

Interestingly, some competitive athletes are among today's greatest ascetics. Asceticism was traditionally a practice left only to people committed to the religious life. Ironically, the lure of success and money in modern sports has changed that. But there is more to sports than competition and commercial success.

There is good reason to believe that athletes at peak moments touch their quantum modality. As mentioned earlier, many athletes report the slowing down of time; for example, a baseball outfielder will tell you the reason he can catch that fast ball is because he actually sees it quite well, as in a slow-motion replay (for other examples see Leonard 1990). The explanation is that the reaction time of athletes in such acts is shortened considerably from the usual secondary-awareness processing time for motor action. This reduced reaction time takes athletes closer to primary awareness, which produces joy and a feeling of exhilaration.

The vast majority of athletes do not achieve commercial success.

Nevertheless, they enjoy their sports because of this enhanced encounter with the quantum self. In a certain sense they become attached to what creativity theorists call the "flow" experience. And this is not just for athletes. Who has not felt exhilarated occasionally by physical work such as gardening or even housework? There is flow in physical work.

The encounter with the quantum self is always creative; thus in every such encounter there is the possibility of creativity, including creativity of the vital-physical body complex. The accomplishments of modern athletes make it clear that cultivating the human body has great creative possibilities.

Unfortunately, however, organized sports give little attention to integrating the joy of body creativity with the rest of the athlete's life, which is constricted by the mental ego-structure. There is, however, an ancient system, developed mainly in China and Japan but now popular all around the world, that is designed precisely to integrate the creativity of the body with that of the mind. I am, of course, speaking of the martial arts.

Martial Arts

Competitive sports use the quantum modality of the self but only insofar as it is identified with the mind-brain complex. Since the brain controls the body through the endocrine and other systems, this is useful; athletes are able to use their bodies in creative ways, no doubt. But an even better way is to learn to access the body's own "mind"— the correlated vital counterparts of physical body conglomerates. The martial arts do this.[4]

Martial arts grew out of systems of self-defense systems for non-violent people. In defending yourself you may have to do something violent, which is generally counter to your spiritual philosophy. But can you do it without violence in your mind? You can if your emotions are integrated, if you have controlled access to your emotions, if your instinctual emotion does not invade your thought pattern. The sword kills, but that doesn't require anger in the mind. This is the general idea.

In a great martial arts story, a samurai warrior is winning a battle with the man who killed his father. But as he corners his enemy and is about to plunge his sword into the man's body, his victim spits into his face. The warrior suddenly lowers his sword and walks away from his adversary. What happened? When the man spat at him, anger and hatred rose in the samurai's mind, and it would be wrong to kill with anger and hatred in mind. This is the general goal of martial arts: to be a warrior who embodies a profound access to and control of emotions and of the movement of the vital body.

Prominent in martial arts thought is the concept of controlling chi, or vital energy. The beautiful dance of tai chi and the wonderfully aesthetic movements of aikido are expressions of this control of chi.

Recall that there is a quantum-system plus measurement-aid apparatus in the cell similar to that in the brain. As consciousness collapses the states of this system along with those of the vital body, it identifies with the system self-referentially, a self-reference that distinguishes life from its nonlife environment (akin to the subject-object split). For an organism with a brain, the self-identification arising from the collapse in the machinery of the brain overwhelms that arising from the collapse in the rest of the cells of the body. But ultimately, it is the same consciousness that causes both, and through it we have influence over bodily mechanisms and disease processes. Our task is to remember our forgotten vital-physical body ego identity and integrate it with our brain-mind ego identity. This requires the creative process.

"See first with the mind, then with the eyes, and finally with the torso and the limbs," wrote the Japanese philosopher of the body Yagyu

Tajima. When we have controlled access to chi (the quantum movement of the vital body that is correlated with the quantum movement of matter in the cells of the body), and when we experientially realize that the consciousness that collapses the modes of chi and the modes of the cells is the same consciousness that collapses those of the brain and the mind, then we begin to perceive with the whole physical-body/vital-body/brain-mind. The purpose of tai chi, aikido, and the East Indian system of yoga—in particular, hatha yoga and the breathing exercises called pranayama, the practice of which in its simplest form is following the inflow and outflow of breath—is to unite the physical-body/vital-body identities of consciousness with one another and with the brain-mind-based identity. *Yoga* in fact means union.

It is interesting that some hatha yoga postures (*asanas*, in Sanskrit) resemble animals and are given animal names for that reason; they help us relive our evolutionary past and to release repressions that may still be with us. In samadhi, hatha yoga postures sometimes occur spontaneously, suggesting such a release. In the same vein, hatha yoga may help us regress to the time that we spent in our mother's womb and to work out some of the repressions that took place in that phase of our lives. Some of the positions assumed in hatha yoga have an uncanny similarity to fetal positions. There is also a biological theory that the development of the human embryo reflects the entire history of the evolution of living forms.

The Body Centers of Emotion: The Chakras

Let's now delve into the subject of emotions in some detail. Psychologist William James wisely distinguished between thoughts and emotions and said they are independent of one another. Why are they independent? James did not address that question, but with the concept of vital and mental bodies we can do so succinctly: thoughts and emotions arise from different sources.

Confusion is created in modern minds because of the influence of materialism. Emotions arise concomitantly with changes in the physical body and are felt along with these changes; but there is no need to speculate, as materialists, that these physical changes are all there is when we emote. Physical body changes are just movements of molecules, like the movement of electrons on a TV screen. There is no story inherent in either. Your mind provides the story line, the meaning, for the movement of electrons on your TV screen. So also, you provide the story line, the software functions such as survival, etc., for the movement of molecules in your physical body with your vital body.

The vital body movements accompany the physical changes and represent the "living" behind the physical movement; this is what we experience as the feeling content of emotions. In the language of quantum physics, in every emotional event consciousness simultaneously collapses not only the physical changes but also the vital changes that are correlated with them (and also, usually, correlated changes in the mind).

It may surprise you that the vital movements are not as unfamiliar as you may think. Have you ever wondered why on Valentine's Day we send cards with pictures of the heart on them? There is a myth that St. Valentine is the reigning persona on the subject of romance. True. But why does the myth use the symbology of the heart?

Mythology is the history of the self. When we don't remember because of prevailing fads of thinking (such as materialism, currently), myths remind us. And what does the Valentine mythology of the heart coupled with romance remind us of? Think back to your first experience of romance. You felt it in your heart, but not all of what you felt was physical. Sure, the heart beat faster, maybe even missed a few beats occasionally—those phenomena were physical. But along with the physical there was an indescribable feeling, wasn't there?

Feelings are subtle because we experience the total thing, all at the same time; we don't experience the vital and the physical separately. The same is true of thoughts; we usually experience thoughts in language, but that is part of the physical representation of thought. But we all know that thought exists without language. Every one of us has experienced silent thoughts, the sound of silence, the meaning that percolates without the clothing of language. Of those experiences mental creativity is made.

Similarly, in the case of romance, do you know now what I am talking about? No, romance does not exist in the brain or in the mind; but it does not exist in the physical heart, either; the physical heart is simply a blood pump. The emotive quality of romance, and compassionate love also, comes from the vital correlates of the physical changes in the region of the physical heart that consciousness simultaneously collapses and experiences.

The West mythologized the movement of the vital body in romance via the St. Valentine's Day heart. The East went scientific. Easterners identified the heart as a chakra, a special center for feeling vital energy associated with romance as well as some of our most noble emotions: love, kindness, sacrifice.

The heart chakra is not the only one that you have felt. When you are nervous or anxious, where do you feel it? In your gut, your stomach area ("butterflies in your stomach," but it's not all physical, not all due to lack of oxygen in that area)—the navel chakra in the Eastern tradition. This chakra has to do with the emotions of ego-survival—jealousy, anxiety.

The third-eye chakra is located between your eyebrows. When you are concentrating, when you are one-pointed in your curiosity and your desire for knowledge, you can easily feel the vital energy between your eyebrows. People in India, when they engage in hard spiritual practice, cover their third eye with sandalwood paste in order to cool it down from the concentration of vital energy, which is accompanied by the feeling of physical heat. Indian women wear a *bindi* to cover their third eye for the same reason.

There are seven such major chakras (fig. 16). The lowest chakra is located at the base of the spine (connected with basic survival-related emotions—feelings of insecurity, fear); the second one is located at the gonads (connected with contexts of reproduction, lust). The third and fourth are the navel and heart chakras. The fifth chakra is located at the throat and concerns the desire to communicate. The sixth chakra is the third eye. The seventh chakra, the crown chakra, is located at the top of the head. It corresponds to our desire to integrate, parallel to the integrating function of the brain.

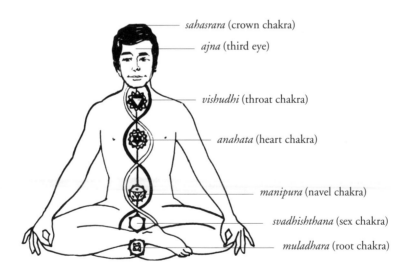

Fig. 16. The chakras

I think that the chakras are those regions of our body where quantum collapse of the physical takes place in correlation with collapse in the vital body. In other words, these are the places for important mapping (the making of software representations) of the vital body onto the physical.

As a result of the map-making, there are conditioned movements at each of these chakras. With a little practice, you can perceive the movement of prana at a chakra, in addition to physical movements, when you concentrate your attention there. These movements of prana are felt as winds or currents, even tingles. And they are conditioned movements. The easiest conditioned movements to feel are the ones connected with single cells located all over our skin. You can feel them right under the skin after a good massage or a shower. The purpose of yoga is not to feel these conditioned movements, but to go beyond them to creatively regain access to our vital body. The conditioned movements, associated with the mind, may help you to get acquainted with prana, but you have to do more.

Shadow Cleansing

There is good medical evidence that at least in the West, before taking up the journey of creative discovery of the vital body, it is best to engage in what Carl Jung called shadow cleansing. In Jungian terminology, the shadow archetype represents individually and collectively repressed mental and emotional material in the individual and collective unconscious.

The complement of the conditioned movement of prana is the creative, quantum movement of prana, called kundalini shakti in the literature. The Sanskrit word *kundalini* means coiled up, and *shakti* means energy. *Kundalini shakti* refers to latent prana, to be released with the creative quantum leap of the vital body from the guidance of the mind to the direct guidance of the intellect. The release of kundalini shakti refers to the pranic movement that accompanies the quantum leap of the vital body from the guidance of the mind to the direct guidance of the intellect.

Hindu mythology describes kundalini as a latent power that lies coiled at the base of the spine (the root chakra) and in our sexuality (the second chakra); this energy is released for our creative use if and when it rises to the head chakra. Thus, rising kundalini is a metaphor for the creativity of the vital body, in which our various vital-body ego identities at the various chakras—our fragmented vital body—are integrated. When the vital energy "rises" to the crown chakra, we also achieve a union of the vital-physical ego identities with the brain-mind, arriving at integration.

But in the West, in recent years, many spontaneous kundalini raisings have caused distress, even trauma, to the subject (Greenwell 1995). The kundalini phenomenon has been known in the East, especially in India and Tibet, for millennia, but harm caused by raising of kundalini is practically unheard of except in the relatively recent case of Gopi Krishna (Krishna 1978).

I think that these traumatic effects of raising kundalini are due to the repressed shadow of the Western psyche. Eastern culture is emotionally but not mentally expressive. In the West, by comparison, there is more mental freedom for children and adolescents and less conforming to authority. But the Western child is taught to suppress emotion, partly because of the good-evil split in the Judeo-Christian heritage (negative emotions are wrong) and partly because of the orientation of the materialistic West toward accomplishment and efficiency (emotions are not efficient).

So cleansing of the emotional shadow is essential for the average Westerner if the latent kundalini is going to rise creatively and effectively. How does one cleanse the shadow? For mental shadow cleansing, regular psychotherapy may be effective, combined with a meditative, witnessing attitude toward the repressed material as it comes up. For emotional shadow cleansing, the more recently developed technique of bioenergetics is more effective.

How does bioenergetics work? When we are defensive, we tense our muscles. In childhood trauma, some of our skeletal muscles tense up and do not fully relax again, but retain the body-memory, just as the mind retains the mental memory of such trauma. A memory can be said to be held in a muscle when the muscle is fixated in a certain position and cannot relax (Wolf 1986).

Each muscle—an array of long cells that are up to one foot in length—contains many cell nuclei and many small fibers called myofibrils. Myofibrils contain repeating units called sarcomeres, which are arranged lengthwise along the long cylindrical axis of the muscle. The bioenergetics of the muscle has to do with the free flow of calcium ions. When a muscle is tensed during a trauma, the muscle sarcomeres are flooded with calcium ions. After the trauma, some of the calcium may remain in the sarcomere, maintaining tension in the muscle. This is now a memory of trauma in a particular muscle.

Now suppose the memory is repressed. Quantum mechanically, this means that if this state comes up in a superposition of possibilities in thought and emotion, consciousness is not going to choose to collapse it. So this particular muscle is not going to be reactivated by normal body-mind-vital-energy processes to get the opportunity of functioning fully again.

Muscles with locked-in memory can, however, be felt during massage work, and a skillful therapist may be able to relax the muscle in the patient's body. How does this healing happen? The quantum theoretic answer is nonlocal collapse. The healer may visualize her own muscle in that body area, tense it, and then relax it. More effectively, the healer may project good chi or vital energy to the affected area. If the therapist's body muscles and/or vital energy are correlated to the patient's through healing intentions, consciousness may collapse the patient's muscles at the same time as the healer's into relaxation and good health.

The Creative Transformation of the Body

In the spiritual traditions of India, the world's cradle for research and new ideas in spirituality, there are two dominant approaches to spiritual attainment. The one most familiar, called the right-handed path, or the path of light, is based on ideas of transcending our ego-conditioning. It is what I call inner creativity; it centers on the mind. But there is also tantra—often called the left-handed path, or dark path. Tantra talks about transcending sexuality, quite literally: the goal of tantra is to raise the kundalini from the root, sexual, and navel chakras to the crown chakra.

A close look at the metaphor of kundalini rising through the chakras will help the reader to see my point. The lower three chakras, located at the base of the spine, the genitals, and the navel, pertain to the libidinous and conditioned vital-physical ego identifications. The fourth chakra is located at the heart. Engaging in sex makes us romantic because vital energy is felt in the heart chakra as well (with sexual release, the vital energy rises to the heart chakra, says the traditional description). The opening of this chakra, visualized as the rising of the kundalini to this chakra, is considered the first important breakthrough in tantric practice. The opening of the heart experientially signifies the flowering of compassion. Why? The emotions associated with the heart chakra are usually tainted by mental conditioning, which brings "me" and "my" into the equation of love (love with possessiveness—I love you because you are my significant one). The opening of the heart chakra signifies freeing love from association with the mental ego.

Could it be that the creative breakthrough in the opening of any chakra is not only the possibility of creative control of the associated emotion(s) but also the realization that we are not limited to our identity with the brain-mind ego? Consciousness assumes an identification with the vital body in correlation with the physical body through collapsing possibility waves of the vital body along with those of the physical body (for example, at the chakra points). This is the same consciousness that experiences our thoughts. Wouldn't a direct realization of the vital-physical ego identity lessen the mental ego-identity, creating a shift away from mental ego-centeredness? I believe this is what happens with kundalini rising and its eventual integration.

The final destination of the rising kundalini is the chakra located at the top of the head (*sahasrara* in Sanskrit—the thousand-petalled chakra). Metaphorically, this signifies, in my opinion, the complete realization of the unity in consciousness of the physical-vital and mind-brain identities.

Now we can understand what we do in physical hatha yoga and in tantra practices. Ordinarily, we are totally identified with our minds, as mapped onto our physical brains. The right-handed path or path of light emphasizes the creativity of the mind (which may or may not involve the intellect). In contrast, the left-handed or dark path of tantra emphasizes creativity of the correlated vital-physical body. In these practices we engage in hatha yoga—its postures and breathing techniques—in order to shift the conditioned center of our identity from the mind to the correlated vital-physical body; we do movements to activate and feel our chi, as in tai chi; we energize our ki with the practice of aikido; we activate our vital energy through sports and dancing. Prana, chi, ki, and vital energy are, of course, the same thing: the quantum modes of movement of the vital body. Ordinarily, we experience the vital energies only with the help of the mind; for example, mental visualization of a lover will stimulate vital energies in the heart chakra. However, when we directly experience a mode of prana, chi, or ki at a chakra without the intermediary of the mind, a sudden insight takes place. Now we are reclaiming the vital-physical body identity. This is justifiably called the opening of a chakra. The Indian tradition visualizes the opening of a chakra as the creation of a new path to it from the root chakra; this new path is called the *sushumna nadi*.

The raising of kundalini and its subsequent integration is said to come with unusual powers of control—not only of emotions but also of many body functions. Many autonomic functions can now be controlled, such as the rhythms of the heart; Elmer and Alice Green's book *Beyond Biofeedback* reports their experiments with one kundalini master (Green and Green 1977). There are kundalini masters who can transduce temporary movements of prana by mere touch (the phenomenon of *shaktipat*, popularized in the West by Swami Muktananda), a glorious display of quantum nonlocality involving the vital body. There is genuine opportunity here for the future evolution of human creativity.

We live our lives in part under the tyranny of the mind—how our mind looks at and uses our instincts to influence the body. Take the case of fear. Fear is an essential instinct without which we cannot survive. But do we need fantasy fear? This fear, created largely by the mind (as when you see a stranger in the dark), also guides our behavior, creating unnecessary surges of adrenaline and imbalances of the sympathetic nervous system. The opening of the root chakra helps rid us of the fantasy fear. Similarly, the opening of the second chakra frees us from mental fantasies about sex.

The rising of kundalini thus signifies returning the conscious control of our instincts to where it belongs, not the mind but the vital body (and, as psychiatrist Uma Krishnamurthy [2000] reminds us, ultimately the intellect, which sets the contexts of the movements of the vital body).

The pervading myth of tantra is that when a man's kundalini rises to the crown chakra, the path of the male semen is reversed and he becomes *urdhareta*, a person whose semen moves upward. You can see that this is a metaphor for gaining control over the sexual instinct. (And this is not male chauvinistic; the spiritual literature of India describes women urdharetas, meaning that these women had acquired control over sexuality.)

The path to the kundalini-rising experience consists of practices of the body, such as yoga postures and breathing techniques. Breath is a whole-body function; oxygen must travel to literally every cell of the body. Furthermore, breath is a function that is autonomic but over which we have limited conscious control. Could it be that by practicing pranayama we are trying to shift from our conscious self-identity based in the brain-mind (associated with collapsing the possibility waves of the mind, such as thought, and those of the brain, which maps the mind) to the correlated, normally unconscious self identity based in the vital-physical-body (associated with the collapse of quantum possibilities of the vital body in correlation with important body organs, including the brain)?

What is the goal of pranayama but the slowing down of breath? What does slowing of the breath accomplish? Just as meditation slows down the brain and the mind (that is, it slows the collapse of the possibility waves in both), pranayama slows down the physical body organs and thus the collapse of the chakras associated with them. Slowing down reduces secondary-awareness processing and frees us from our slavery to conditioning. Thus pranayama has the same effect on the vital centers that meditation has on the mind.

I must tell you about my first direct experience of kundalini. This was in 1981; I was a guest speaker at a workshop given by the dolphinologist John Lilly and his wife Toni at Esalen Institute in Big Sur, California. The East Indian guru, Bhagwan Shri Rajneesh was very popular then, and one morning I was participating in "dynamic" meditation to a Rajneesh music tape—a combination of first shaking your body vigorously, then slow dancing, followed by a sitting meditation. Shaking the body was unusually invigorating. When the music changed to signify the beginning of slow dancing, we were instructed to dance with closed-eyes. But I bumped into somebody and opened my eyes, and lo! a pair of beautiful bouncing breasts engaged my stare. I closed my eyes immediately. Unfortunately, closing my mental body was a different matter. The mental picture of bouncing breasts and my ensuing embarrassment, plus the fear of bumping into somebody else, preoccupied me.

When the slow dancing ended, I was relieved. I sat down to meditate and concentration came easily. It was then that I felt a strong current rising along my spine from my lower back to about the throat area. It was extremely refreshing—utter bliss.

Since I did not know much about kundalini at the time, I did not pay much attention to it or work with the energy that became available. Later, at a workshop with physician Richard Moss, I had deep experiences of prana, but I still didn't comprehend their importance. Only since I have associated further with the yoga experts in India have I delved into pranic energization in a disciplined way. Even my limited experience has convinced me that there is an important phenomenon of creativity here that is of considerable significance if we are truly to become whole.

The Yoga of Becoming Whole:
The Integration of Body, Mind, Spirit

In India, yogic healing consists of a manifold approach to who we are. In the Upanishads there is a description of the five bodies of a human being: the physical, vital, mental, theme (or intellect), and bliss bodies (see chapter 7). Accordingly, Indian medicine is divided into the study of five healing modalities: diet, herbs, and hatha yoga (asanas, or postures) for the care and healing of the physical body; pranayama for the care and healing of the vital body; repetition of a mantra for the care and healing of the mental body; meditation and creativity for the care and healing of the theme or intellect body; and samadhi, or absorption into oneness, for the care and healing of the bliss body. Indian medicine is yoga—the art of becoming whole.

What does being whole mean? In Indian psychology, three qualities of the psyche, the previously introduced gunas, are recognized. Roughly speaking, the gunas correspond to unconscious drives: tamas is due to behavioral conditioning from our psycho-social-cultural environment; rajas is akin to the Freudian libido and arises from vital-body and genetic conditioning of mainly sexual origin; sattva is the drive (from the collective unconscious) toward creativity or illumination of the darkness of ignorance brought about by tamas and rajas. Being whole involves transcending all the gunas, all of our unconscious drives. First, we transcend tamas, the drive of the personal unconscious due to mental conditioning, through spiritual practices and inner creativity of the mind. Second, we transcend rajas, the drive of the vital-physical body unconscious, with creativity of the vital-physical body. When rajas is under our conscious influence (through the intellect, which is beyond the mind), our desires arise only as needed to carry out the necessary vital body functions, not because of mind games.

Thus, we can more easily integrate one major cause of conflict: the split between good and evil. The possibilities are unlimited.

And at the third or final level, we transcend even sattva, creativity—the drive of the collective unconscious. Then we are whole. Then creative ecstasy or joy, *ananda*, is our natural, everyday state.

Notes

1. One brilliant exception is Larry Dossey (1990).

2. In addition to those in Chopra (1990), many other cases of spontaneous healing can be found in Dossey (1990), O'Regan (1987), and Moss (1984).

3. Dossey (1990) has emphasized that the nonlocal healing effect of prayer is an example of quantum nonlocality.

4. For an excellent review of martial arts and other body-related spiritual practices, read Murphy (1992).

Liberation

INNER CREATIVITY is a journey of transformation. Every time we realize a truth about ourselves or cognize a state that enables us to shift our identity toward buddhi and away from our ego, we are engaging in inner creativity. We progress along our spiritual path usually through insight—the creative "ah-ha!" But the theory of quantum creativity allows two more epistemological possibilities. First, in quantum creativity there is a stage of unconscious processing—processing without awareness or subject-object split. Is it possible to know directly that we are the unconscious processor of our insights? This would be cognition from beyond maya, consciousness without a subject and without an object (nirvikalpa samadhi; see chapter 10). Second, according to science within consciousness, consciousness is the ground of being—an idea that resonates with what the great philosopher-sage Shankara said, echoing the Upanishads: consciousness is one without a second. Can we directly know this original, eternal, unblemished existence, which the Indian tradition calls turiya?

There are two perspectives from which to look at consciousness and its manifestations. From one perspective, spiritual experiences, including all savikalpa samadhis, can be neatly understood as the play of discontinuous quantum leaps to states of awareness in which the subject-object split tends to narrow and the quantum self is increasingly experienced. Consider the proverbial example of a rope mistakenly perceived as a snake. In experiences of savikalpa samadhi we discover deeper truths about the snake, as it were, and these transform our lives.

The second perspective is from beyond the subject-object split. Identifying with consciousness itself, without an object and a subject, is realizing that what appears as a snake is only a rope. With nirvikalpa samadhi ego-bondage is forever broken. And turiya is the great insight of consciousness of which all other insights of outer or inner creativity are mere glimpses, no more than partial.

Why is the great insight of turiya the end of all seeking? If you know the truth that you are the ground of all being, you also know that the world is an epiphenomenon, that the ego is not your identity, so identification with it can drop. If you directly know your self as the knower, the known, and the field of knowledge, where is the charm in further cognition in your ordinary ego state of consciousness or even the exalted states of samadhi? So identification with the ego can drop. When you are cradled with all sentient beings in limitless love, what is the egoic need to seek love in a particular relationship? It has no place, and the ego dissolves in that eternal sea of love. If appropriate action flows effortlessly, why identify with the limited free will of the ego?

Nirvikalpa samadhi is the answer to another essential spiritual quest—perpetual unblemished happiness that exists without any effort. But even nirvikalpa samadhi is a special state, a temporary being in wholeness. Beyond it is turiya, in which being is permanent albeit dynamic. Arriving in turiya signals liberation from the bondage of the ego, liberation from all the seeking. It is said that only with turiya is one totally rid of the fear of death, because only with turiya does one go beyond the birth-death-rebirth cycle of existence.

What is it like when you are in nirvikalpa samadhi, when you are the unconscious processor of your experience? Franklin Merrell-Wolff, who described his "imperience" as consciousness without an object and without a subject, was quite specific:

> The first discernible effect on consciousness was something that I may call a shift in the base of consciousness. . . . I knew myself to be beyond space, time, and causality. . . . Closely associated with the foregoing realization, there is a feeling of complete freedom. . . . I did not attempt to stop the activity of the mind, but simply very largely ignored the stream of thought. . . . The result was that I was both here and "There," with the objective consciousness less acute than normal. (Merrell-Wolff 1995)

Krishnamurti put it beautifully when he described insight as simultaneously being in stillness and being in movement, but without a causal connection between the two (Krishnamurti 1995). Being "There" at the still point, at the gap between events, nothing happens. Being here, there is movement, but the movement cannot be causally connected to the stillness. In between "here" and "There" are the discontinuity and tangled hierarchy of quantum measurement.

And what is turiya? It is a not special state of consciousness, but it is attained in the ever-present and forever-new primary state of awareness that is causally prior to all other states of awareness. Once we "wake up" to the wisdom of turiya, that awareness of the primary self never ceases. One never comes "out" of that awareness. Consider what Ramana Maharshi said about turiya:

It flashed through me vividly as living truth that I perceived directly, almost without thought process. "I" was something very real, the only real thing about my present state, and all the conscious activity connected with my body was centered on that "I." From that point onwards the "I" or Self focussed attention on Itself by a powerful fascination. Fear of death had vanished. Absorption in the Self continued unbroken from that time on. Whether the body was engaged in talking, reading, or anything else, I was still centered on "I." (Ramana 1978)

Another realized sage, who stated the difference between nirvikalpa samadhi and turiya in his writings, is Swami Shivananda of Rishikesh:

There are two kinds of . . . nirvikalpa samadhi. In the first the jnani (wise person), by resting in Brahman, sees the whole world within himself as a movement of ideas, as a mode of being or a mode of his own existence, like Brahman. Brahman sees the world within Himself as His own imagination (*sankalpa*). So also does a jnani. This is the highest state of realization. . . .

In the second variety the world vanishes from view and the jnani rests on pure attributeless Brahman. (Sivananda 1987)

How Long Does It Take to Be Liberated?

There is a long-standing question in the tradition: Why should the final insight—that consciousness is the ground of all being and we are that consciousness—take time? Can't one just "see" or realize the truth when one first encounters it in the scriptures or from a teacher, and that's that? There is a beautiful story to support the position that liberation can happen to anyone at any time. Narada, the great celestial angel, was passing by two mortals. One was a *sadhu*, a renunciate, in meditation. He asked, "O Narada, when shall I arrive?"

Narada said, "I have an appointment with God soon. I'll find out."

The second person was inhaling deeply from a marijuana pipe. He had the same question, "When shall I arrive?"

Narada laughed but promised him also that he would ask God.

When Narada returned, he first went to the renunciate. "Well, what did God say? How many years longer need I meditate?"

"You have to meditate for three more lifetimes," said Narada.

"Well, if nothing's going to happen in this birth, I may as well give up and have some fun," thought the renunciate, and he abandoned his practice.

The marijuana addict was also eager to hear from Narada. "Well?"

"See that tree over there? See all those leaves? That many lives it will take for you to arrive," said Narada.

"Really? I'll arrive, too?" exclaimed the fellow, and he began dancing. And at that moment itself he arrived at turiya and came to know his true nature.

We can realize the truth at any moment, just like this man, and be liberated. For most of us, however, realizing the truth is part of a protracted process of inner creativity, and that takes time. Realizing the truth is always beyond intellectualization, free of any ideas about it; and it is always a sudden insight, even when it is realized with the help of someone else or the scriptures.

Another controversy in the literature is whether there is any need for further transformation after the great insight into the nature of being. Knowing the ultimate truth about consciousness is paradoxical. Truth *is*; everyone is always in consciousness as the ground of being.

Ignorance is an illusion. The rope looked like a snake, but now you know it is rope; it was always rope, never a snake. Thus knowing the truth, what is the need to change anything? Once we know that consciousness alone is real and lose all doubt about the epiphenomenal nature of the manifest world, our identification with a particular body-mind complex remains a mere functional necessity. This is what sets us free from ego-bondage. When this happens, we are liberated. There is no need to transform our outer behavior. The marijuana smoker in the story can go on smoking marijuana; if he is not attached to the behavior and is always happy, what difference does it make? Similarly, there is a Zen saying: Before enlightenment, I chopped wood and carried water; after enlightenment, I chop wood and carry water. So liberated beings need not have many saintly qualities. And vice versa—developing saintly qualities is no guarantee of liberation.

But in many recorded cases, such as Hui Neng, Sri Aurobindo, Krishnamurti—the list is long—even after realization there is a period of maturation. How is this so? One explanation is that the realization was incomplete, only a partial insight—only savikalpa or nirvikalpa samadhi, not turiya.

Incomplete realization may also be the explanation for scandals we sometimes hear about concerning spiritual teachers. When one does not identify with the ego, why would one succumb to purely temporal temptations that would undermine one's effectiveness as teacher? This is especially important in the West, where people tend to hastily declare that they are liberated when what they have experienced is savikalpa samadhi.

The mystic-saint Chaitanya spent many years after his realization longing for union with God, which suggests that he had not arrived in turiya. He was expressing the pain of the inevitable separation from the whole due to samsara, the divine play of the world. With nirvikalpa samadhi one attains fullness; when one returns to ordinary states of waking, dream, or sleep, one misses that fullness. Much of Chaitanya's life story illustrates this perpetual tension of not attaining fullness in spite of attaining fullness while in the human condition.

Ramakrishna felt it necessary to try out the methods of many spiritual traditions. He experienced each as a path to nirvikalpa samadhi. In the process he became stabilized in the wholeness of consciousness, a condition where the bliss of undivided wholeness recurs regularly in ordinary waking awareness—called *sahaja*, easy, without effort; no effort is needed to go from "here" (movement) to "There" (stillness). And then Ramakrishna resumed the attitude of a devotee of the Divine Mother.

When Franklin Merrell-Wolff's wife died in his later years, Franklin fell apart. What was happening with him if all attachment drops away with realization? Clearly he had experienced nirvikalpa samadhi; he was not established in turiya.

The Buddha, who grew up in the Hindu tradition, identified the goal of the spiritual journey as not samadhi but *nirvana*—the cessation of the flame of desire. *Nirvana* is another term for turiya, which is beyond all forms of samadhi, including nirvikalpa.

Thus we see that people referred to as realized mystics in the literature differ in their realization. For some, the dropping of the ego happens instantaneously. These are the clear cases of turiya, liberation, or nirvana. For others, letting go of the ego-identity takes longer. For still others, it may have to wait until death. In other words, there is a process of maturation for spiritual enlightenment, as for all creative processes. The theory of creativity theory demands it, and the data seem to agree.

The point is that savikalpa or nirvikalpa samadhi does not stabilize easily in the human condition. Franklin Merrell-Wolff told me that after he cognized the state of consciousness without an object, he would attempt to enter it again, but it took effort. As he aged, the effort required became increasingly greater, so he stopped trying.

Until turiya is realized, even the enlightened are not beyond the grip of the experience of separation due to maya. There is a saying that maya is too strong even for the realized, as illustrated in another Narada story. As a realized being, Narada is always in God's company. One day he wants to know why maya is said to be so strong. God smiles. Soon they come to a river, and God tells Narada to take a dip. Narada takes a dip, comes up, sees a beautiful maiden, falls in love, gets married, and has children. Then one day a flood arrives and sweeps away Narada's house, wife, and children. Narada is lamenting aloud when he hears God's voice, "Are you done with your dip in the water yet?" Yes, maya is strong.

There are recent examples of masters in whom the nirvikalpa state did stabilize: Ramakrishna, Anandamayi Ma, Krishnamurti, Sri Aurobindo, to mention several. In all these cases there was a period of maturation. During this period, it is natural for adepts to experiment with other methods, other paths. A jnana insight resolves a particular doubt about the nature of reality, but it hardly prepares you for relationship issues. You can still falter; you can make mistakes. But all of these you see as more "grist for the mill."

In Hinduism, the manifestation stage of inner creativity is subtly acknowledged by recognizing that "hearing" the truth (*shravana* in Sanskrit) is followed by contemplation (*manana* in Sanskrit), and if that is not enough, by further meditative practice (*nididhyasana* in Sanskrit) until identification with the ego drops.

Samadhis are initiations to further purification of the body-mind complex. Purification, as we have seen already, transforms us and undermines the ego. You cultivate desirelessness, as Buddha did. If your physical body/vital body/mind/brain have become integrated in the sense discussed in chapter 13, you are free from the mood fluctuations of ordinary states of consciousness. Eventually, purification gives way to surrender. Surrender of accomplishments catapults your jnana practice into a natural embrace of spiritual joy. Similarly, the practice of bhakti now becomes sweet (*madhuram* in Sanskrit). Sweet, sweet surrender. Karma yoga is now the practice of the will of God; you act as the causal connection between the act in the world and God.

Ramakrishna used the analogy of a salt figurine dipped into the ocean to describe the process of surrendering. The figurine dissolves; its separate structure and identity no longer exist, but its function, the saltiness, remains even though merged with the ocean. This is the goal. The challenge is to not run away from the ambiguities that arise on the way toward this goal, not escape into an action-oriented agenda, but to remain aware of the movements of consciousness as they manifest reality.

At the cremation grounds in India, an attendant stands by the pyre with a stick. If a part of the body somehow escapes the fire, the man is there to push it back in with his stick. When the body is fully burnt, however, the stick itself is thrown into fire. If identification with the ego drops during one's lifetime, one is a free being while alive (*jivanmukta* in Sanskrit). If not, freedom comes with death (*videhamukta* in Sanskrit).

Concentration and awareness meditation are used in the meditation path of inner creativity; so also, there are advanced meditation practices that can take one to consciousness beyond the subject-object split. The same meditations can be used to become stabilized in sahaja samadhi. In these meditations we are asked to be attentive to the gap between two thoughts or two breaths, or even between two states of consciousness, like waking and sleep. Idealist science explains the basis for these practices: The manifest world comes into being moment to moment through quantum collapse; it is not continuous. In between the apparent continuity of awareness, there are gaps in which there is only consciousness. Hinduism offers the famous 112 meditation techniques given by Shiva himself for quantum leaping to these gaps (see the appendix in Reps 1957). What you meditate upon is the jump from being "here" in manifest awareness to being "there" in the gaps. Why are these techniques to be practiced only when the mind is under control to some degree? Because, secondary-awareness processes bring about a continuity in awareness that is very hard to penetrate until we learn not to pay attention to them or until they are abated to a degree.

There are also strategies for surrendering the ego. In Tibetan Buddhism, there is a form of meditation called *dzogchen* in which one is attentive to a "presence" rather than to objects in awareness. In Christianity, there is a similar form of meditation known as "practicing the presence of God." Following the thread of underlying happiness in yourself will take you to the presence. This practice also is advanced in nature: how can you meditate on the presence unless the intuition is strong in you that there is perpetual happiness beyond the superficial mood swings of pleasure and pain?

Swami Sivananda advocated the practice of seeing the world as dreamlike. The dream state of consciousness is useful in advanced stages of practice because in this state one can more easily realize that all the dream characters are but the dreamer. Bringing this realization to our waking awareness is a huge step toward wholeness.

Beyond Liberation

For one who is liberated, there is no more rebirth. This makes scientific sense. The Upanishads say that after liberation all that remains is *prarabdha karma*, the cause-effect propensities intended to be worked on in the current lifetime. Science within consciousness agrees. The job of the quantum monad is not done until the propensities brought about in this birth are used to fulfill its worldly mission as well. So prarabdha must run its course during the rest of the life for the liberated individual. Does this involve a productive, eventful life? Or is liberation a retirement from further action?

The Buddha was not finished in his spiritual journey with the attainment of samadhis and liberation, Hindu style. Abuse—people experiencing samadhis and then claiming to be liberated—must have been common in his day just as it is today. Refusing to equate samadhi with liberation, the Buddha must have asked: What good is samadhi if there is nothing to show for it? After much meditation and practice of equanimity, resolving to sit under the bodhi tree until enlightenment came, the Buddha arrived at the cessation of the flames of desire, nirvana. After his nirvana, pondering what to do and wondering who would understand his teaching about the cessation of desire, the Buddha received the injunction from the gods to teach, which he did for many years. That was his prarabdha.

Thus liberation by no means signifies retirement from life. It may be just the opposite. I have a vision. I believe that for some liberated beings of our age, their prarabdha may take them to extend the creative play of the divine further and to lead humanity to new heights of creativity—supramental creativity.

Supermind

The philosopher-sage Sri Aurobindo felt that stabilization in sahaja samadhi, or liberation, opens the door to investigation of the supramental, to going beyond the causal laws of the theme body of consciousness that govern the physical, vital, and mental bodies (Aurobindo 1955). A liberated being, if God so wills, can act supramentally in ways that we call miracles. Always in harmony with the will of the Whole, such a being can create a material body in which to manifest at will; choose immortality, both in the body and without, as necessary; levitate, in clear violation of material laws.

Mental creativity stays within the laws of science. The paranormal phenomena that we investigate today are called *paranormal* because of the limited context of traditional science. In the new science, making good models for the understanding of the paranormal within more general laws would be normal practice.

The new science also opens up to us the exploration of the creativity of the vital body. This will continue to create much new understanding of our health and well-being and will lead to new insights into how the "miracles" of spontaneous healing work. For the "miracles" of mind-body healing—healing cancer, for example—are also within the laws of the theme body.

But supramental creativity, as in true miracles—creating at will, from nothing—is beyond all laws of any science we know.

The Vedantin Satyanarayan Sastry likes to quote to me the *Yoga Vasishtha*, in which there is reference to manifesting physical material forms from thought. He suggests that the involution of consciousness (see chapter 7) must consist of the process of condensation from subtler to grosser forms, much as water vapor condenses into liquid water that condenses into solid ice. I counterargue that since Sastriji is a chemist by training, he naturally tries to model everything according to chemistry. The condensation model cannot work because it violates the principle of the conservation of baryon number, which says that the number of baryons in the world (such as protons and neutrons) is a constant. Thoughts don't have baryon number. To create baryons of ordinary matter from thought would require the simultaneous creation of baryons and antibaryons. These antibaryons would, however, annihilate ordinary baryonic matter, creating havoc.

Is the *Yoga Vasishtha* wrong, then? After pondering this for many years I have reached the conclusion that the rishis of the *Yoga Vasishtha* were hinting at how supramental creativity works. First, we become liberated; we become established in speaking truth (*vaksiddha* in Sanskrit); our will (*sankalpa* in Sanskrit) becomes aligned with God's will. In this journey of liberation an integrated path, as Aurobindo envisioned, should help.

Next, we learn to hold our thoughts, visualizing them for prolonged periods. Since the laws of our theme collective, the *vijnanamaya kosha*, are no longer compulsory against our sankalpa, we may be able to manifest the thought form.

Are we humans destined to become superhuman investigators of supermind—gods, in this sense—at some stage of our evolution? The Sufi poet Rumi wrote:

> I died as a mineral and became a plant
> I died as a plant and rose to animal
> I died as an animal and I became a man.
> Why should I fear?
> When was I less by dying? (Rumi 1988)

When we "die" as mental humans, perhaps we will become supramental, superhuman beings. But prerequisite to this, the journey of liberation must be undertaken in massive numbers—something that can happen only if spirituality becomes a vital concern of all humanity.

A Quantum Physicist's Guide to Enlightenment

S O HERE WE ARE. We have accomplished the promised integration of science and spirituality. Spiritual metaphysics—consciousness is the ground of all being—works as the basis for a new paradigm of science. The old science finds its place in the limit of conditioned behavior. The job of the new science is well defined: it comes into play whenever creativity is involved. The past work of spiritual traditions gives valuable guidance for the new science as data, as scaffolding for new concepts. The new science is helpful in sorting out the validity both of spiritual cosmologies and of the techniques and technicalities of the spiritual paths that define the various traditions.

This chapter was inspired by conversations and correspondences with an intelligent woman, a non-science professional, who joined me on a spiritual odyssey to India, where I gave a series of lectures on Vedanta, quantum physics, and the proposed integration. This woman voiced excellent questions; my intent is to address these again here.

I field these questions on spiritual enlightenment in the context of several steps or stages of growth along what Ken Wilber calls the spectrum of consciousness. Do note, however, that the stages are neither linear nor compulsory. They are not necessarily experienced in the sequence I present them. There are a few fortunate people in history who have bypassed some of the stages and gone more directly to liberation.

Stage One

Q: Talk of stages of spirituality or of a spectrum of consciousness makes me nervous. Are you saying that there is a hierarchy of beings, that some people are "more conscious" than others?

A: I am saying that some people are more conscious than others in some sense, but it's subtle, and it is not a hierarchy. If you are an adult who cares for children, do you feel hierarchically superior to them? You could, but adults who are well-adjusted usually don't. The spectrum of consciousness is similarly developmental, not hierarchical. We all travel the learning journey of our quantum-monad identity for many lifetimes, but some of us are old souls. Some people have done some of the introductory-level stuff before, so they breeze through it this time around to reach the more advanced levels of education. Instead of feeling superior to others, these people feel compassionate; they are anxious to give a helping hand.

Q: Surely you are idealizing. I have encountered arrogant spiritual teachers who clearly look on their students as inferior.

A: I am not denying that there are such teachers. That they exist is unfortunate and is due to the ego inflation that can take place in the initial stages of the awakening of buddhi. However, there is a safe-guard against permanent ego inflation. Ultimately, self-consciousness comes to us via a tangled hierarchy. The further we go toward the quantum self, the more we realize that there is no ego to inflate.

The following story illustrates what I am saying. A clergyman who took on a teaching assignment on an island found three elderly pupils who he particularly liked. They were sincere, honest, and good, but they were uneducated and didn't even know how to say the Lord's Prayer properly. So he taught them, and taught them well—to his satisfaction, he thought, as he was leaving the island in his boat. Sud-denly he saw a strange sight: three people were walking over the water toward his boat. His prize pupils! One of them said, "Sorry to bother you again, but we have forgotten how to say the Lord's Prayer. Would you teach us once more?"

Now, who was teaching whom?

Q: When would you say stage one of the spiritual path begins?

A: Stage one begins when you discover or acknowledge that you are unhappy. This is no small thing. It is a very important self-discov-ery, because the many distractions we have these days make it easy to sweep any unhappiness under the rug. But the time comes when sweep-ing no longer works.

It was at a nuclear physics conference where I had partied till the wee hours that it dawned on me. I had downed an entire packet of antacids, and still the acidity did not abate. I was sufficiently intoxi-cated, but the alcohol failed to assuage the jealousy toward my fellow physicists that had been tormenting me the whole day. I had good company but not enticing enough to mask my boredom. The question arose in my deepest core: why do I live this way? This is how I entered stage one. Most people begin similarly.

A few fortunate ones, of good karma, surely, come to stage one by way of what creativity researcher John Briggs calls "nuance," a sensitive experience of the joy of the world—a secondary awareness of the quantum self, in the language of the new science. If you were blessed by nuance in your early life, you may breeze through stage one.

Q: So I am at stage one. The problem is, I am still a materialist, or, according to your terminology, probably a dualist, believing in the primacy of both matter and God. I believe that who I am is the product of my brain. I also believe that spirituality is good for me. I love to read, especially books that confirm both of these beliefs. Books that conflict with my beliefs, such as yours, confuse me. They touch me in a certain way, but—

A: You are looking for some good brain food to give you a quick recipe for happiness or, at least, a temporary shelter against suffering. Or, if you are coming to spirituality due to an experience of nuance, you look for brain food with the idea of validating, maybe even repeating, your joyful experience. You are reading books like this for ideas on how to proceed. This can be somewhat disorienting, because every time you read a good book with hints about spirituality and happiness and reality, you feel convinced that it is on to something, even when the books differ from each other and from your belief system. Why can't all these books be right? Why do you have to make choices? Which is the right recipe?

Q: Some of the books I read discourage me from engaging the intellect. Instead, I must feed my heart, these books urge. Go love somebody, be in relationship, they insist. I don't know. Are they making a valid point? I like to read those books, but I also like the other books.

A: Yes and no. Notice what you are actually doing. Instead of reading "heady" books, you are now reading "hearty" books. But still, you are only reading.

It is like the cartoon of a guy reading *The Joy of Sex* while his girlfriend tries to elicit some affection. "Knock it off," he says, "Can't you see I'm reading?" The divine is ready to make love with you, and all you want to do is read books about it.

The cartoon's point also applies to books on meditation that spend many pages on the folly of following spiritual paths when all you need to do is meditate, just sit. This was the mystic Jiddu Krishnamurti's big draw. He wrote some hundred books telling people to just be aware. And what do many of his readers actually do? When they feel confused, they read one more Krishnamurti book! But practicing awareness? No, they are not ready for that yet.

Q: I am also interested in drugs for my mind expansion. In fact, some of my most alive moments come when I am on a psychedelic drug. Is it wrong to use drugs? Will drugs lead me to enlightenment?

A: You are also using drugs as brain food, quick recipes for exalted states of consciousness. Drugs are not necessarily bad, mind you (even Patanjali mentions them in the context of yoga), but they too often produce a dependency that later becomes a hindrance. Notice how spiritual traditions handle drugs, always with respect and ritual. That is the proper way, and never as recreation, if your objective is spirituality.

Drugs are popular because some of them do produce instant "spiritual" experiences. They open the so-called limbic gate, and the predominant activity of the brain shifts to the limbic brain. When the limbic activity overwhelms the neocortex, the tyranny of conditioned thinking loses its grip and attention is given to the preconscious secondary-awareness processes; then it is easy to fall into the joy of increasingly primary-awareness experiences, or at least, flow.

Drugs allow you to "feel spiritual," to experience the immediacy and joy of altered states of consciousness without requiring a commitment to transform. But their strength is also their weakness. Sooner or later, you notice that you depend on drugs for your spiritual joy. You like the "high," but you also dread the boredom of the "low." You begin to tire of the roller coaster ride.

Some drug experiences may fit exotic ideas in New Age books that you read: parallel universes, imaginal realms, a holographic universe, alien encounters, quantum brain, and so forth. Who needs old-fashioned spiritual practices, such as meditation, when you can hobnob with aliens of a parallel universe by reading a book or taking a drug?

But you may begin to notice that not everything in your drug experience is exotic. Strangely, the experience also gives you a glimpse of a simplicity that you read about in books on meditation. So if you treat them with respect and ritual and moderation, drugs can be useful in the spiritual journey. Can they take you all the way to enlightenment? Unlikely, but not impossible.

Q: How about books?

A: There is no harm in reading. Most New Age authors are creative and are not trying to mislead you. If you sort through enough authors, you are bound to come across those who can inspire you to the next stage of investigation.

In sum, initially in your search to banish unhappiness you are frantic; unable to commit, you are easily attracted toward temporary highs brought about by external stimuli such as books or drugs. Even these transitory tastes of spiritual joy eventually begin to dissolve your lack of commitment, your fear of spiritual practices. You begin to suspect that the source of your spiritual joy may well be yourself, just as the spiritual traditions say. You are now ready for the second stage.

Stage Two

Q: When does the transition from the first stage to the second stage happen? What is the signature of the second stage?

A: In stage one you want to want spirituality; the second stage begins when you want to explore spirituality, or God, if you will. You are still not sure that God or consciousness is "for real," but you are willing to give old-fashioned spirituality a chance. You also find it encouraging that, in this new age, some folks seem to offer old-fashioned spirituality in fairly uncomplicated and seemingly effortless forms.

So you may take initiation in transcendental meditation and start practicing twenty minutes of meditation twice each day. Or you may become a Krishna devotee, chanting the Krishna mantra two thousand times first thing every morning. Or perhaps you become a Sufi, whirling away your ego in the dervish dance. You may go to a Buddhist monastery, sit in zazen, and watch your thoughts or breath. You may return to your roots and start attending services at your local church or synagogue.

You have become more serious in your pursuit of spiritual happiness. Whereas before, your commitment to a particular teacher or teaching extended only a few days or until the next book came along, now you are willing to follow a practice for weeks, even months.

Q: You are right. I do have more commitment than before. But here is my problem with commitment: Each time I begin a new practice, for a few weeks the practice brings me a native joy and relaxation that I have not known before. Very exciting. But then, just when I think I've found the particular practice that will lead me to salvation, the joy dries up. So that's why I move on to the next practice with the next group. But the same story repeats. Fortunately, the spiritual supermarket is huge, and there are so many things to try. But I sometimes wonder how long it will take me to find the right path.

A: I've got news for you. You are not going to find the right path this way.

Q: Why not?

A: The practice dries up not because it is not right for you, but because of conditioning. The ego makes every practice routine after a while. A routine practice is just more ego stuff. It cannot take you beyond ego where happiness is.

Q: You may have a point there. What do you think of New Age workshops? I love attending them.

A: You've discovered workshops. Good! Charismatic workshop leaders seem to know your number, your fickleness of pursuit, your lack of commitment, and they call you on that. Yet they are willing to labor with you to help you break through to a new high. You like that; there seems to be more honesty. But your real attraction is from a different source. You want to be like the leader—so cool, so highly developed in consciousness. You feel bigger than yourself when you are in his or her proximity. And you also soar by the end of the workshop, don't you?—so expanded in your consciousness that your significant one has a hard time communicating to the "new" you when you return home. Right?

Q: Right! But the feeling of expanded consciousness does not last long. When my workshop leader is out of sight, the practices I did with him or her seem to lose their magic. Why is that?

A: The workshop and its leader have an effect on you that is a lot like magnetic induction; as soon as the magnet is gone, you are back to your ordinary "iron" state. You may try doing a repeat workshop to repeat the magic, but the second time often isn't as charmed.

Q: That's what I find. Fortunately, there is always another workshop, another teacher for me to hear. But is there someone who will make me into a permanent magnet? They do say, when the disciple is ready, the right guru arrives. Why shouldn't that apply to me?

A: You are not there yet. Before, in stage one, you were a voracious reader; now you are an experience junkie. Downgrading intellect, you enjoy a certain touchy-feely mushiness. You don't go to workshops primarily because you seek personal growth, enlightenment. This change from intellect to emotion has lead you to experiment with expanded relationships, and where better than in workshop settings?

The psychologists Amy and Arnie Mindell lead an exercise at conferences on consciousness just for fun in which they ask people to line up in four categories according to their motivations for attending the conference. First, the serious researchers are called together—a substantial group. The second group consists of humanitarians, those who have come to better equip themselves to serve humanity—again a substantial group. The third group, the personal growth enthusiasts, is the largest; and the fourth, people looking for significant relationships, claims only a few. Now Amy and Arnie ask people to switch groups to their second choice. The people in the first two groups interchange quite a bit, but their total sizes remain virtually the same. The biggest shift occurs in the last two groups, when many in the personal growth group enlarge the relationship group.

Q (sheepishly): You probably are right. I can see myself and my problems more clearly now. What do I do?

A: Here is the real problem: If your contexts have not changed, if the learned repertoire of your adult ego still holds sway, how can you explore the meaning of new experiences? Your tendency invariably is to repeat old patterns.

The seduction of workshop-expanded consciousness may even lead to old-fashioned affairs, which cloud your intent and broadcast pain to all involved. Frequently, the experience ultimately reveals itself as a tragicomic, melodramatic distraction.

Q: And I still don't change?

A: Right. You are left substantially where you were before. You have replaced drugs with meditation, chanting, or Sufi dancing. Instead of intellectual exploration of the world of books, you now prefer to explore the experiential world, but so what? You have remained virtually the same, as self-centered as before.

Q: Is it hopeless then? How do people ever move on from this situation?

A: Sooner or later, understanding dawns. It is here that emotional experiences sometimes work better than a purely intellectual pursuit of spirituality. Perhaps it is through an increased depth of meditation, which reveals to you your boundaries and how you perpetuate them by always looking outside yourself for a solution to your suffering. Perhaps a teacher at a workshop makes a timely comment that penetrates. Perhaps a touch of vital creativity or a bit of kundalini experience expands your heart beyond the "me" and "my" that ordinarily dominates our heart energy. But one way or another you recognize your divided loyalty and see the limits of your compartmentalized, half-hearted attempt at spirituality.

Why haven't you changed? Because you're afraid of what will happen to you if you change. At a workshop, in response to the workshop leader's appeal to surrender the ego, I once blurted out in complete sincerity, "But I want to be there when it [enlightenment] happens." So you keep one foot in your materialist worldview so that if spirituality does not work, you can always return to your previous life, a known quantity.

And many who thus play it safe do return to their previous lives after their "midlife-transition" forays into consciousness research. Many never continue to stage three of spiritual exploration.

Q: I want to go to stage three. What has to happen?

A: There is a story about a husband who has brought his pregnant wife to the hospital to give birth. Seeing his wife suffer, the husband is sympathetic: "Honey, are you sure you want to go through with this?" So long as you are like this husband, you are stuck. If you are like the wife, things begin to happen.

You will hit the books again in search of new conceptual understanding to facilitate a decisive leap into consciousness exploration. Now you may be drawn toward books that talk about transformation, about consciousness as primary. You may begin reading transpersonal psychology or the works of Carl Jung not as brain food but for clues in the science of transformation. You may even revisit a few of the traditional Good Books. You may be drawn toward ideas of creativity; you may think about quantum-leaping the abyss that separates your ego and the elusive quantum self.

Q: I can see that. This is already happening to me.

A: Now is the time to explore the various paths with all those exotic Sanskrit names that you previously avoided (there are no short cuts!): jnana yoga, bhakti yoga, karma yoga, raja yoga, and tantra. These paths are common to all traditions. You must begin to complement your meditation practice with the practices prescribed in these yogas.

You may go to a Zen teacher and ask for a koan to solve. When reading about Zen koans is no longer mere intellectual play, changes can happen. You recognize that chanting provides more than emotional richness in your life; it kindles your bhakti—a two-way, tangled-hierarchical relationship with God. With this deeper understanding, chanting once again has the same kind of softening effect it had in the beginning but lost because of conditioning.

Perhaps for the first time in your life, you begin to regard serving another as a worthwhile endeavor. What have you got to lose except your selfishness? Serving only "numero uno" does not satisfy as much as serving another, as you begin to find out.

Your meditations no longer are merely a scheduled routine; you discover creativity and freedom in meditation. Meditative awareness or the mantra of your concentration practice begins to operate spontaneously at times other than meditation. You recognize the freedom that meditation is bringing you; you slow down in your approach to life; your tendency to react reflexively diminishes. Now you have the privilege, more than once in a while, of saying "no" to conditioned behavior. You have become open for quantum leaping.

Q: That sounds good. But I am a little surprised that as a scientist you are not keen on developing new paths to the spirit for this new age.

A: Somebody once asked me about using the virtual reality of a computer game to explore consciousness. That is as New Age a method as you can think of, but I am afraid it won't work. Identified with our ego, we already live in a virtual reality. Exploring a computer-generated virtual reality only augments the ego's separation.

The new science helps us see that the nature of the ego's separation from the wholeness of the quantum self is conditioning and simple hierarchy. Regarding the first, the job is to get over conditioning and into creativity and to establish a good balance between the two. Regarding the second, the job is to discover tangled hierarchy in relationship and then find a good balance. The first is achieved through creativity of the mind (jnana yoga), the process of cognition (raja yoga), and creativity of the vital-physical body (tantra); the second through bhakti yoga and karma yoga. This does not preclude devising new techniques, but the yogas will be the same; we will still practice becoming more creative and more loving. Do not let the Sanskrit names fool you; these paths are universal.

Q: If I become a true practitioner of inner creativity following one of these paths, or maybe all the paths—a kind of integral yoga—then what?

A: Then you have a burning question: Is there God or not? Is consciousness the ground of all being or not? You may ponder your question for hours. At other times you may sag in discouragement: what's the use? There must be a causal answer to the questions of the world, a mathematical model that materialists will eventually figure out.

What you learn from quantum physics, science within consciousness, and experimental metaphysics is now invaluable. These systems of knowledge can give you faith in sudden discontinuous change.

Then one day, when you least expect it, you arrive at certain knowledge—a sudden insight, a samadhi, a satori, even consciousness without subject-object split—that leaves no doubt that consciousness defines your life. Your frantic search—Is the spiritual path useful? Is spirit a vital part of me?—has found fruition. You have now broken through your ego-identity. Your buddhi is awakened. You have creative access once again to your theme body, as if you are born into a second childhood. And new themes await your exploration. You are ready for stage three.

(If nirvikalpa samadhi is experienced at this stage, the following stages of the spiritual journey may still continue. However, they are looked upon as the manifestation of the insight gained in nirvikalpa samadhi. In rare cases, turiya may cause instant transformation and no further stages are necessary. Life is then lived according to one's prarabdha—the karmic propensities for this life.)

Stage Three

Q: So tell me, what happens once buddhi is awakened?

A: With awakened buddhi comes a sense of freedom and personal power that never existed for you before. This propels you to creative exploration as never before. You no longer seek out the "doable" problems in your given expertise—problems that you engage simply because they are within your power to solve, not because you are truly curious about them. For the first time in your life, you investigate the world as it is, with all, or at least some, of its complexity.

Q: I have heard that many people develop special abilities called siddhis.

A: Some people do develop paranormal abilities—telepathy, clairvoyance, and such. That is very simple to understand; with access to the quantum self, experiences of quantum nonlocality come more easily. If you were a healer before, now you are a healer with empathy, with a special sensitivity to your patients that borders on the paranormal; you are open to quantum nonlocality.

Q: Would you say that many people become teachers, even at this stage?

A: Yes. You may want to use your personal power to awaken people to consciousness, to spirituality. You may become a spiritual teacher, giving lectures and workshops with that purpose. You may even accept a few people to personally guide.

You may write. You have a privileged view of the inner machinations of the world. From this vantage point, creative solutions to important problems come easily, and wanting to write about them is only natural. If you are a scientist, you may become involved in paradigm shifts. Changing the worldview is no easy matter, and it demands your dedication.

Q: Sounds like fun!

A: It is. But one has to be alert. Are you judging fellow creatives for their limited approaches and for not appreciating your wisdom? As a teacher, you would clearly bring a certain freshness to your teaching, a certain power that touches your students. When you see another teacher who does not seem to have that fresh spark, do you tend to leap out and criticize this teacher and his or her teaching? Say you were a physician before your awakening; you are used to good living. What's wrong with making an equally good living in your new vocation as a spiritual teacher? Nothing. But are you attached to your high living? How do you treat a deserving student who cannot pay?

You live in America, where the American dream reigns. Stay aware lest you be caught up in it. If the American dream comes to you, and you can take it or leave it, that is one thing. But it is quite another thing to get caught up in chasing the never-ending dream. No, you won't necessarily backtrack to become a materialist, even if you shamelessly compromise yourself and your truth for the American dream. But this will arrest your further progress on the path.

Q: Are there signs to watch for so we can avoid these pitfalls?

A: Watch your humility level. Who is the doer behind your success? Whose will is it that propels your actions? Are you thinking that you are a great woman, a great man, a great spiritual teacher? Do you wonder that other people don't appreciate your wisdom, just because you are not as loud as some in beating your own drum?

Face the truth. Truth always sets you free. Do some of your ego-based values still continue? Are you competing rather than cooperating? Are you accumulating extra money for the sake of security and power, or at least comfort, rather than living with what is sufficient?

Watch yourself in relation to the opposite sex. Do you still nurture adolescent romantic illusions? Romance is fine, but weaving illusions that draw on external gratification is not; it is a carry-over of conditioned patterns. Do you exert your personal power for pursuing sex? Do your relationships continue to be hierarchical?

Watch the level of silence within you. Do your actions most often spring forth from the depths of inner silence, or do you continue the materialistic tendency of expanding horizontally through unnecessary actions?

Watch your vital energy. Do you still have mood swings that depress you periodically? When your heart expands, do you feel compassionate or patronizing?

Watch your mental processes preceding an action. Do you continue to act from the mind, from reasoning? Are you willing to wait until an intuition tells you how to act? In other words, do you continue the classical-physics practice of heeding only the local causes, or are you open to quantum nonlocality?

Q: I would think that at the third stage people are so stabilized in awareness that they would automatically see through these tendencies and make necessary corrections. Why don't they?

A: There is a tendency when we awaken in buddhi to give up rigorous practice because we think we are enlightened, we think we've made it all the way and have arrived at liberation. But if unhappiness still lurks at the edges, if you are still bound by the preferences of perpetual cycles of pleasure and pain, how authentic or complete is your liberation?

Q: So unhappiness is something to watch for?

A: Yes. It is the telltale remnant of ignorance. Along with seeking. If you are liberated, what is there still to seek? Why would you be oriented toward accomplishments? This is the question one has to ask oneself with utter honesty.

Q: Are you saying that not doing hard practice brings the ego right back?

A: There certainly is an increased tendency toward tamas—psychosocially conditioned behavior. One has to be aware of that tendency in order to keep tamas subdued. We have to draw on the warrior inside, gather our personal power, get over our tamas. It helps to go back to good books once again or find an advanced teacher in order to become stabilized in buddhi.

Q: I never realized that the ego is so persistent.

A: Living in the world, living in the body, constitutes a continual temptation to succumb to conditioning and to accept limitation. We all have the repressed tendencies that Jung called the shadow, personal as well as collective. It is time to do some shadow cleansing. Reading Jung and working with a Jungian therapist may help. If we surrender with the right intent, God (Mother Kali represents this aspect of God to Hindus) will do the cleansing for us. But we have to ask, we have to be humble. We have to dismount from our high horse.

At this stage, our onward movement may also be arrested because of aspects of our psyche that never got integrated—if not personal ones, surely the collective ones, our anima or animus, for example. This integration may need to be given priority. Didn't Jesus say (Guillaumont et al. 1959), "When you make the male and the female into a single one, so that the male will not be male and the female (not) be female . . . then shall you enter (the kingdom of heaven)?" Quantum happiness is not cheap; it requires a tangled hierarchy in our relationships. Without the integration of anima or animus, the tangled hierarchy of relationship will always elude us.

Q: I get it! What is the way to Carnegie Hall? Of course. It is practice, practice, practice.

A: Yes, but creative practice. A conditioned practice will not do the job.

With creativity, with patience, with humility, with warrior energy—all designed to purify our sattva—the natural urge for illumination appears once again in full force; integration begins and you return to the spiritual path. You dismount from your high horse of false liberation. Grounded in humility, you are now ready for stage four.

(If one began stage three with the experience of nirvikalpa, or if any of the sudden leaps in the processes of individuation involved this experience, then the seeking drops at this point. But other vestiges of ego identification may still remain. Only turiya exempts us from ego identification.)

Stage Four

Q: What is the telltale sign of reaching stage four?

A: When your personality is integrated, a stage that Carl Jung called individuation, you have reached stage four. Your male and female aspects are integrated; your ways of knowing, sensing, thinking, feeling, intuiting have reached a balance.

Being in stage four is truly wonderful. You have personal power, you are open to quantum creativity, you have inner fortitude, and yet you have not the slightest impulse to chase after achievements or disdain those that come to you. Your humility is simple and profound. You are not shy in necessary exposure, but you do not court publicity. You make a comfortable living that does not compromise your freedom, your being, or your principles. Your relationships are tangled hierarchical, and you are constantly observant against any remaining ego glitches.

In stage four, you are vigilant about the ego, about tendencies to habituate, and maintain regular practice skillfully and diligently. You may try to be creative in sleep, to see if you can remain aware at the juncture of wakefulness and sleep. You may practice sleep yoga to arrive at nirvikalpa samadhi. In your waking awareness, you may practice the presence of the quantum self.

Don't forget skill, however; without it, any practice loses its creative edge and becomes conditioned!

Now you are mostly joyful when you work, when you are engaged with the world and in your relationships. You are sensitive and responsible. You are peaceful, with a good balance of the quantum self and the ego in your self-identity. In other words, you no longer identify much with the ego, which is more and more merely functional.

Q: So why continue spiritual practice, then?

A: Strangely, although nothing is lacking, you notice that your actions are not always appropriate. Some of your projects still bite the dust of unfulfillment, exposing the limited nature of your wisdom in undertaking them. Some of your relationships still don't break through to tangled hierarchy, but remain frozen. A few shadows still linger in the back of your closet. And you still suffer, if from nothing more than boredom. You can philosophize: Didn't Nietzsche say "Against boredom, even the gods themselves struggle in vain?" But you know in your heart that the permanent antidote to boredom is spiritual joy, which is always available; you only need to dispel the cloud of ignorance that still covers it.

Q: So boredom is the telltale sign of not having reached liberation!

A: We have to watch how we are when we are by ourselves. Are we restless? Do we have to kill time with "Dear Abby" or a crossword puzzle? Do we need some nice music to soothe our mood? Are these our props against boredom? Do we feel antsy about having enough energy to return to work?

Your mind has slowed down compared to how it was before, but not enough. What you need is the practice of nondoing. You are familiar with nondoing in connection with creativity: remember "do be do be do"—alternate doing and nondoing (being), conscious and unconscious processing that takes us to creative insight? But that is only an introduction to nondoing, because creativity is still about action (external or internal).

Can you imagine practicing nondoing for nondoing's sake—just quieting down the mind only to have a quiet mind, not as fuel for more activity? You have done enough mental creativity! Now it is time to practice the equanimity of mind that Buddhists call *samata*. And in truth, there is method to this apparent madness. You are moving toward a sense of appropriate action. Appropriate action requires a silent mind. Appropriate doing requires a nondoing, unattached, witnessing mind. It calls for a quantum leap from the thinking mind to what Aurobindo called the intuitive mind. That is nature's law.

Q: Please say more.

A: Let's have an example of nondoing meditation. Lao Tzu, a great exponent of this practice, used to walk in the morning in silence with a friend. One day, the friend brought another man, after warning him against talking, to walk with the great Lao Tzu. The sight of the sun rising over the river was very beautiful, and the newcomer expressed his pleasure, "What a beautiful sunrise!" Neither Lao Tzu nor his friend said anything. When they returned, Lao Tzu took his friend aside and said, "Please don't bring your friend to walk with us again. He talks too much."

Q: How does one practice nondoing?

A: First, you reduce unnecessary engaging in external stimuli. Second, you develop witnessing (*sakshibhava* in Sanskrit) of your internal awareness. Initially, this is mostly the witnessing of thoughts. As you practice nondoing of the mind, you become more aware of the movements of your vital body. You also become aware of the play of vital energy behind your restlessness and mood swings. You realize that you need to investigate the vital-body movements connected with negative emotions and have creative access to them in order to stabilize them.

This is the most serious practice at stage four. You could have rested on your laurels, and many do. And why not? Societies have an insatiable need for doers, so all societies glorify doing and condemn nondoing. But doing at the service of the ego causes much of the harm in the world: the unnecessary exhaustion of resources and the destruction of the environment are two examples. Doing in the service of others is good, but without the wisdom of appropriateness, the good that can come even from service to others is limited.

If it is God's will, one day you arrive at equilibrium in nondoing. This may happen for some only after much creative exploration of vital energy. Your kundalini awakens and is duly integrated. This gives you ready access to positive emotions, such as love, with which to transform negative emotions. The actions of body-mind-spirit become harmonized as both tamasic and rajasic tendencies are tamed. A nondoing mind is neutral as to good and evil. These dichotomies no longer bother the psyche. Archbishop Desmond Tutu exemplified this state in his conduct of amnesty hearings in South Africa.

Q: So how far is stage four from stage three? And how far is it to liberation?

A: At stage three, the purification of sattva from the tendencies of tamas (arising from behavioral conditioning and the unconscious urges from the personal and collective unconscious) was the important goal. Once vital-body and genetic conditioning (rajas or libido) is dealt with, transcending all three gunas (tamas, rajas, and sattva) begins to take place. In stage four, the important goal is silence from the mental and vital energies. You are getting ready for the true goal of spirituality—complete liberation from all ego-bondage.

Q: What is the key element in complete liberation?

A: A pig and a chicken are looking for breakfast. The chicken wants to stop at a restaurant that has a big sign "bacon and eggs." The pig refuses. When pressed by the chicken, the pig explains, "For you, eggs are just a contribution; for me bacon is total commitment." For liberation, likewise, it is total commitment for you, total surrender of your will to the will of the divine, the quantum self.

Liberation comes through an experience of nirvikalpa samadhi or a direct leap to turiya. Nirvikalpa samadhi eventually leads to complete liberation, after a period of maturation. Given all the growth that goes with maturation, at some point identification with the ego drops instantly, discontinuously, and there is only turiya. Now you are ready for stage five, living as a liberated individual (*jivanmukta* in Sanskrit).

Stage Five

Q: How does a liberated person live?

A: This is perhaps one of the most esoteric questions, and I will be brief because I cannot speak from personal experience.

The first thing is that a liberated being lives happily. Happiness is always with us, but our concern for "I" limits our ability to recognize the constant presence of happiness and fully enjoy it. When the "I" is not, as for a liberated person, happiness is—even enjoyment of happiness is. Paradoxical? Who is there to care?

Second, the job of the quantum monad is done or will be done as soon as the rest of the prarabdha karma is lived out. A liberated person is stable in the wisdom that all is God's will and that one is not separate from God. All of this person's actions are appropriate, in the sense that they create no internal conflict. In this person's eyes, perfection reigns, whatever is the case.

Q: What accounts for the huge differences we find in the behavior of enlightened beings?

A: Do we find this? Most of the differences in behavior are due to differences of degree of enlightenment—savikalpa samadhi, nirvikalpa samadhi, or turiya. However, it may be true that different liberated persons hear different tunes. Some are satisfied to be *pratyeka buddhas,* meaning those who are interested in liberation of only their particular quantum monad. Others, prompted by profound compassion, want to do everything within their power to help the rest of humanity arrive at liberation. This is the bodhisattva ideal—"forever and everywhere shall I live and strive for the redemption of every creature throughout the world." For others, spiritual practice continues until turiya expresses itself in unprecedented creativity. This is now supramental creativity, which appears in the manifest world as miracles, in apparent violation of physical laws.

Q: This is a subject that fascinates me. Tell me more.

A: Creativity in stage three is mental, or at best a quantum leap to the intellect, meaning that a new context of mental activity is discovered—a new physical law, a new style of art, a new love story, and so forth. There are, of course, vital and physical accessories to the mental discovery, but they do not involve new contexts ($E = mc^2$ is expressed using the same mathematical language as before).

At stage four, creativity involves the vital body; jumps in the context of movement of vital energy are symbolized by the rise of kundalini shakti. Extraordinary feats are performed by individuals whose kundalini is integrated, but these feats, on close scrutiny, do not involve any new context for the movement of the physical; they operate within established physical laws. (Heart rate can be speeded up at will, for instance, but the energy for it still comes from physical food.)

In stage five it is the contexts of physical movements, the physical laws, that can be transcended. Now there is complete mastery of the theme body. This is supramental and supravital creativity.[1]

Q: Please give examples of supramental or supravital creativity.

A: Beings at this level can levitate at will, can materialize physical objects from nothing, can be at two places at the same time, can survive without food. In other words, they create miracles, which scientists everywhere abhor, but for which there is ample evidence; Jesus rising from the dead is a dramatic example. Actually, scientists need not be fearful, because these individuals, completely attuned to the will of

God, do no harm to the physical world (they are not capable of it), nor do they adversely affect the karmic play of other beings. As the *Course in Miracles* puts it, "Miracles reflect the laws of eternity, not of time"— so laws they do reflect.

The end. I have told you all I know and some things that I only intuit. *Tathastu* (so be it).

Notes

1. Patanjali maintains that siddhis, the power to perform miracles, can be attained through arduous practice of *samyama*, stabilization of *dharana* (concentration), *dhyana*, (a single flow), and *samadhi* without attaining liberation; but this is not desirable because it hinders the spiritual progress of the practitioner and is also dangerous for the world.

The Politics of Integration

To THE MODERN MIND, one of the most disconcerting things about religions is the constant bickering that goes on among them regarding matters such as the nature of God, the soul, and the purpose and meaning of human life and how to fulfill them. Every religion seems to have its own story line, which the followers defend.

A scientific approach solves some parts of the story-line problem. Religions that originate with one person—for example, Buddhism, Christianity, and Islam—tend to deify the founder in one way or another. Was Buddha's enlightenment greater than the enlightenment of a modern Buddhist? Was Jesus completely God and completely man—a condition impossible for anyone else? Was Muhammad the greatest of all prophets? Can science resolve such controversies? Yes and no. Yes, because science gives us larger contexts for questions, contexts in which the questions lose many of their parochial teeth. No, because science usually has little to say about an individual person or event.

In what new context can we think about Buddha's enlightenment? In the new science, awakening is understood to occur when an individual realizes the falsity of the ego identity and intuits that all is one consciousness and the apparent world is the play of the quantum self. But there are levels of possible maturation within this realization: How completely does the realized person identify with the quantum self? Is all dualism between his or her will and God's will gone? Do miracles happen around the enlightened person, signifying control over the theme realm? Does the enlightened person recall past lives? How oriented is he or she to appropriate action?

Ken Wilber—correctly, I think—attributes these different layers of maturation within realized existence to a spectrum of consciousness. Everyone is capable of experiencing the entire spectrum, and everyone will in time. The founders of religions were special individuals because they arrived at liberation in this lifetime and divine will manifested in their lives with such fullness that their teachings continue to this day.

Are these special people God-human—fully God and fully human? They can be called that because their actions reflect appropriateness. They are true to their godliness because they do not identify with their ego-individuality. Yet they are true to their humanness because they retain their ego functions.

But science cannot answer questions like: was Jesus the only God-man, or, was Muhammad the greatest of all prophets? We can only hope that a scientific approach makes the narrowness of such beliefs so obvious that few people will accept them. In any case, the spiritual journey itself purifies the devotee of this superiority/inferiority orientation.

We can also ask: Now that we have a science within consciousness, is religion even needed? If it is not, then the entire question of the unity of religions disappears.

Can Science Replace Religion?

I was giving a talk on the new science within consciousness in the living room of my friend Larry Brown in the small town of Jackson, California. It was a small gathering, just enough people to fill a living room, so the discussion after the talk was lively. A local chemistry teacher especially startled me with his question.

"Aren't you talking about public faith, faith obtainable through public experiments?"

I was startled by the use of the word *faith* in this context. But, of course, he was right. When Alain Aspect's experiment verified quantum nonlocality and elucidated the concept of a transcendent domain of reality, it built a public faith in all of us. Before Aspect, transcendence had to be taken on private faith until direct intuition of it transformed it to private fact. But now we can go from public faith to private fact. Sure, artists and mystics have always brought from heaven a modicum of inspiration to help us with our faith, but only science has the ability to demonstrate heaven with public experiments.

If private faith in transcendence is no longer needed, suppose, for the sake of argument, that the new science and experimental metaphysics were able to provide public verification for most spiritual concepts. Then would there be a need for separate enterprises of religion and science? Isn't the job of religion to guide people in their faith?

One quick answer is that no science can verify the ultimate ontological issue: consciousness as the ground of being. That has to be verified directly by each spiritual aspirant, which generally requires guidance from teachers, communities, and traditions. However, this is the most esoteric of issues, not the entire focus of most exoteric religions. So, how does one justify these religions?

In the foregoing, I have emphasized the personal aspect of the spiritual search, but there is also a social aspect, the need for a spiritual community. As Jesus said, "When two or more are gathered in my name, there I am in the midst of them." Community enhances our personal practice. Exoteric religions also support people in living morally, provide spiritual counseling and therapy, and offer guidance in inner creativity, including the creativity of the vital-physical body. Organizations engaged in science—universities and research institutes—can complement but not replace the exoteric religions. Let there be trade between the two types of organizations. Let religious organizations get information from the new science, and let the new scientist complement his or her personal spiritual search and research by sharing with spiritual communities—the religions.

The New Scientist and Spiritual Transformation

There is a story about an encounter over lunch between Krishnamurti and the famous physicist Nobel laureate Richard Feynman. Rather, I should say, nonencounter, because they met, but they did not dialogue. Feynman, who had come to visit his friend David Bohm, was enormously charismatic, so the conversation at the lunch table revolved around him. When the lunch broke up, Krishnamurti was walking back to his room, and the chef was walking with him. Suddenly Krishnamurti made the observation that Feynman was a very unhappy person (Krohnen 1997).

Was Krishnamurti reading Feynman's mind during the luncheon? I don't know, and that is not my point. Rather, my point is that this observation could have been made practically about every scientist—past, present, and future. It was true of Newton and even of Einstein (certainly in his younger days). Many of the scientists who are investigating consciousness in the West are generally unhappy. They are competitive, they are accomplishment-oriented, and they are stressed to the hilt. So if the investigation of consciousness is supposed to bring us happiness, you have to wonder what kind of consciousness these people are studying. The answer is obvious. These scientists are looking at consciousness objectively; they are studying object-directed awareness. They have made no commitment to personal transformation through their investigation.

People often ask me if other scientists looking through this wonderful quantum visionary window see the same possibility of integration between science and spirituality that I see. If not, why not? If so, when can we expect some genuine movement among scientists toward the integrative paradigm? The answers to these questions are all tied to the question of the commitment of the individual scientist to transformation.

Most scientists today do science for career motives. Many who dream of a paradigm shift want to discover that one new idea that will bring them instant fame and fortune. The paradigm that integrates science and spirituality within consciousness is not based on a new idea. Thus these scientists are reluctant to accept that the "new" idea for the paradigm shift they seek—the idea that consciousness is the ground of all being—has been around for millennia. Yet once one sees the validity of this idea, the authenticity of the quantum window also becomes clear.

To appreciate the primacy of consciousness a scientist must investigate consciousness directly. Not only with concepts, not only through public experiments in experimental metaphysics (important as these are), but also through direct experience. Consciousness is closer than our jugular vein, said the great sheik Ibn 'Arabi. But we have to look at ourselves.

I will tell you another personal anecdote. I was having a discussion about my own and related work with a great physicist who, like me, investigates consciousness through quantum physics. After we spent the day together, he very kindly invited me to his house. At the dinner table, he asked me what, if any, profound proof have I found for God in my personal experience. I told him that I have learned to love my wife, and that I am happy most of the time. He was not impressed.

Traditional objective science demands from its practitioners strict objectivity: scientists must not become subjectively involved with their field; that is, they may change the field of their practice, but they must not allow their research to change them. One must argue compellingly for the scientists of the new science to radically extend their methodology in this regard.

Scientific investigation requires both theory and practice. But even with experimental metaphysics, the study of the nature of consciousness involves aspects that must be approached purely experientially. Prime examples are the two-self nature of our being and the idea of transformation of ego-identification. Scientists will continue to miss the very profound insight that consciousness is the ground of all being if they don't delve into transformation. Consciousness researchers Willis Harman and Christian de Quincey (1994) agree with me:

> The point is that the transformation in experience which the scientist would undergo while exploring consciousness is essential for the kind of direct and deep insight required to gain knowledge of the psyche. Without that, the scientist would be blind to the phenomena and processes under investigation. Such "inner vision" is the starting point—the sine qua non—of any true consciousness science; it is the source of data which, later, the scientist can build into a communicable model.

Should We Unite All Religions?

If spirituality is scientific, if there is ontological and cosmological unity behind all spiritual traditions, then is there any purpose in having separate religions? Why not just have one universal religion?

A similar issue arises with regard to cultures. Should we encourage cultural diversity? Isn't it less confusing if we have one unified culture? A country of diverse immigrant populations, such as the United States, envisions a "melting pot" culture, a one-culture stew richly flavored with the seasonings of different cultures. But anthropologists and sociologists have now realized that the melting pot is not feasible after all, because one culture inevitably dominates. A culturally diverse population, instead, must be a whole cloth in which the weave includes distinct patterns that reflect the contributions of individual cultures. We understand the advantages of diversity in biological evolution; we must recognize that true cultural diversity can provide similar advantages to human societies.

Likewise, we must retain our diversity of religions. Every religion reflects the culture in which it developed and the traditional paths (knowledge, love, action, meditation, kundalini, etc.) as defined by that culture. People are attracted to different paths and accordingly are best served by different religions. Respecting the diversity of all religions need not obscure the underlying unity.

Hinduism is a good example of diversity within unity. Hinduism is defined not as a religion but as part of the culture of a people who discovered spirituality to be an important and eternal part of life. Within this broad notion of spirituality many teachers and many teachings exist. The different schools bicker with one another, but all are accepted under the broad umbrella of Hinduism. This is a useful model for the religious diversity within unity that science within consciousness so clearly establishes. Within a scientific approach, religions will always have a creative component; they need never become pulpits of bigotry, as sometimes happens now. They will change as the science changes and the cosmology gets better. Religions will also change as the culture changes, and with it, the people that the religion serves.

Should We Integrate Church and State?

Secularism—the separation of church and state—is now the tradition in the West. When the Western worldview accepted the Cartesian mind-matter split, secularism worked. It ensured freedom of religion from possible state influences. It also ensured that public education would be free of a particular religious dogma.

Secularism has been a good thing in the West because the Christian church, the dominant religion, is authoritarian. The public schools needed to be protected. Now, however, public education needs to be protected not only from the dogma of the church but also from the dogma of scientism. Children rightfully are not taught with any seriousness that God created the world in six days (classical creationism), but they are being taught the failing dogma that everything is made of atoms, implicitly including mind and consciousness.

If both religion and science were free of dogma, secularism would not be needed. With science within consciousness firmly in place and spirituality recognized as an unquestionably important part of being human, there would be no need to separate church and state. It would be like trying to separate economics and politics. But that time has not arrived yet.

The failure of the old science is clear. So is the danger of scientism. What we need to do to avoid the perils of scientism is to open up questions concerning reality, metaphysical questions, to alternative views beyond materialism, such as the spiritual view of the world. Discussions on philosophy should not shy away from spiritual philosophies. Even more importantly, students should be allowed to learn to look at their selves, to meditate, especially in view of their intense exposure to media-manipulated images of themselves. Meditation should not be excluded from the public school curriculum because it has traditionally been a part of spiritual practice.

Perhaps the greatest immediate impact of a science within consciousness is to reassure everyone concerned that a dialogue between science and religion is safe, is timely, and is fruitful. Our children do not need to be protected from this dialogue. Let them learn about atoms and molecules, but let's not teach them that there is nothing but atoms and molecules. Let them be exposed to alternative views of mind and consciousness, of themselves. Let them learn techniques of investigation beyond the intellectual and experimental techniques of today's materialist science, techniques of inner investigation that span physical and vital body, mind, intellect, and consciousness—indeed, the entire great chain of our being. Let's continue to emphasize reading, writing, and arithmetic, the three R's that will assure young people's success in the outer arena of life, but let's complete their education with the three I's—intuition, insight, and inspiration—which will bring them happiness. Most importantly, let's respect our children enough to teach them all the facts and all the opinions, controversy notwithstanding, and let them choose their own worldview. We owe them that.

References

Almeder, R. (1992). *Death and Personal Survival: The Evidence for Life after Death.* Lanham, MD: Rowman and Littlefield.

Aspect, A., J. Dalibard, and G. Roger. (1982). "Experimental Test of Bell Inequalities Using Time-Varying Analyzers." *Physical Review Letters* 49, pp. 1804-7.

Assagioli, R. (1976). *Psychosynthesis: A Manual of Principles and Techniques.* New York: Penguin.

Aurobindo, S. (1955). *The Synthesis of Yoga.* Pondicherry, India: Sri Aurobindo Ashram.

Bache, C. M. (1990). *Lifecycles: Reincarnation and the Web of Life.* New York: Paragon.

Balsekar, R. (1989). *The Final Truth.* Redondo Beach, CA: Advaita Press.

———. (1993). *Consciousness Speaks.* Redondo Beach, CA: Advaita Press.

Banerji, R. B. (1994). "Beyond Words." Preprint. Philadelphia: St. Joseph's University.

Barrow, J. D., and F. J. Tipler. (1986). *The Anthropic Cosmological Principle.* New York: Oxford University Press.

Bass. L. (1971). "The Mind of Wigner's Friend." *Harmathena* 112. Dublin: Dublin University.

———. (1975). "A Quantum Mechanical Mind-Body Interaction." *Foundations of Physics* 5, pp. 155-72.

Bateson, G. (1980). *Mind and Nature.* New York: Bantam.

Becker, C. B. (1993). *Paranormal Experience and the Survival of Death.* Albany: State University of New York Press.

Bell, J. S. "On the Einstein-Podolsky-Rosen Paradox." *Physics* 1, pp. 195-200.

Blake, W. (1981). *Poetry and Prose.* Berkeley: University of California Press.

Blavatsky, H. P. (1968). *The Secret Doctrine.* Los Angeles: Theosophy Co.

Blood, C. (1993). "On the Relation of the Mathematics of Quantum Mechanics to the Perceived Physical Universe and Free Will." Preprint. Camden, NJ: Rutgers University.

Bohm, D. (1951). *Quantum Theory.* Englewood Cliffs, NJ: Prentice Hall.

_____. (1980). *Wholeness and the Implicate Order.* London: Routledge and Kegan Paul.

Briggs, J. (1990). *The Fire and the Crucible.* Los Angeles: Tarcher.

Buber, M. (1970). *I and Thou.* Translated by W. Kaufmann. New York: Charles Scribner.

Byrd, R. C. (1988). "Positive and Therapeutic Effects of Intercessor Prayer in a Coronary Care Unit Population." *Southern Medical Journal* 81, pp. 826-29.

Capra, F. (1977). *The Tao of Physics: An Exploration of the Parallels between Modern Physics and Eastern Mysticism.* New York: Bantam.

Chalmers, D. (1995). *Toward a Theory of Consciousness.* Cambridge: MIT Press.

Chopra, D. (1989). *Quantum Healing: Exploring the Frontiers of Mind-Body Medicine.* New York: Bantam.

Cousins, N. (1989). *Head First: The Biology of Hope.* New York: Dutton.

Cranston, S., and C. Williams. (1984). *Reincarnation.* 2 vols. Pasadena, CA: Theosophical University Press.

Davies, P. (1989). *The Cosmic Blueprint.* New York: Simon and Schuster.

Dayananda, S. (1993). *Introduction to Vedanta.* New Delhi: Vision Books.

Dennett, D. (1991). *Consciousness Explained.* New York: Basic.

d' Espagnat, B. (1983). *In Search of Reality*. New York: Springer Verlag.

Dossey, L. (1990). *Recovering the Soul*. New York: Bantam-Doubleday.

Eccles, J. (1994). *How the Self Controls Its Brain*. New York: Springer Verlag.

Einstein, A., B. Podolsky, and N. Rosen. (1935). "Can Quantum Mechanical Description of Reality Be Considered Complete?" *Physical Review* 47, pp. 777-80.

Eldredge, N., and S. J. Gould. (1972). "Punctuated Equilibria: An Alternative to Phyletic Gradualism." In *Models in Paleontology*, ed. T. J. M. Schopf. San Francisco: Freeman.

Elsasser, W. M. (1981). "Principles of a New Biological Theory: A Summary." *Journal of Theoretical Biology* 89, 131-50.

_____. (1982). "The Other Side of Molecular Biology." *Journal of Theoretical Biology* 96, 67-76.

Evans-Wentz, W. Y., ed. (1960). *The Tibetan Book of the Dead*. Oxford: Oxford University Press.

Feynman, R. P. (1981). "Simulating Physics with Computers." *International Journal of Theoretical Physics* 21, pp. 467-88.

Gallup, G. (1982). *Adventures in Immortality*. New York: McGraw Hill.

Goldberg, B. (1982). *Past Lives, Future Lives*. New York: Ballantine.

Goswami, A. (1989). "The Idealistic Interpretation of Quantum Mechanics." *Physics Essays* 2, pp. 385-400.

_____. (1990). "Consciousness in Quantum Physics and the Mind-Body Problem." *Journal of Mind and Behavior* 11, pp. 75-96.

_____. (1993). *The Self-Aware Universe: How Consciousness Creates the Material World*. New York: Tarcher/Putnam.

_____. (1994). *Science within Consciousness: Developing a Science Based on the Primacy of Consciousness*. Research Report. Sausalito, CA: Institute of Noetic Sciences.

_____. (1996). "Creativity and the Quantum: A Unified Theory of Creativity." *Creativity Research Journal*, pp. 47-61.

_____. (1997a). "Consciousness and Biological Order: Toward a Quantum Theory of Life and Its Evolution." *Integrated Physiological and Behavioral Science* 32, pp. 75-89.

_____. (1997b). "A Quantum Explanation of Sheldrake's Morphic Resonance." In *Scientists Discuss Sheldrake's Theory about Morphogenetic Fields*, ed. H. P. Duerr and F. T. Gottwald. Germany: Scherzverlag.

_____. (1999). *Quantum Creativity: Waking Up to Our Creative Potential*. New York: Hampton Press.

Grant, V. (1985). *The Evolutionary Process: A Critical Review of Evolutionary Theory*. New York: Columbia University Press.

Green, E., and A. Green. (1977). *Beyond Biofeedback*. New York: Dell.

Greenwell, B. (1995). *Energies of Transformation*. Saratoga, CA: Shakti River Press.

Grinberg-Zylberbaum, J., M. Delaflor, L. Attie, and A. Goswami. (1994). "Einstein-Podolsky-Rosen paradox in the Human Brain: The Transferred Potential." *Physics Essays* 7, pp. 422-28.

Grof, S. (1992). *The Holotropic Mind*. San Francisco: Harper San Francisco.

Grosso, M. (1994). "The Status of Survival Research." *Noetic Sciences Review* 32, pp. 12-20.

Guillaumont, A. et al., trans. (1959). *The Gospel according to Thomas*. San Francisco: Harper & Row.

Harman, W., and C. De Quincey. (1994). *The Scientific Exploration of Consciousness: Toward an Adequate Epistemology*. Research Report. Sausalito, CA: Institute of Noetic Sciences.

Hawking, S. (1988). *A Brief History of Time: From the Big Bang to Black Holes*. New York: Bantam.

Helmuth, T., A. G. Zajonc, and H. Walther. (1986). In *New Techniques and Ideas in Quantum Measurement Theory*, ed. D. M. Greenberger. New York: New York Academy of Science.

Herbert, N. (1986). *Quantum Reality*. New York: Dutton.

————. (1993). *Elemental Mind*. New York: Dutton.

Ho, M. W. (1994). *The Rainbow and the Worm: The Physics of Organisms*. Singapore: World Publishing.

Hofstadter, D. R. (1980). *Goedel, Escher, Bach: The Eternal Golden Braid*. New York: Basic.

Humphrey, N. (1972). "Seeing and Nothingness." *New Scientist* 53, p. 682.

Huxley, A. (1970). *The Perennial Philosophy*. New York: Harper Colophon.

Iyer, R. (1983). *The Jewel in the Lotus*. New York: Concord Grove Press.

Jahn, R. (1982). "The Persistent Paradox of Psychic Phenomena: An Engineering Perspective." *Proceedings of the IEEE* 70, pp. 135-70.

Jastrow, R. (1978). *God and the Astronomer*. New York: Warner.

Joy, W. B. (1979). *Joy's Way*. Los Angeles: Tarcher.

Jung, C. G. (1971). *The Portable Jung*. Edited by J. Campbell. New York: Viking.

Kamenetz, R. (1994). *The Jew in the Lotus*. New York: Harper Collins.

Kimura, M. (1983). *The Neutral Theory of Molecular Evolution*. Cambridge: Cambridge University Press.

Krishna, G. (1971). *Kundalini—The Evolutionary Energy in Man*. Boulder, CO: Shambhala.

Krishnamurthy, U. (2000). *Yoga and Mental Health,* to be published

Krishnamurti, J. (1995). *On Truth*. San Francisco: Harper San Francisco.

Krohnen, M. (1997). *The Kitchen Chronicles: 1001 Lunches with J. Krishnamurti.* Ojai, CA: Edwin House Publishing.

Kuhn, T. S. (1970). *The Structure of Scientific Revolutions.* Chicago: University of Chicago Press.

Leonard, G. (1990). *The Ultimate Athlete.* New York: North Atlantic.

Libet, B. (1985). "Unconscious Cerebral Initiative and the Role of Conscious Will in Voluntary Action." *Behavioral and Brain Science* 8, pp. 529-66.

Libet, B., E. Wright, B. Feinstein, and D. Pearl. (1979). "Subjective Referral of the Timing for a Cognitive Sensory Experience." *Brain* 102, p. 193.

Lockwood, M. (1989). *Mind, Brain, and the Quantum.* Oxford: Basil Blackwell.

London, F., and E. Bauer. (1983). In *Quantum Theory and Measurement,* ed. J. A. Wheeler and W. Zurek. Princeton: Princeton University Press.

Lovelock, J. E. (1982). *Gaia: A New Look at Life on Earth.* Oxford: Oxford University Press.

Lucas, W. B. (1993). *Regression Therapy: A Handbook for Professionals.* New York: Deep Forest Press.

MacGregor, G. (1992). *Reincarnation in Christianity.* Wheaton, IL: Theosophical Publishing House.

Marcel, A. (1980). "Conscious and Preconscious Recognition of Polysemous Words: Locating the Selective Effect of Prior Verbal Context." In *Attention and Performance* 8, ed. R. S. Nickkerson. Hillsdale, NJ: Lawrence Erlbaum.

Margulis, L. (1993). "Reflection." In *From Gaia to Selfish Gene,* ed. C. Barlow. Cambridge: MIT Press.

Maslow, A. (1968). *Toward a Psychology of Being.* New York: Van Nostrand Reinhold.

May, R. (1976). *Courage to Create*. New York: Bantam.

McCarthy, K., and A. Goswami. (1993). "CPU or Self-Reference? Can We Discern between Cognitive Science and Quantum Functionalist Models of Mentation?" *Journal of Mind and Behavior* 14, pp. 13-26.

Merrell-Wolff, F. (1995). *Philosophy of Experience*. Albany: State University of New York Press.

Mitchell, M., and A. Goswami. (1992). "Quantum Mechanics for Observer Systems." *Physics Essays* 5, pp. 526-29.

Moody, R. (1976). *Life after Life*. New York: Bantam.

Moss, R. (1981). *The I That Is We*. Berkeley, CA: Celestial Arts.

———. (1984). *Radical Aliveness*. Berkeley, CA: Celestial Arts.

Motoyama, H. (1971). *Theories of the Chakras*. Wheaton, IL: Theosophical Publishing House.

Moura, G., and N. Don. (1996). "Spirit Possession, Ayahuasca Users, and UFO Experiencers: Three Different Patterns of States of Consciousness in Brazil." *Abstracts of Talks at the Fifteenth International Transpersonal Association Conference, Manaus, Brazil*. Mill Valley, CA: International Transpersonal Association.

Murphy, M. (1992). *The Future of the Body*. Los Angeles: Tarcher.

Nagendra, H. R., ed. (1993). *New Horizons in Modern Medicine*. Bangalore, India: Vivekananda Kendra Yoga Research Foundation.

Netherton, M. (1978). *Past Lives Therapy*. New York: Ace.

Nikhilananda, S., trans. (1964). *The Upanishads*. New York: Harper and Row.

Nuland, S. B. (1994). *How We Die*. New York: Knopf.

O'Regan, B. (1987). "Healing, Remission, and Miracle Cures." *Institute of Noetic Sciences Special Report*.

Oshins, E., and McGoveran, D. (1980). ". . . Thoughts about Logic about Thoughts . . .: The Question of Schizophrenia." *Proceedings of the Twenty-Fourth Annual North American Meeting of the Society for General Systems Research*, pp. 505-14.

Osis, K., and E. Haraldsson. (1977). *At the Hour of Death*. New York: Avon.

Pasricha, S. (1990). *Claims of Reincarnation: An Empirical Study of Cases in India*. New Delhi: Harman Publishing House.

Peace Pilgrim. (1982). *Peace Pilgrim: Her Life and Work in Her Own Words*. Santa Fe, NM: Ocean Tree Books.

Penrose, R. (1989). *The Emperor's New Mind*. Oxford: Oxford University Press.

_____. (1994). *Shadows of the Mind*. Oxford: Oxford University Press.

Piaget, J. (1977). *The Development of Thought: Equilibration of Cognitive Structures*. New York: Viking.

Radin, D. I., and J. M. Rebman. (1996). "Deep Interconnectedness and Group Consciousness: Exploring the Limits of Mind-Matter Interaction." In *Proceedings of Presented Papers for the Thirty-Ninth Annual Parapsychological Convention*, pp. 219-45.

Ramana, Maharshi. (1978). *Talks with Ramana Maharshi*. Edited by T. N. Venkataraman. Madras, India: Jupiter Press.

Ray, P. (1996). *Noetic Sciences Review* 37, Spring issue.

Reich, W. (1949). *Character Analysis*. 3rd ed. New York: Orgone Institute Press.

Reps, P. (1957). *Zen Flesh, Zen Bones*. New York: Doubleday.

Ring, K. (1980). *Life at Death*. New York: Quill.

_____. (1992). *The Omega Project*. New York: Quill William Morrow.

Rogers, C. R. (1959). "Toward a Theory of Creativity." In *Creativity and Its Cultivation*, ed. H. H. Anderson. New York: Harper.

Rumi, J. (1988). *The Branching Moments.* Translated by J. Moyne and C. Barks. Providence, RI: Copper Beech Press.

Sabom, M. B. (1982). *Recollections of Death.* New York: Harper and Row.

Sancier, K. M. (1991). "Medical Applications of Qigong and Emitted Qi on Humans, Animals, Cell Cultures, and Plants: Review of Selected Scientific Research." *American Journal of Acupuncture* 19, pp. 367-77.

Schmidt, H. (1993). "Observation of a Psychokinetic Effect under Highly Controlled Conditions." *Journal of Parapsychology* 57, pp. 351-72.

Schuon, F. (1984). *The Transcendent Unity of Religions.* Wheaton, IL: Theosophical Publishing House.

Searle, J. R. (1994). *The Rediscovery of the Mind.* Cambridge: MIT Press.

Seymour, C. R. F. (1990). "The Old Gods." In *Angels and Mortals,* ed. M. Parisen. Wheaton, IL: Quest.

Sheldrake, R. (1981). *A New Science of Life.* Los Angeles: Tarcher.

Simonton, O. C., S. Matthews-Simonton, and J. J. Creighton. (1978). *Getting Well Again.* Los Angeles: Tarcher.

Sirag, S. (1993). In *The Roots of Consciousness,* ed. J. Mishlove. Tulsa, OK: Council Oaks Books.

Sivananda, Swami. (1987). *Vedanta (Jnana Yoga).* Rishikesh, India: Divine Life Society.

Sogyal Rinpoche. (1993). *The Tibetan Book of Living and Dying.* San Francisco: Harper San Francisco.

Stapp, H. P. (1993). *Mind, Matter, and Quantum Mechanics.* New York: Springer.

_____. (1994). *A Report on the Gaudiya Vaishnava Vedanta Form of Vedic Ontology.* San Francisco: Bhaktivedanta Institute.

_____. (1995). "The Hard Problem: A Quantum Approach." *Journal of Consciousness Studies* 3, pp. 194-210.

Stevenson, I. (1974). *Twenty Cases Suggestive of Reincarnation.* Charlottesville: University Press of Virginia.

_____. (1977). "Research into the Evidence of Man's Survival after Death." *Journal of Nervous and Mental Disease* 165, pp. 153-83.

_____. (1987). *Children Who Remember Previous Lives: A Question of Reincarnation.* Charlottesville: University Press of Virginia.

Stuart, C. I. J. M., Y. Takahashy, and M. Umezawawa. (1978). "Mixed System Brain Dynamics." *Foundations of Physics* 9, pp. 301-29.

Tarnas, R. (1991). *The Passion of the Western Mind.* New York: Ballantine Books.

Taimni, I. K. (1961). *The Science of Yoga.* Wheaton, IL: Theosophical Publishing House.

Varela, F. J., E. Thompson, and E. Rosch. (1991). *The Embodied Mind.* Cambridge: MIT Press.

von Neumann, J. (1955). *The Mathematical Foundations of Quantum Mechanics.* Princeton: Princeton University Press.

Walker, E. H. (1970). "The Nature of Consciousness." *Mathematical Biosciences* 7, pp. 131-78.

Wallas, G. (1926). *The Art of Thought.* New York: Harcourt, Brace, and World.

Wambach, H. (1979). *Life before Life.* New York: Bantam.

Wheeler, J. (1983), "Law without Law." In *Quantum Theory and Measurement,* ed. J. Wheeler and W. Zurek. Princeton: Princeton University Press.

Whitman, W. (1969). *Leaves of Grass.* New York: Avon.

Wickramsekera, I., S. Krippner, J. Wickramsekera, and I. Wichramsekera II. (1997). "On the Psychophysiology of Ramtha's School of Enlightenment." Preprint.

Weil, Andrew. (1995). *Spontaneous Healing.* New York: Knopf.

Wigner, E. (1962). In *The Scientist Speculates*, ed. L. J. Good. Surrey, U. K.: Windmill Press.

_____. (1967). *Symmetries and Reflections*. Bloomington: Indiana University Press.

Wilber, K. (1977). *The Spectrum of Consciousness*. Wheaton, IL.: Quest Books.

_____. (1980). *The Atman Project*. Wheaton, IL: Theosophical Publishing House.

_____. (1981). *Up from Eden*. New York: Anchor Press/Doubleday.

_____. (1982). *The Holographic Paradigm and Other Paradoxes: Exploring the Leading Edge of Science*. Boulder, CO: Shambhala.

_____. (1993). "The Great Chain of Being." *Journal of Humanistic Psychology* 33, pp. 52-55.

_____. (1996a). *A Brief History of Everything*. Boston: Shambhala.

_____. (1996b). "How Big is Our Umbrella?" *Noetic Sciences Review* 40, pp. 10-17.

_____. (1997). "An Integral Theory of Consciousness." *Journal of Consciousness Studies* 4 (1), pp. 71-92.

Wolf. F. A. (1984). *Starwave*. New York: Macmillan.

_____. (1986). *The Body Quantum*. New York: Macmillan.

_____. (1990). *Parallel Universes*. New York: Simon & Schuster.

_____. (1994). *The Dreaming Universe*. New York: Simon & Schuster.

_____. (1996). *The Spiritual Universe*. New York: Simon & Schuster.

Zohar, D. (1990). *The Quantum Self*. New York: William Morrow.

INDEX

Quest Books
encourages open-minded inquiry into
world religions, philosophy, science, and the arts
in order to understand the wisdom of the ages,
respect the unity of all life, and help people explore
individual spiritual self-transformation.

Its publications are generously supported by
The Kern Foundation,
a trust committed to Theosophical education.

Quest Books is the imprint of
the Theosophical Publishing House,
a division of the Theosophical Society in America.
For information about programs, literature,
on-line study, membership benefits, and international centers,
see www.theosophical.org
or call 800-669-1571 or (outside the U.S.) 630-668-1571.

Related Quest Titles

The Yoga of Time Travel, Fred Alan Wolf

Head and Heart, Victor Mansfield

Science and the Sacred, Ravi Ravindra

From Atom to Kosmos, L. Gordon Plummer

Beyond the Postmodern Mind, Huston Smith

To order books or a complete Quest catalog,
call 800-669-9425 or (outside the U.S.) 630-665-0130.